EXHIBITING SCOTLAND

EXHIBITING SCOTLAND

Objects, Identity,
and the National Museum

ALIMA BUCCIANTINI

University of Massachusetts Press
Amherst and Boston

Copyright © 2018 by University of Massachusetts Press
All rights reserved
Printed in the United States of America

ISBN 978-1-62534-329-1 (paper); 328-4 (hardcover)

Designed by Jen Jackowitz
Set in Palatino Linotype and Museo Slab
Printed and bound by Maple Press, Inc.

Cover design by Rebecca Neimark, Twenty-Six Letters
Cover photo: *Erik*, one of the eleven Lewis Chessmen, c 1150–1200 AD,
© National Museums Scotland.

A catalog record for this book is available from Library of Congress.

British Library Cataloguing-in-Publication Data
A catalog record for this book is available from the British Library.

An earlier version of chapter 1 was previously published as "Moving the Nation: Taking the Smithsonian to Scotland" in *Studies in Ethnicity and Nationality* 12, no. 1 (2012): 101–17, published by John Wiley & Sons Ltd. a revised and expanded version here is printed by permission of John Wiley & Sons.

For my beloved grandfather Charles Bucciantini,
who has never stopped asking when he would see this book

Contents

Preface: The Museum as Performance Space ix

Timeline of Museum Names xi

Acknowledgments xiii

Beginnings 1

Chapter 1
The Smithsonian Inspires: 1984 19

Chapter 2
Scotland, for Scotland: 1989 48

Chapter 3
Creating a National Narrative: 1998 77

Chapter 4
Objects Connecting Nations: 2005–2006 101

Chapter 5
Objects Unifying the Nation: 2007 134

Chapter 6
Changing Nation, Changing Museum: 2008–2011 166

Conclusion 191

Notes 199

Index 225

Preface

THE MUSEUM AS PERFORMANCE SPACE

I have always been interested in stories. What are the stories that we tell ourselves about our communal history and identity? How do we present and save those stories for the future? This book looks at the museum as a space that not only holds and protects artifacts but one that uses objects to create dynamic stories about the nation it represents.

I came to the museum through an interest in nationalism studies. This field sometimes lacks a sense of time, as nationalist fighters appeal to the "epic past" without caring when, or even if, that epic past actually existed. Museum studies, on the other hand, lacks a sense of time for other reasons. Much of the (wonderful) reading I encountered treats the museum as a timeless collection, or as a building erected at a certain moment, or as a place visitors spend an afternoon—but few address what happens in the longer term. Where were the stories built from a selection of artifacts that stayed on exhibit for a month or six months or six years? More crucially, where were the voices of the people who curated the exhibitions?

This book tells the story of one institution, from 1780 to 2017. In doing so, it first shows the power of individual objects to tell distinct stories at different moments of museum history. When circumstances and curators dictate, objects can become icons. Second, it demonstrates the power of the exhibition, both temporary and permanent. Exhibitions and their associated marketing are moments for curatorial staff and their museums to reevaluate how they want to present themselves. Lastly, the book tackles the ever-changing museum itself and the ongoing question of if and how Scotland should represent itself in a national museum—and the complicated issues, in turn, of what that museum would collect, look like, and be called.

Exhibiting Scotland starts in 1780 because that is when the conversation about collecting and displaying a national heritage began. Yet it was not until 1985 that the National Heritage (Scotland) Act established the foundation of what was then to be called the Museum of Scotland. The building itself did not open until 1998. This centuries-long span of time is part of what makes Scotland fertile ground for a book about national museums. The country is both old, having been independent prior to the 1707 Union of the Parliaments that united it with England, and new, exercising some independent governing powers in 1997 when the Scottish Parliament reopened. Throughout this period, the nation has used the national museum as one space to present itself both to outsiders and to those within the nation.

Scotland has been negotiating its national identity and the stories it tells about itself to the world since 1707. It is, I think, no mistake that it was Scotland that gave us Sir Walter Scott, father of historical fiction. I want to shine a light on the work done on these stories by curatorial staff and the ways in which narratives in museum space are changeable and ever-changing, contingent on forces within and without museum walls. *Exhibiting Scotland* is an attempt to tell the long history of a unique institution within a unique nation.

Timeline of Museum Names

There have been many changes to the names of the institutions covered in the text over the time covered. Unless otherwise stated, the museums are referred to by the names they were called at the time. A reference sheet and timeline is provided here.

1780—The Museum of the Society of Antiquaries is formed by the Society of Antiquaries of Scotland and moves around various venues in Edinburgh

1854—Founding of the Industrial Museum of Scotland

1858—The Society of Antiquaries of Scotland opens the National Museum of Antiquities of Scotland (NMAS)

1864—The Industrial Museum becomes the Edinburgh Museum of Science and Art

1904—The Edinburgh Museum of Science and Art becomes the Royal Scottish Museum (RSM)

1985—Formation of the National Museums of Scotland, which formally unifies the National Museum of Antiquities of Scotland and the Royal Scottish Museum under one corporate umbrella

1985–2001—The National Museum of Flight, the National War Museum, the National Museum of Rural Life, and the National Museum of Costume (closed in 2013), which are located at sites throughout central Scotland, are joined under the auspices of the National Museums of Scotland. At some point the Royal Scottish Museum begins branding itself as the Royal Museum of Scotland

1998—The Museum of Scotland opens next to, but apart from, the Royal Museum of Scotland

2006—Official creation of the National Museum of Scotland, with the unification of the Royal Museum of Scotland and the Museum of Scotland. The corporate umbrella organization National Museums of Scotland becomes the National Museums Scotland

2011—A revitalized "Royal Museum" half of the National Museum of Scotland opens after major renovation work and rehanging

2018–2019—The last of the new galleries in the Royal Museum half of the museum opens to the public

Acknowledgments

So many people in so many countries have contributed knowledge and support to this project. Words will indubitably fail me as I attempt to detail exactly how much.

I could not have done this work without the help of current and former staff of the National Museum of Scotland. Any omissions or errors of interpretation are mine alone. Thanks to Dr. David Caldwell, Dr. Hugh Cheape, Dr. David Clarke, Dr. George Dalgleish, Dr. Geoff Swinney, Jane Carmichael, Catherine Holden, and Dr. Michael Lynch for agreeing to be interviewed. Thanks also go to Kerryn Fraser, Alex Hinton, Katie Stevenson, and the current staff of Scottish History and Archaeology for speaking to me during my 2017 research trip and providing feedback and last-minute materials. Perhaps the most useful of all the National Museum of Scotland staff since 2005 have been the wonderful museum librarians; they remember me regardless of if I was in last week or two years ago. I could not have done this without them. The library is my favorite space in Edinburgh, and I miss it, and the people in it, all the time.

Marla Miller, editor of the Public History in Historical Perspective book series, provided unflagging support, which included reading the full manuscript several times. Her clarifying comments made this a much better book. Executive editor Matt Becker at the University of Massachusetts Press helped me over many hurdles on the way to publication and has been endlessly patient. Thank you for that. Comments from the two anonymous peer reviewers of the manuscript helped to show me what I was missing.

Dr. Stana Nenadic and Dr. Nick Prior were there at the start of this research and deserve much of the credit for anything good that exists within it. The ongoing discourse they provided between history and theory is one I hope to model in the future. The community of Scottish history at the University of Edinburgh was immensely helpful and supportive, especially my cohort in Buccleuch Place. While I am glad to have been able to write this book without wearing gloves to type, the camaraderie and intellectual space of that time was a unique gift. I value all of you.

"NaMu: Making National Museums" was a series of six conferences that rotated between Leicester, United Kingdom; Linköping, Sweden; and Oslo, Norway, and brought together scholars and professionals on issues concerning national museums between 2006 and 2008. The people I met at NaMu events all played a part in the shape of this work, whether they know it or not. Dr. Linda Andersson Burnett has the distinction of being both an Edinburgh and NaMu friend, and she has probably had the most influence here, but the whole project, spearheaded by Peter Aronsson, Arne Bugge Amundsen, and Simon Knell, was important.

Andrea Burns encouraged me to submit a book proposal to the University of Massachusetts Press, and my engagement with the National Council on Public History (NCPH) has been critical to my quick education in the field of public history since my move back to the United States. Thanks to the lovely women of the NCPH who have welcomed me with open arms. Special thanks as well go to my graduate assistants in the Public History department at Duquesne University, Lauren Van Zandt and Emily Davis, who are each started on brilliant careers, helped along, I am sure, by the time they spent helping on this very book. I am honored to have worked with you.

My family and friends have been patient and loving throughout this long process. The most loving thing they did was never ask about the timeline, so thanks for that. I said it would be done eventually, and here it is.

EXHIBITING SCOTLAND

Beginnings

After Dolly the cloned sheep, the object docents at the National Museum of Scotland are most asked to locate for visitors is the walrus ivory chessman biting the top of his shield in a berserk rage.[1] He's known as Erik and is something of a mascot for the museum. In a children's guidebook published in 1998, he hops happily out of his case and leads readers around the exhibits, popping in and out of pages and time periods, unconstrained by the rules of the chessboard.[2] Erik is part of what's known as the Lewis Chessmen in the museum's collection, and this role as guide is just one of the many he has played since he entered the collections in 1888, not to mention his pre-museum life, which may have started as early as the twelfth century. Erik and his fellow nameless chess pieces are engaging and have a deep and mysterious past, so it is easy to understand why he would come to take a starring role as museum ambassador. But what of all the other thousands of artifacts in the museum? How did they get there and what do they do once there?

Objects are all around us. As societies, we create, use, refashion, and discard objects continuously. However, some objects—those from the past, those belonging to important leaders, those made of rare materials, or just those we like the look of—we tuck away in museums. Museums are for special objects, or so we tell ourselves. Once the objects are in the museum they are catalogued, assigned numbers, and displayed in exhibition halls with labels beneath them. They are on show for all the visitors to see or stored safely away until their moment arrives.

But why do we do this? Why remove certain objects from the normal flow of their lives and place them in museum spaces? What does that do for society? Much has been written about what visitors perceive and understand when they view these objects.[3]

One of the eleven Lewis Chessmen in the collection of the National Museum of Scotland, this one is known affectionately as Erik and is something of a mascot for the museum. © National Museums Scotland.

Through that, we have come to understand that each viewer approaches each artifact with his or her own predetermined experiences and expectations. These perceptions also depend on whether visitors see artifacts on their own, with friends, with

Beginnings 3

family, or with a school group. But visitor studies and reception theory is not my aim here. My question is larger.

Why have objects in museums at all? Objects are the means through which curators and other museum professionals create the stories museums tell. And it is these stories that make museums important civic places. Some scholars have written about museums as monumental buildings or as institutions of civil society.[4] They are that. But more than those things, they are places of narratives, of stories, and it is the objects within them that make the stories possible.

While there are many possible types of stories museums can tell, it is one of the largest that I focus on here—the national story. This is because the national museum and the national stories that it tells are some of the most influential and complicated of all museum enterprises. While other sorts of museums use their object collections to tell stories of transportation or textiles or Texas, a national museum has to gather a collection of artifacts that is broad enough to tell the story of an entire nation. Then, the curatorial team has to arrange them into exhibitions that reflect the nation as it is, was, and might be.

Nationalism—the feeling, as Ernest Gellner famously put it, that the boundaries of the state and the nation should be congruent—has long been sustained and supported by stories.[5] Whether these are the epics of times gone by, or romantic novels and plays, or simply the history we learn in school, nationalism relies on stories and performance to make people feel attached to their nation. The stories presented within the exhibition halls of a museum are no different. They are just built using objects rather than words, and created by curators rather than writers. Museums are spaces where national narratives are produced and consumed.

This connection between national museums and the production of national narratives can be seen especially clearly when you look at the timing of both. While the word "nation" appeared in many languages, including English, before the end of the eighteenth century, it then came to be used as we do today—for a group of people larger than a known list, bound together through shared identity.[6] At this same time, private collections were becoming public museums across Europe. Such a confluence was not mere historical coincidence. Public displays of national collections sustained and built fledgling national identity, which in turn encouraged the idea that nations should have national museums, and the two continued hand in hand.[7]

All of this is true in a general sense, but to get a particular idea of how museum objects craft national museum stories, which create and sustain national identity, I look to Scotland as a compelling example. The National Museum of Scotland is at once both old and new. Its founding collection and founding curators date back to 1780, when the Society of Antiquaries of Scotland began. However, the building itself, and the first government recognition for a museum of Scottish national history, did not come until 1997. The museum has continued to grow since then.

The history of the "national" museum is also intertwined with that of a wider industrial museum. Many new Scottish industrial products had been shown at the Great Exhibition of 1851 in London. Once the initial excitement over the exhibition waned, thoughts turned to creating a permanent, similar institution in Edinburgh to continue educating working-class Scots about the industrial arts. It opened in 1864 and was initially called the Industrial Museum of Scotland.[8] At first, it included substantial natural history collections and within a decade was renamed the Edinburgh Museum of Science and Art.[9] In 1904 it became the Royal Scottish Museum (RSM), by which point it encompassed artifacts from natural history, ethnography, and many other disciplines. There was never one overarching narrative and no concern with the particular history of the nation. This non-national, or indeed more universal, identity of the RSM remained and was even strengthened after the creation of the Museum of Scotland. Anything not directly related to the history of Scotland in the collections of the museum created by the Society of Antiquaries of Scotland, known as the National Museum of Antiquities of Scotland, had been transferred to the depositories of the RSM, and vice versa, after the 1985 formation of the overarching corporate organization known as the National Museums of Scotland, which amalgamated the National Museum of Antiquities of Scotland and the Royal Scottish Museum under the one national umbrella. By the opening of the Museum of Scotland in 1998, this universal/national spilt had been embedded in the stones of the new dual building. The words "The World to Scotland—Scotland to the World" were carved into a circular stone placed at the threshold between the old museum building, which housed what was by then known as the Royal Museum, and the new Museum of Scotland.[10] Visitors would pass back and forth between the two, literally stepping over the difference in approaches between the two spaces.

However, in 2006 that difference was erased in nomenclature, as the whole structure on Chambers Street was given the new name "National Museum of Scotland" and the Royal Museum and Museum of Scotland names were removed. Much of the former Royal Museum was then closed for major refurbishment, as part of what would be called the Royal Museum Master Plan, a fifteen-year-long, £80-billion project, which was first unveiled in 2004. The grand opening of the new, reimagined National Museum building occurred on July 29, 2011. The first, and largest, stage of the project provided new ground-level access to the former Royal Museum and rehung ten galleries to "make more explicit the connections between the international collections and pioneering Scots who collected, created, and acquired them, and the relationship between the new displays and those in the Museum of Scotland building."[11] The project continues, with galleries in the former Royal Museum space being rehung and reopened every few years. The last few—in East Asia and Ancient Egypt—are scheduled to open in 2018–19.[12]

From 1780 until now, the National Museum has repeatedly changed its name, its mission, and how it thought of Scotland. Thus, this institution provides a canvas on which to analyze the ways that museum exhibitions, made of varying arrangements of artifacts, reflect changing national identities. It is not only the National Museum of Scotland that evolved from 1780 until the present day. Scottish nationalism as well has undergone shifts during this time. Each of these changes has been reflected in the exhibitions put on, the artifacts chosen to star in them, and the museum as a whole. Looking at the curatorial intent behind each of the changed exhibitions helps to illuminate the process by which events outside the museum influence decisions inside the museum. This book looks at a series of moments in the life of a complicated museum, where objects, the exhibitions they were in, and the nation where it happened all intertwined. The fight for a national museum helped Scottishness, and increased Scottishness can be seen in the changed museum.

Focusing on curatorial intent, rather than visitor perception and reception theory, is important in this case for several reasons. First, it adds an important and overlooked perspective to our understanding of the function of museums. Second, and perhaps even more importantly, it helps to illuminate the series of active decisions that are made every time an object is labeled, displayed, or moved.

As visitors or observers, we tend to think that museums are static spaces. Metaphors of the museum as "attic" or "treasure trove" reinforce this idea of unchanging dustiness where objective historical truth is displayed. However, everything that is displayed in a museum is the result of dynamic choices and shifting social, political, and economic circumstances both within and outside the museum walls. So, looking at the ways in which the exhibitions at the National Museum of Scotland have altered over time can show how the often-volatile national context outside influenced national narratives within.

The more than two-hundred-year life of the National Museum also demonstrates how major museums operate within an international network. They learn from each other, loan artifacts and whole exhibitions to each other, and partner with each other. This is important because this process allows us to see how the narratives of national objects are altered when they are displayed outside their normal context. It also shows the trends in museum display at a given time—an important but underexamined consideration. Finally, it allows us to look at the politics of museum partnerships. How are they established, and how do they mirror or challenge national politics?

In order to fully understand the interplay of nationalism politics and the museum, this book looks at Scotland and its museum at multiple levels. First we must consider the level of the individual object and its story since the foundation of the museum is its artifacts. Next we must understand the level of the exhibitions, which are created from those objects and how they change over time. Finally, we must examine the museum itself and how it is named, housed, funded, and recognized by the Scottish nation and the larger British state.

Scotland

Scotland has long had a unique, and changing, relationship to the British state. In the medieval and early modern period it was a separate kingdom that just happened to occupy the northernmost third of what we now consider the island of Great Britain. Its primary trading and cultural links were with Scandinavia and the European continent rather than England. This began to change in 1603, when Elizabeth I of England died without an heir, leaving James VI, who was already king of Scotland—and the son of Elizabeth's cousin Mary Stewart—to become James I of England as well. The Union of the Crowns was the first move in the slow unification of the two countries, but nothing really changed in this first step other than to heighten latent Catholic-Protestant tensions in Scotland.[13] James was a Protestant, which is why he could be king of England, but his mother, Mary, had been a devout Catholic, and many of her Scottish supporters took her son's defection from the church, and the country, badly.

In 1707 Scotland ceased to exist as an independent state. However, unlike other sections of the United Kingdom, such as Wales or Ireland, Scotland chose union. Or at least the elites and aristocracy did, after weighing the benefits of being part of the larger British economy, military, and especially the growing British Empire. Scottish leaders negotiated a deal wherein

Scotland would give up its parliament and military but keep its own system of education, church, legal system, and banks. This negotiation was different from colonization and allowed for the maintenance of a level of Scottish identity manifest through civil institutions that is usually not seen without a full state.[14]

While in general the Union was seen as beneficial, especially to those sons of middle-class Scots who now took well-paying jobs overseas with the empire, there was still lingering resentment with the absence of Catholic leadership. The last Catholic monarch, Mary Stewart (also known as Mary, Queen of Scots), had not merely died; she had been plotted against, imprisoned, and eventually beheaded. There was a faction in Scotland, which grew after 1707, who felt that members of the Stewart dynasty were the only true leaders of Scotland. These were known as the Jacobites.

Popular culture has sometimes portrayed the Jacobites as nationalists, but even the longest and most all-encompassing of the Jacobite rebellions—known as the "Rising" or the "Forty-Five," which continued from July 1745 to April 1746—pitted Catholic Scottish Highlanders against Protestant Scottish and English military officers. This was a fight over religion and regionalism, not Scottish national identity.

Charles Edward Stewart landed in Glenfinnan, on the west coast of Scotland, to retake his "rightful" throne on August 19, 1745. He gradually gathered the support of sympathetic Catholic Highlanders. At first the campaign was a success, although Stewart was not a natural commander. The Jacobite army made their way to Edinburgh and then south of the Scottish border to Derby on December 4 before facing any serious resistance. The British were not expecting a real fight from the ragtag Jacobites, but once the Scots crossed Hadrian's Wall, which was traditionally, if not legally, considered the border between England and Scotland, the British reconsidered.[15]

By April 16, 1746, the Jacobites had been chased back to the desolate surroundings of Culloden Moor, in the Northwest Highlands. The majority of the remaining fighters were malnourished, and many had deserted what by that point seemed a losing cause. Those who were left were slaughtered on the moor by the British forces. Meanwhile their prospective leader, Charles Edward Stewart, watched some of the action from behind the lines while picnicking before making a hasty exit to Europe, dressed as a peasant woman. The Jacobite dream was over for good.

It was after this defeat that "Scottishness" as we know it today really began—from opposition. It is often easier to define what you are through what you are not, and the implementation by the end of 1746 of what were known as the King's Laws served that purpose. The Act of Proscription banned Highlanders from possessing weapons, the Dress Act outlawed the "wearing of Highland Dress," and the Heritable Jurisdictions Act eliminated the inherited feudal power of Highland chiefs.[16] With these new laws, the British government attempted to clarify what was "civilized" Britishness and what was "savage" Scottishness. In doing so, however, they also identified an easy set of signifiers for anything different from Britishness. The authorities moved what had been just the territory of those on the edge of the nation, the Highlanders, to that of the majority and made it stand for the whole.[17]

As the laws remained in place but the brutality of the Jacobite rebellion faded, the lure of the forbidden made these things romantic and tempting—and useful. Scottish soldiers soon filled much of the growing British Army, and they identified themselves with their regimental tartans. They were especially sought after for so-called rough postings because of their supposed martial spirit and hardy fighting nature. As long as the fighting was in the service of Britain, it was welcome—and draped in tartan.[18] This sense of a Scotland with a unique identity within a larger Britain is what Graeme Morton calls "unionist nationalism."[19] It is also what the supporters of the original Union of the Parliaments envisioned when they negotiated to maintain Scottish law, education, religion, and banking while merging other powers.

Unionist Nationalism on the Streets

By the late 1700s the government-sponsored bodies of Scottish identity were doing well. Scottish universities were drawing students from across Europe as Edinburgh became a center of Enlightenment philosophy and thought. Scottish banks and law were similarly centers of excellence, and the Scottish church maintained its separation from the Church of England. But what of that indefinable essence of nationhood? What about national history and material culture?

On November 14, 1780, David Stewart Erskine, Eleventh Earl of Buchan, called together a select group of Edinburgh elites for an extraordinary meeting at his house destined to address these issues.[20] Once the crowd was assembled, the earl read to them his meticulously prepared *Discourse Delivered at a Meeting for the Purpose of Promoting the Institution of a Society for the Investigation of the History of Scotland and Its Antiquities*. In this he lamented the lack of a "regular society for promoting antiquarian researches . . . in this part of Great Britain."[21] He wanted to start one, spurred on by what he saw as an unacceptable lack of attention to Scottish "relics," which were leaving the country and being sold to foreigners both English and other. He had much to say about the presence of a similar society in London from 1707, and was anxious that Scotland not fall behind or cause all of its antiquaries and collectors to engage solely with the southern society.[22] Erskine also mentioned that there had been several attempts to create a society in Scotland, some as early as 1572, but that each had dissolved prior to gaining a royal charter. He suspected that these early societies "failed on account of their having no house in property, nor any private interests to care for their books, museum, and other necessary appurtances; and that having met in taverns, their meetings degenerated into convivial and anomalous conversations."[23] It was clear that the earl had in mind a much more serious affair than those that had come before.

In his *Discourse* the earl spoke of several motivations for forming the society at this particular time. First, he talked of the interest in Scottish antiquity across Europe due to the current popularity of the poems of Ossian. These fragments of supposedly ancient epic ballads of the Highland chief Ossian and his son Fingal were great favorites with the leaders of Europe in the 1760s, and the earl refers to them admiringly as artifacts of Scottish history and tradition.[24] The Ossianic fashion served to highlight the wealth of interest that could be evoked by the Scottish past. He also wished to correct previous scholars of the past, usually monks, and save the scarce remnants of vanishing civilizations. William Smellie, one of the first members of the new society and the first curator of its collections, gave a few other reasons for the timing of the foundation in his edited version of Erskine's remarks. Smellie noted that "till we were happily united with England, not in government only, but in loyalty and affection to a common sovereign, it was not, perhaps, altogether consistent with political wisdom, to call attention of the Scots to the ancient honors and constitution of their independent monarchy. Not many years have elapsed since the jealousies of the two nations were succeeded by a warm and mutual attachment to the same family and constitution."[25]

Scottish history, having been leveraged powerfully by the Jacobites not much earlier, had become a fraught field of study. However, by the 1780s Smellie and others believed that the divisions of the recent past were healed enough to allow academic, rather than pointedly political, interest in the past. The earl hoped that his incarnation of the Antiquarian Society would concern itself with the whole body of antiquarian studies. He saw the society and its museum as a way to study "public virtue and national utility."[26] This distinctive Scottish identity, however, could only be accepted widely after the Union with England had been solidified. Now that the present situation of Scotland was settled, and the Jacobite risings had been definitively crushed, men like the Earl of Buchan could afford to celebrate the past.

After hearing the earl's *Discourse*, the crowd agreed that there should be a further meeting on November 28, 1780, and at a third meeting on December 18 the Society of Antiquaries of Scotland was formally constituted. They have been running ever since.[27] Almost immediately the members of the society began collecting whatever objects people were willing to give them, and the earl went on a hunt for a space in which to display the fledgling collection.[28] Some sort of museum of Scottish history was born.

Toward a Public Institution

For years the Society of Antiquaries and its museum stumbled from house to house in Edinburgh, trying to find a permanent home. The collections expanded, but display space and public access were severely limited and little work was put into cataloguing or examining the contents of the collections. Curators were by and large amateur enthusiasts with other primary employment, and their pay and length of tenure reflected this. However, in the middle of the nineteenth century—the heyday for museums of national history across the world—the museum in Scotland changed. The society had started as a private association, but by the early 1840s, it had begun petitioning the British government for grants and public recognition, continuing to do so at regular intervals despite continual rejections. It was thought that governmental support would shore up the shaky finances of the society while also letting them take on a stronger public role. The museum was becoming increasingly popular with the public, welcoming four thousand people in 1841 and more in the following year, including Prince Albert himself.[29] Gradually, however, the feeling grew in the society that it was not just government funding they should be seeking but a wholesale movement of the collections to public and state control.

By 1848 the society was campaigning hard for a place in a new building being planned for the foot of the Mound in the center of Edinburgh.[30] The Mound is the entryway to public Edinburgh, where the medieval and Reformation-era Old Town meet the neoclassical and Georgian New Town. It is an artificial hill constructed of debris removed when the Nor' Loch was drained to build Princes Street Gardens and is a symbol of the Enlightenment improvements that led Edinburgh to be called the "Athens of the North." A home here would give the Antiquarian Society and their museum legitimacy and embed them in the physical space that was being created to reflect the intellectual conversations of the time. The Edinburgh New Town, now a UNESCO World Heritage Site, was built in stages between 1767 and 1890 and is seen as one of the first urban planning projects.[31]

The society wanted to move to this overtly public and established building not only for reasons of rent and space but also because their presence would signify that the museum enterprise had moved beyond a private endeavor into something that had benefits for the whole of a much larger society. As the building on the Mound was also to host the National Gallery, the ties of shared space would raise in status the museum of the Society of Antiquaries above some of the competing museum projects in Edinburgh at that time. Institutions such as the museum of the Royal Society and the collections of the University of Edinburgh were long adversaries of the Society of Antiquaries, and being able to claim space next to the National Gallery would have strengthened the antiquarians' claim to the preeminent museum in the city and nation.

The Society of Antiquaries had expressed their displeasure at being unable to secure government funding for a permanent museum in 1844, when they wrote that they considered "the refusal of their application . . . as a slight offered to Scotland and they cannot help comparing the support which scientific institutions in Scotland receive from the government with the munificent grants made to those in England, and still more so to those in Ireland."[32] The society members believed that Scottish nationhood, as seen through its material culture and history, should be supported by the British government.

By this point there was no longer any apparent threat of Scottish separatism. In fact, King George IV himself had made a triumphant visit to Edinburgh in 1822, where he wore a full tartan suit and was greeted by all the Scottish elites in their kilted best.[33] Twenty years later, Queen Victoria bought her Highland retreat, Balmoral Castle, and ignited a trend for all things "Highland."[34] The Society of Antiquaries, however, would continue asking for government support for the museum for years to come, and they would continue to be ignored.

To further bolster their case for national status, the Society of Antiquaries turned to Daniel Wilson, an artist and archaeologist who had been recently elected to the society. He took charge of the collections, attempting the first comprehensive and scientific cataloguing of the contents. There had long been links between the Society of Antiquaries of Scotland and similar groups in the Scandinavian countries. Grimur Thorkelin, an important Icelandic scholar, had been a correspondent and friend of the Earl of Buchan starting in 1783, a relationship that led to ongoing dialogue between the two and multiple trips to visit and compare artifacts and museums.[35]

This pattern of scholarly antiquarian connection outlived the earl and continued to develop into the late nineteenth century. Members of the Society of Antiquaries of Scotland were especially interested in the building of the Danish National Museum of Antiquity, which opened in 1819. Scandinavian archaeologists Christian Thomsen and Jens Worsaae developed a theory of "seriation" to categorize museum artifacts.[36] Their tripartite division of objects into categories of Iron Age, Stone Age, and Bronze Age allowed what they believed to be the natural evolution of human society to be seen most clearly.

First curator of the National Museum of Antiquities Daniel Wilson admired the Scandinavian system and agreed with its theories of evolution. However, the system was meant purely for prehistoric artifacts and thus did not accommodate many of the objects in the society's holdings, such as a "Maiden" beheading machine given to the society in 1797. This fearsome object is an early form of guillotine that was in use for public executions in Edinburgh from 1564 to 1710. Therefore the schema had to be expanded somewhat, and Wilson became increasingly interested in the social basis of objects—and especially in the importance of comparison among cultures and times. He thus catalogued every object by its intended use and home location, as well as the underlying tripartite division, which he soon expanded to take on other categories of materials and 'ages' of history.[37]

The final product of this work, the *Synopsis of the Museum of the Society of Antiquaries of Scotland*, was completed in 1849 and distributed to all members of the society, as well as sold in the museum. Two special copies were sent to Balmoral for Queen Victoria and Prince Albert.[38] The catalogue was also printed in the first volume of the *Proceedings of the Society of Antiquaries of Scotland* in 1852. There it was joined by a list of what was known to be coming into the collections in the near future and several articles on the state of archaeological research in Scotland.[39] The creation of the catalogue and the *Proceedings* served to emphasize the national scope of the collections and its importance to the people of Scotland and the United Kingdom as a whole.

A National Museum?

In part, this mission to secure new housing and increased public support was successful, and in 1851 the Society of Antiquaries was offered rent-free accommodation in the Royal Institution building (now the Royal Scottish Academy) at the foot of the Mound on Princes Street. A year later, it also finally received state recognition. With that, the collections moved to the jurisdiction of the government and Scotland had, for the first time, a national museum. When the museum finally opened in its new quarters in 1859, it was under a new name, or names: formally it was the National Museum of Antiquities of Scotland, though it was also known as the Museum of Antiquities, and was most commonly referred to as the Antiquarian Museum.[40]

Names of museums tell observers much about how an institution is being framed for the public, and through that, something about which narratives are going to be given priority within its exhibition space. Changes in naming often reflect changes in status and role for a museum within the national context, and looking at how a museum is titled at any moment in time can show which aspects of itself the nation is choosing to make most public. This first attempt at naming the collection of Scottish historical artifacts was especially critical, however, merely because it *was* the first.

Previously the museum had been without an official title. It had been commonly known as the museum of the Society of Antiquaries of Scotland, largely in order to separate it from the other major Edinburgh institution, the Chambers Street museum of the Royal Society of Edinburgh. This name, unofficial as it was, reveals how the museum was seen at the time—as the auxiliary activity of a scholarly association. It could remain under that name regardless of which location it moved to, as it was the society that was important, rather than the museum or its contents.

However, with national control and the move to a recognized and iconic new home, the museum began to exist as an institution. It was connected to, and yet separate from, the society that had inspired it. The new name helped to cement the idea of the museum as a national institution and to give it an identity that was more public and widely accessible, as well as allowing it to emulate other European museums of the time in London, Paris, and elsewhere.[41] London's British Museum, the Louvre in Paris, Washington, DC's Smithsonian Institution, and the State Hermitage Museum in Russia all used simple, declarative names that tied them to a place or a donor, not to a scholarly organization. The Antiquarians were well-traveled men, and they knew the worldwide museum context in which they operated.

But was this yet a national museum, just because it was controlled by the government and accessible to the public? In 1891 the National Museum of Antiquities of Scotland moved into their biggest and most permanent home to-date, the newly built Findlay Building. This ornate red brick building in the heart of the modern New Town of Edinburgh was built in 1889 by the newspaper baron John Richie Findlay. He wanted to support the creation of a National Portrait Gallery but was also a member of the Society of Antiquaries, so he recommended that the space be split between the two museums. Thus, by 1891 the Findlay building held the National Portrait Gallery and the National Museum of Antiquities of Scotland. By this point the museum had some level of British government funding, had been around in Scotland for two centuries—most recently in very prominent, historically and culturally important locations—and was calling itself a national institution. However, there was never a sense of the National Museum of Antiquities using its collections to say anything about the particular history of Scotland, even when it received its new home and new, national naming. Instead, it clung to the tripartite divisions and anthropological comparison of Daniel Wilson. The museum also kept to the longstanding policy of collecting everything and anything it could.

The naming of the place echoed these ideas. The National Museum of Antiquities of Scotland was a solid official title but also hid many ambiguities. As the collection turned into the twentieth century, it was a *national* museum and it was the museum of *antiquities*, not the museum of the nation. The institution was being presented as the museum of a collection, rather than that of an idea or a community. There was no cohesive narrative of Scottishness within the collection presented but rather a constellation of separate artifacts.

Benedict Anderson has written that "museums and the museumizing imagination are profoundly political."[42] Only when the story of the nation has been put into a form where the average people who make up the nation can see it, and see themselves in it, can the nation truly exist. Thus, the act of negotiating which particular narratives will be in a museum is an act of nation-creation, and the school trips and Sunday jaunts around the galleries are ways in which identity is solidified.[43] Because the time of nation-building overlapped so closely with the zenith of the formation of national museums, we have come to believe that a national history museum is, in the words of one curator, "something that should be part of any civilized nation's approach to its history and their culture."[44] In this world where national identity and national states are so normal as to be nearly unnoticeable, there are a series of necessary symbols of the nation. The museum, like the national assembly and flag, is one of these.[45]

This was worrying to the increasingly vocal campaigners that were assembling outside the museum, looking for a more recognized Scottish nation. Although the British Museum is not a museum of Britain so much as a museum of the glories of British enterprise, other sub-state nationalisms within and without Britain had long presented their histories in material form to reinforce their claims of existence. By the twentieth century, Ireland and Wales had vibrant national museums supported by the British state.[46] Across Europe, other nations that would soon begin agitating for nation-state status had opened museums as first steps in their quest for international recognition. The Czechs, Hungarians, Serbs, and Poles were just some to see the power of collecting and displaying national historical narratives in order to solidify claims to self-determination. The National Museum in Prague was founded in 1818, and the Hungarian National Museum started slightly earlier, in 1807. Later in the century, the Serbian National Museum was founded in 1844, and the National Museum Krakow had followed in 1879.

This pattern of recognizing and institutionalizing national identity through the formal building of a national museum developed over the nineteenth century throughout Europe. Scotland had long been deeply embedded in a European social and cultural context because of its central role in the Enlightenment, so cultural and political figures were well aware of events across the continent. By the twentieth century, Scots were more than ready to start using their long history of collecting to do some political agitating. The gentle statements of nineteenth-century antiquarians might not be enough anymore. Add to that, two major museums in one space got cramped quite quickly. Formal complaints by curatorial staff and institutional supporters about a lack of space for the proper display of objects in the National Museum of Antiquities of Scotland were presented to the government in 1929, 1951, 1981, and 1985, and informal murmurings about the same were a constant presence around Edinburgh.

So, what happened with those complaints? A brand-new, purpose-built National Museum of Scotland did finally open in 1997, but how did we get there, and where did things go from there? It is very rare to have a new national museum open in the end of the twentieth century. What forces inspired this story? What were the intertwining threads of material culture, museum exhibitions, and Scottish national identity politics that led to this new institution?

1
The Smithsonian Inspires
1984

Artifacts are central to how national museums create and recreate narratives for public consumption. Most often we think of these artifacts as being displayed in permanent exhibitions in their home nations, very rarely, if ever, changing. However, the temporary exhibition (an exhibition that is on display only for a limited time) and the traveling exhibition (one that goes from institution to institution) can offer extended opportunities for new artifactual narratives. Sometimes exhibitions can be used for other reasons as well.

Perhaps oddly, the place to start this story is in the United States with a book called *Treasures of the Smithsonian*. This book, published by the Smithsonian Institution Press, highlights all the best parts of the Smithsonian collections.[1] In essence, the book serves as a blueprint to an exhibition. In the early 1980s, as Scottish curators and campaigners were trying to fight for their own national museum, they decided to host a "blockbuster" traveling show from the United States in order to demonstrate what could be done by a well-supported national museum service. The 1983 book, through a series of interwoven coincidences, big personalities, and lots of effort, became the temporary show *Treasures from the Smithsonian Institution at the Royal Scottish Museum,* which was seen in Edinburgh between August and November 1984.

Creating a Blockbuster

As of April 2017 the Smithsonian Institution comprises nineteen distinct museums and galleries, and one zoological park, which together make up America's national museum service.[2] The majority of the Smithsonian museums are arranged around a strip of land between the Washington Monument and the Capitol Building in Washington, DC, known as the National Mall. The museums are colloquially known as "America's Attic" or "America's Treasure Chest," sobriquets that the institution itself embraces.[3] The objects, now numbering in the many millions held by various corners of the Smithsonian, vary from famous works of art to natural history specimens, relics of exploration to frontiers of land and space, and items of national and global historical import. Items from all these categories came to Scotland under the auspices of *Treasures from the Smithsonian*. During its four-month run the exhibit had 100,000 visitors and was considered one of the centerpieces of the Edinburgh International Festival that year.[4] Tracing how, and why, a collection of 260 objects were chosen, transported, and displayed in the rapid space of seven months—from an initial call in January 1984 through opening on August 11—illuminates the political pressures present in 1984. The fact that this exhibition was held at the Royal Scottish Museum also helps demonstrate some of the complications of the museum world in Edinburgh.

The Royal Scottish Museum is a place of many names. It was founded in 1855 as the Industrial Museum of Scotland, inspired, as many world museums were, by the Great Exhibition at the Crystal Palace in London in 1851. In 1864, before opening, the museum was renamed the Museum of Science and Art. It finally opened in May 1866. In 1904 it became the Royal Scottish Museum, also known as the Royal Museum of Scotland. Throughout this transition, though, the public seems to have generally referred to the museum as the "Scottish Museum" or the "Chamber's Street Museum" for its perceived contents and its location in the city.[5]

The Appeal of the Temporary Exhibition

Visitor figures show that more people visit large national museums for the first time during a temporary exhibition than at any other time.[6] This is true at the National Museum of Scotland as well as at other similar museums.[7] Such mass appeal can be a great benefit for museums. The host institution gets increased attention, as does the lending institution. These exhibits allow flexibility, so that displays and their intended messages can be changed to suit particular predicted audiences, a feature that is often lacking in permanent installations. Temporary exhibitions can also address topical issues, as they are only expected to last for a few months. These multiple layers of flexibility make the temporary exhibition a good forum for using objects to elucidate specific cultural points.

Usually it is the host or lender of the exhibition who uses the temporary exhibition to show a different side to the artifacts, and through them perhaps a different culture or idea.[8] However, because of another other cultural force associated with *Treasures from the Smithsonian Institution*—the Edinburgh International Festival—a third view was additionally being imposed onto the artifacts. Frank Dunlop, the director of the festival, told an American newspaper that he had asked the Smithsonian to participate because "I want to show Europeans, who tend to think there is no American culture, how wrong they were, how many good things existed."[9] There were, therefore, three levels of expectation and narrative imposed on *Treasures from the Smithsonian*. The lender wanted to showcase the "diversity" of its collections, the festival wanted to say something about the wealth of American culture, and the host, the Royal Scottish Museum (RSM), wanted to promote itself as an internationally important institution. The first two goals were fairly easily met by the shape and contents of the exhibition itself. The third, in both its reasoning and fulfillment, was harder to achieve and assess.

The temporary exhibition of American artifacts in the RSM reveals the power of such exhibitions to confer legitimacy.

Because of the larger shadow cast by the Smithsonian Institution, the RSM gained attention and prominence both nationally and internationally. The Smithsonian benefited as well, of course, but the most important beneficiary was the RSM and, more significantly, the idea of internationally important museums in Scotland. Although the RSM called itself the "largest comprehensive museum in Europe" when filling out a facilities report for the Smithsonian prior to being approved as a host institution, within Scotland and the United Kingdom its presence and mission had long been overshadowed by the London museums.[10]

In the early 1980s Scotland was only just beginning to actively define itself as "different" from the rest of Great Britain. Beginning with her election in 1979, Prime Minister Margaret Thatcher's administration had provoked distinctly different voting patterns in Scotland than in the rest of the country. In the 1979 election, Scotland voted 31 percent Conservative compared to the rest of the country's 44 percent, and the discrepancy worsened in the following elections. By 1983 Scotland gave the Conservatives only 28 percent to the whole's 46 percent, and in Thatcher's last term it was down to 26 percent compared to 46 percent nationally.[11] As support for the Conservative Party waned, the Scottish National Party gained a larger voice in politics. The discovery of oil in the Scottish North Sea had raised the prospect of economic independence, and the Scottish National Party was quick to capitalize on anti-Thatcher feeling, with signs at rallies proclaiming, "It's Scotland's Oil." The feeling of misuse only grew when the British government began levying a new poll tax in Scotland a year before enacting it in the rest of the country. All of these forces, among many others, made the 1980s a time when Scots began to see themselves in a new light.[12]

Bringing an internationally important exhibition—one that had been designed particularly for Edinburgh and was going to be seen nowhere else—was a cultural coup that helped the RSM stake a claim to a national recognition equal to that of London-based museums. The presence of objects normally associated with more internationally known institutions imbued the halls of the RSM with some of their aura. Important museum artifacts routinely bring their power with them in this way. Once they have entered into the rarefied world of the museum they have an authority that remains with them even outside their normal spatial context. By being able to show these famous artifacts off, the RSM got some of their "star power" for a while. Being able to attract a major exhibition such as this one may have also helped strengthen the ongoing negotiations between Scottish and British authorities over the issue of a national museum for Scotland. Although conversations about this topic had been occurring sporadically since the eighteenth century, the question took on new weight in the Thatcher era with the resurgence of Scottish nationalism and general dissatisfaction with British governance. Funds for a new home for the Scottish collections were promised but then pulled in 1976 because of cuts to public spending across the country.[13]

Official reports of the RSM assert that there was a "delegation from Washington who proposed to bring a major exhibition from the Smithsonian to Scotland" in January 1984.[14] At the same time a change in direction at the Edinburgh International Festival, then in its thirty-seventh year, took place. Frank Dunlop had been appointed as the new director to shed the previously stuffy, elitist air of the festival and attract shows that were more geared to a populist audience. This may explain why the exhibition catalogue claims the exhibition came about after a call from Dunlop to the Smithsonian, in contrast to the RSM's report, with the RSM only becoming involved later.[15] The catalogue narrative omits some intriguing details and obscures the complicated dialogue that surely led to the connections between America and Scotland.

Some of these connections are embedded in the fabric of the Smithsonian and were used to justify the exhibition. The official institutional review of the exhibition notes, "In 1784, James Smithson, benefactor of the institution which bears his name, travelled to Scotland at the suggestion of Benjamin Franklin. The decision to bring 'Treasures of the Smithsonian Institution' to Edinburgh *could be* seen as a bicentennial celebration of this event."[16]

There is a nice symmetry in this logic, and such an anniversary seems worth celebrating with an event to further connect two nations. However, the use of "could be" is slightly mystifying. Another official review, intended for the wider public's eyes, put forth this bicentenary idea more strongly, as did many media reports. One in particular even expanded the story, and with it the sense of connection and indebtedness between the Smithsonian and Edinburgh. It reported, "It's 200 years since the British scientist James Smithson visited Edinburgh and then followed Boswell's walk through the Highlands, William Thornton, future architect of Washington's Capitol by his side. Smithson never visited America, but it's felt that Thornton was among those who influenced him to bequeath his fortune to founding the Smithsonian."[17]

Interestingly, however, there is no mention of this supposedly critical bicentenary in the exhibition catalogue or any other official publications, beyond media reports. In fact, though many newspaper articles do mention the Smithson visit to Scotland, some observers were less than happy about the neat justification.[18] The London *Times* ran a very positive review of the exhibition several days after it opened but began the article by sliding in some sly comments, saying that "the excuse for it [the exhibition] is, rather flimsily, the Bicentenary of James Smithson's visit to Edinburgh."[19]

The Smithsonian's own publications presented the Smithson story as more of an interesting aside to an exhibition already fated to happen anyway, saying, for example, that "a Smithsonian Institution link was found in an expedition to Edinburgh and the Highlands made 200 years ago by a group of scientists, including young James Smithson, the English chemist whose bequest served to create the Institution."[20] Even the press release issued by the Smithsonian to announce the exhibition made a more casual link between the bicentennial and exhibition, quoting its director as saying, "It seems especially appropriate that this year, on the two-hundredth anniversary of our founder James Smithson's visit to Edinburgh, that the Smithsonian, the national museum of the United States, participate in this international arts festival."[21]

This made it sound as if it was just fortuitous timing—and indeed, that was probably the case. However, museum officials are increasingly responsible for marketing their museums and exhibitions, and the Smithson story was marketing gold. It strengthened the connections between loan and host exhibition and set up a history of shared culture that increased the value of sending American objects to Scotland. Even Queen Elizabeth received a version of the story when the secretary of the Smithsonian wrote to ask for the pleasure of her company at various events. For Her Majesty, Ripley expanded the story, writing that James Smithson had traveled in Scotland with William Thornton, later to be the designer of the U.S. Capitol, and a French abbé as tutor. Benjamin Franklin had recommended the abbé to the men when they met him in Paris.[22] The RSM press release expanded the details, saying that the men were "encouraged by Benjamin Franklin to have some first-hand experience of the country whose name was associated with enlightenment."[23] These stories seem to be factually true, but the ways in which different versions were used to frame the exhibition can show the complex links between luck and reason that combine in creating a temporary exhibition.[24]

While the chronological coincidence of James Smithson's trip to Scotland provided some impetus to the exhibition, it also came out of a complex interplay of political forces within neither the host nor loan institution but rather the largely silent third partner in the enterprise, the Edinburgh International Festival. The festival was started in 1947 to enrich cultural life in Britain and has been, and remains, a major source of tourism income for the city and Scotland in general.[25] However, by the early 1980s the organizers fielded increasing complaints that the festival had become too elitist and had betrayed its root mission to expose the whole of the population to culture.

Frank Dunlop was appointed the head of the Edinburgh International Festival in the summer of 1983. He was asked to take the festival in some new directions, reinvigorate its programs, and hopefully eliminate concerns about elitism. Shortly after his appointment, Dunlop sent a letter to S. Dillon Ripley, then the director of the Smithsonian Institution. In this, Dunlop introduced himself then moved on to the main point: he had heard that the Smithsonian might want to have a first international traveling exhibition and could he offer Edinburgh as a venue? He outlined the ways in which the Edinburgh International Festival would provide everything that the Smithsonian desired in an exhibition venue, and how their presence would be of mutual benefit.[26] This was an important voicing of the power differential between Edinburgh and the Smithsonian. As the much larger partner in any potential joint venture, the Smithsonian had to be reassured that they would not be lowering their status by participating. This is a theme that reappeared repeatedly over the course of planning, mounting, and analyzing the exhibition.

Links between the United States and Britain had also been strengthened because of the personal friendship and ideological agreement between President Ronald Reagan and Margaret Thatcher. There was also a general U.S. desire to continue building bridges with Western Europe at the height of the Cold War. Given this, the Smithsonian's venture to Edinburgh fit in well with events in both nations and advanced goals on both sides of the Atlantic.

The Smithsonian was happy to increase their international and European profile, the International Festival wanted a large and crowd-pleasing central exhibition, and there was the fortuitous matter of James Smithson's Scottish trip. However, there was also a less obvious reason for the show's staging in Edinburgh, one both monetary and personal. This involved the wishes of an American philanthropist, Arthur M. Sackler. He was a successful physician and an avid collector of Asian art and artifacts. He routinely lent objects from his collections to the Smithsonian; right before his death in 1987, his whole collection was donated to the institution, where it now forms the nucleus of the Arthur M. Sackler Gallery.

Understandably, in the early 1980s the Smithsonian Institution authorities were courting Sackler and were consequently open to his suggestions. It seems that he was acquainted with Frank Dunlop and fond of Edinburgh in general. Thus, he supported the idea of a partnership between the Smithsonian and the festival, and when the exhibition was announced, he donated, or arranged for the donation of, much of the money from private and corporate sponsors that allowed *Treasures from the Smithsonian Institution* to be presented free of charge. Sackler and Dunlop worked together to get the exhibition off the ground, and Sackler was quoted as saying that he hoped for further collaboration between the RSM, the Smithsonian Institution, and his collections.[27] Indeed, the Sackler objects were prominently mentioned in many reviews of the exhibition.[28] Certainly Sackler's influence helped encourage the Smithsonian authorities to agree to the exhibition, which was much different than the large-scale traveling exhibitions they usually had created to that date.

After this first contact was made, the details of a proposed exhibition were gradually hammered out. Interestingly, the RSM was not the first choice for location. An internal memo from Ripley to his assistant director, Ralph Rinzler, shows that the Smithsonian officials were relying on Frank Dunlop to procure a hosting location and that a variety of sites—"either the Royal College of Art in the Grassmarket, or the Royal Academy of Art, Princes Street, or perhaps the Royal Scottish Museum (once again in the running)"—were all being considered.[29] It is unclear why the RSM had at first been discarded, as in the end it was deemed the only suitable space. Other venues had already committed their space for the festival or, as in the case of the briefly considered National Museum of Antiquities of Scotland, were thought "both less accessible and less prestigious" than the RSM.[30] In the end, the Smithsonian chose the RSM, and Ripley approached Norman Tebble, the museum director, about it. Ripley first explained the invitation from Dunlop and the proposed scope of the exhibition, before saying, "It occurs to us that it would be as appropriate as it would be eminently desirable if the exhibition could be mounted at the RSM."[31] A month later Ripley wrote to Frank Dunlop, finally formally accepting the invitation to produce a show for the Edinburgh International Festival.[32]

Building the Smithsonian Institution

In its eventual form and narrative, *Treasures from the Smithsonian Institution at the Royal Scottish Museum* echoed much of the

Smithsonian itself. The unique history of the institution and the role it plays in American cultural identity came with its objects to Edinburgh and were one of the components of its success there. The Smithsonian Institution began its life in 1826 when James Smithson left a bequest of $508,318.46 to the people of the United States. Smithson, born in 1765, was the illegitimate son of Hugh Smithson, later to become the Duke of Northumberland, and Elizabeth Keate Hungerford Macie, a widow with royal connections. In his younger years James Smithson was known as James Lewis Macie, and he kept this name until his mother's death in 1800. Afterward he adopted his father's surname. He was a distinguished chemist and mineralogist during his time at Oxford, and was also active in the intellectual and scientific life of London, becoming one of the youngest members of the Royal Society upon his election in 1787. He published at least twenty-seven scholarly scientific papers during his lifetime.[33]

When he died in Italy at the age of sixty-four he left his fortune to a nephew but with the caveat that if the nephew died childless, the money would go to "the United States of America, to found at Washington, under the name of the Smithsonian Institution, an Establishment for the increase and diffusion of knowledge among men."[34] Of course, in practice the endowment of a major cultural institution takes more than willing it to be so. The American government was unsure whether to accept the money in the first place, and when they finally decided to do so in August 1836, they had to battle in British courts against appeals from the mother of Smithson's nephew. U.S. President Andrew Jackson sent Richard Rush as the American delegate for the case, and Rush spent two years arguing in the Court of Chancery against a number of counter-claims from the various branches of Smithson's family.[35]

While the court battles were raging, arguments about the constitutionality—or lack thereof—of accepting the bequest went on back in the United States. In the mid-nineteenth century the United States still had a fairly weak central government, and the doctrine of "states' rights" was considered largely sacrosanct.[36] Therefore, the states, and the individual governments of the states, had more power in decision-making than did the federal government. By accepting a donation on behalf of the entire country, politicians were afraid that the power of the states would be undermined. However, in the end it was deemed constitutional by a committee in the House of Representatives, and Congress accepted the money.[37] In effect, accepting the money and pledging to create a new Smithsonian Institution was one of the first overtly national acts of government. Decisions like this helped solidify a sense of American nation-ness that gradually took over from smaller state or regional identities. Therefore, even before the form of the Smithsonian was decided, it was helping to symbolize American identity.

There was no wording in James Smithson's bequest that expressly designated what the Smithsonian Institution was to do, other than the oft-quoted "increase and diffusion of knowledge." So after the money was accepted and the court case in England won, there were still many details to clarify. Richard Rush collected all of Smithson's scientific collections, library, and research notes; sold off all his other goods; and had the proceeds made into gold sovereigns. Rush and his eleven chests of Smithson booty arrived in the United States in September 1838, and the money was transferred to the U.S. Treasury, yielding the sum that is considered the founding amount for the institution.[38]

In the beginning most scholars and politicians advocated the foundation of a national university—especially one with a focus on science and invention. There were few other models for a national institution to choose from, and this was seen as a way to honor Smithson's own interests by highlighting science learning and teaching. However, other voices fought for an institution of teacher training, or one centered on teaching the classics, so that the knowledge could not be used for military purposes. The discussion gradually widened, and in 1840 a group of politicians formed, calling themselves the National Institute for the Promotion of Science.[39] While they were eventually defeated by the lobbying of academic scientists disgruntled at political intrusion into their world, the National Institute members were the first to raise the idea of a national museum. They wanted to use the

Smithson bequest to showcase artifacts of the American past and its leaders, and to document the natural resources of North America as such items continued to be discovered. The politicians published a manifesto titled *A Plea for a National Museum and Botanic Garden to Be Founded on the Smithsonian Institution at the City of Washington* and presented it at a meeting of the Chester County, Pennsylvania, Cabinet of Natural Science on December 3, 1841.[40]

Between 1840 and 1846 the debate raged on, with suggestions including a national scientific institute, a national library, and a national observatory jostling with the ever-present national university in editorials, public speeches, and on the floor of Congress. Finally, on August 10, 1846, President James K. Polk signed "An Act to Establish the 'Smithsonian Institution' for the Increase and Diffusion of Knowledge among Men." It was an interesting compromise, as it included provisions for

> suitable rooms or halls for the reception and arrangement, upon a liberal scale, of objects of natural history, including a geological and mineralogical cabinet, also a chemistry laboratory, a library, a gallery of art, and the necessary lecture halls . . . all objects of art and of foreign and curious research, and all objects of natural history, plants, and geological and mineralogical specimens, belonging, or hereafter to belong, to the United States, which may be in the city of Washington, in whosesoever custody the same may be shall be delivered [to the Smithsonian] . . . and shall be arranged in such order and so classed, as best [to] facilitate the examination and study of them.[41]

This vague and amorphous definition allowed for at least something of what everyone wanted, while also leaving the shape of the institution flexible enough to handle future changes.[42]

Concepts and Contents

Thus the Smithsonian came to take its central role in American cultural life. It is from this collection and its vast store of information that a traveling exhibition was put together to go to

Edinburgh in 1984.[43] The previous year had seen the publication of a book titled *Treasures of the Smithsonian Institution*. This work brought together beautifully photographed visions of the "best" objects from across the collections, as well as a semi-scholarly look at the role of objects, and the Smithsonian, in American history and culture. The secretary of the Smithsonian, S. Dillon Ripley said in the foreword,

> The truth which lies in objects, so much better than in words, will out, but not necessarily today or even tomorrow . . . so this book of history, the tale of our "Treasures," embodies the perceived truth as seen at the time by those who have shaped the Smithsonian. . . . What could be better than to follow our mandate "for the increase and diffusion of knowledge among men" by telling and retelling this fascinating and evanescent story of how we grew, step by step, into the pyramid of learning represented by 135 years of trial-and-error learning about America and Americans.[44]

The objects selected for the book were meant to convey to the reader a sense of the institution and through that a sense of the nation. Just as at the beginning of its conception the institution helped to solidify national identity, so it continued, but on an increasingly accessible and popular level. The book presented the institution as the "keeper of the nation" but also tried hard to make clear that it was a nation for and of everyone, represented in its mix of collections from both "high" and "popular" cultures.

It was the process of creating the book that made it possible for an exhibition to be designed so quickly for the Edinburgh International Festival. Because objects from all over the institution had already been brought together for *Treasures of the Smithsonian*, it was easier than normal to gather them once again. Label and caption copy only had to be revised, rather than invented. The majority of the Scottish exhibition catalogue is from the earlier book, although it was decided in exhibition meetings that "text for the catalogue will not necessarily adhere to the objects chosen for the exhibition, nor will all illustrations necessarily be in the exhibition. Donald [McClelland, the exhibition coordinator] estimates a ratio of about 30 illustrations from the exhibition."[45] These changes reflected the different context of the exhibition catalogue in Scotland than in the United States; rather than just explaining the particular objects, the *Treasures from the Smithsonian* catalogue had to provide some of the history of the institution and the country it was representing, making it a catalogue with a firmer narrative structure than often seen in such volumes.

What Makes an American Icon?

The catalogue for *Treasures from the Smithsonian Institution at the Royal Scottish Museum* inserted more history and context for the objects and ideas profiled there than its precursor volume. However, the strength of the Edinburgh exhibition was that many of the "treasures" did not need any context in order to be understood. National museums continuously have to decide what makes the objects in their collections belong to that nation. Usually this justification revolves around an object's particular provenance—it can be national if it was used, built, or found in that nation. But the question of which nation can claim an artifact is a fraught one. Appeals for the return of disputed objects are often refuted by saying that certain objects are of general cultural importance and can thus be understood and appreciated by museum visitors whatever their national heritage. The Smithsonian National Museum of American History (NMAH) spends little time explaining the American-ness of any of its objects.[46] As with other large, national institutions, the implicit narrative is that these objects are obviously of the nation, simply because they are displayed within the space of that nation's museum. The larger cultural understanding of many of the most famous of these objects is strong enough to cope with this lack of stated provenance or national tie. Several of these types of objects made the trip to Edinburgh.

Among the objects selected for Edinburgh were the ruby slippers worn by Judy Garland in the 1939 film *The Wizard of Oz*. They had been obtained by an anonymous buyer at an MGM studio in 1970 for $15,000 and were donated to the museum in 1979. Several pairs were made for the film, and the two in the collection of the Smithsonian come from two separate original pairs, rather than having been made for each other. They are in worse condition than some of the other surviving pairs in the hands of private collectors but have always attracted considerable interest at the museum. In one catalogue they are called a "national icon swathed in the magic of its singular aura," and an academic essay posits that they have "become its own symbol, representing nothing so much as its iconic self."[47] When they were first displayed in the 1970s, they were meant to represent the start of the film industry; the technological and social advances in the *Wizard of Oz*, such as the development of color film; and the iconic place that film has taken on in the contemporary world.

Now in the United States they say more about the role of the Smithsonian in collecting the byproducts of American popular culture. The ruby slippers, like a few other objects (such as Kermit the Frog, the puppet from the children's television show *Sesame Street*), have become icons of the museum itself, as well as the ideas they originally were displayed to represent.[48] When in Scotland, and removed from that institutional context, the slippers served more as an object of pilgrimage and awe than as something that connected to any one national or museological idea. Especially in the context of the festival, the slippers were treated as an inspiration for performers and a "must-see" attraction, but spoke more about the international reach of celebrity and Hollywood films than anything particularly American.[49] This globalized narrative was well-suited to the goals of most of the players in *Treasures from the Smithsonian*, as Scottish and tourist audiences were excited to see them, could understand them without a large amount of text or other imposed contextual information, and also probably raised the profile of the Smithsonian in visitor's minds, even if visitors did not learn anything about American history or culture from viewing their display. Other objects more closely entwined in a specifically American discourse did not hold the attention of audiences in the same way.

It is surprising, given the slippers' rapturous review in the exhibition, how close they came to not being included at all. An early object list, which explains the exhibition by saying that "it forms a treasury of world art, history and science with an emphasis on America, through objects selected for their visual beauty and for their contribution to the natural order of life," made no mention of the ruby slippers among the sixty-five objects listed from the NMAH. It did make clear the missions of the exhibition, stating that "it is our hope that the Treasures exhibition will broaden the viewer's understanding of America, and that the objects on display reflect our shared heritage with that of Europe and will mark as well the contributions made by American artists and scientists to the intellectual development of mankind."[50] It seems perhaps that the ruby slippers did not fit the initial ideas of how to represent the contributions of Americans to the world's intellectual development.

The exhibition object list was assembled by asking directors and curators of the then-thirteen different Smithsonian museums to assemble lists of which objects in their collections matched the spirit and mission of the exhibition while also being hardy enough and portable enough to travel. These lists were then submitted to the Smithsonian Institution Traveling Exhibition Service (SITES) and the exhibition team. Mostly they were accepted without question or alteration. However, the curators of the exhibition seem to have wanted to expand the scope into less lofty territory and did this by approaching the NMAH for some of its more popular items.

In a letter, Donald McClelland, the head of the team, requested some objects that had not originally been included in object lists. Among these were the ruby slippers. He wrote, "You will note that to the requested loans from your collections a list of objects has been added that form a statement about Popular American culture. . . . I certainly agree that their inclusion in Treasures would add another dimension for Scotland. . . . The History Museum's loan list and the popular culture list form an important part to the Treasures exhibition. Each object makes a strong statement about our Institution, history, and way of life."[51] Popular culture, as represented through the ruby slippers, was considered to be iconicly American and to have treasure value. As such, they were worthy of inclusion in the exhibition, and perhaps even obligatory. No objections were raised, and a week later the ruby slippers were highlighted as one of the treasures set to come to the Royal Scottish Museum in an official press release.[52] Once the exhibition was actually underway, the slippers received very little in the way of contextual information, but it was not needed. The audience already knew what they were seeing, as they had seen them before in the film, or merely understood them because of their place in the public consciousness that comes out of international entertainment and popular culture. They are a very different type of American icon than others that were brought to Edinburgh, but they encompassed the myriad narrative needs of the exhibition and the institutions involved, being both American and global, rare and accessible.

Presenting the Smithsonian Abroad

Having had such obvious antecedents in the form of the *Treasures of the Smithsonian Institution* book, the temporary exhibition for Edinburgh could be built fairly easily on that existing scaffolding. The final form of *Treasures from the Smithsonian Institution* reflected changes in structure and content to appeal to a more international audience, but its core showed only minor semantic shifts in order to suit the new context. These small changes are seen clearly in even the exhibition's name, though coming to that choice required a long period of deliberation. Originally organizers had wanted to reuse the *Treasures of the Smithsonian Institution* title, at least as a subtitle. The first proposed title was *The Genius of Collecting, the Past to the Future: Treasures of the Smithsonian Institution*.[53] Because of issues of copyright with the book, this was discarded. The next proposed version was *America's Smithsonian: Treasures from the National Museum of the United States*, though this too was rejected, as "a change was needed to avoid the misperception that the Smithsonian Institution is one museum and that we are the United States Government."[54] Other draft titles were variations on the themes of America, treasures, and the Smithsonian, with a compromise finally being reached with the book's publishers to allow a modest change to satisfy copyright—and thus *Treasures from the Smithsonian Institution* was born.[55] The substitution of "from" for "of" may have been a minor one to placate the copyright lawyers. However, it signaled some big changes in the larger narrative goals of the exhibition. The objects' relocation to Scotland had major implications for their meaning and display. Whereas the 1983 book was meant largely to show a nation what treasures it possessed, the journey that the new exhibition took removed these treasures from their national context and embedded them in the heart of another cultural space. The narratives that the selected objects carried with them to Edinburgh had to be recognizable and understandable to international audiences while still retaining a recognizable "American-ness."

Achieving this level of narrative flexibility and strength would have been a difficult task even with all of the millions of objects in the vaults of the Smithsonian. Instead, curators had to pick 260, each of which had to be transported thousands of miles and set up in a space entirely different from the ones they usually occupied. The objects were flown to Scotland by the U.S. Air Force in three cargo planes, and a small army of curators and other Smithsonian staff came as well.[56] The air force had been commanded to help out after the assistant secretary for defense received a letter from the Smithsonian director stating that "as the exhibition represents the Smithsonian and American treasures of great artistic, historic, and scientific importance, we judge the assistance of the United States Air Force to be in the national interest."[57] While in some ways this was a careful manipulation of the situation in order to gain a discount on the sizable cost of transport, it also shows the extent to which the Smithsonian was seen as a guardian of the nation, as integral and important to the country as its defense forces.

Once arrived, the exhibition took over the Royal Scottish Museum's temporary exhibition hall and main entry gallery. It composed a mix of freestanding objects, individual cases, and cases for groupings of objects. There were paintings and prints on the walls, as well as sculptures and machinery. In many announcements Frank Dunlop and Norman Tebble touted the breadth of objects to be displayed, saying that the exhibition made sure there was "something to interest everyone."[58] Treasures at the Smithsonian have long been more about their iconic status in American life and culture. This point was made abundantly clear in the many reviews of the exhibition. When asked how the objects on display were chosen, Donald McClelland, international coordinator of SITES, said that all the objects were selected because of their "significant contribution to the history and culture of our country."[59] The artifacts selected were therefore from the complete spectrum of Smithsonian collections, resulting in a diversity of representation that provided an ongoing source of fascination for many journalists and observers. Ordinary artifacts rested alongside the relics of famous people long dead, the work of well-known artists, celebrity castoffs, and images of important Americans.

While this juxtaposition was perhaps more noticeable in the space of the Royal Scottish Museum, it was not completely out of the ordinary for the Smithsonian. For a variety of reasons the collections of the Smithsonian have always had a haphazard feeling. Unlike many other national museums, the Smithsonian had few or no established collections at its founding besides the scientific specimens of James Smithson. Also, since then, few of its objects have been acquired purposefully. The museum has always had a strong ethic of donation from individual Americans, and of taking and displaying the largest number of these objects possible.[60] Government buildings in the United States such as the Patent Office, the Capitol building, and the National Post Office have all transferred their holdings of objects to the Smithsonian over the years, resulting in everything from relics of presidents and governments to a large number of patent models finding a place in the collections.[61] By sponsoring so many scientific expeditions, the institution has ended up with large numbers of specimens, and by being connected to the federal government it has received objects of importance to the state.[62] The results of these collecting practices and the wide scope and mission of the institution are an encyclopedic collection of objects from all corners of the world that hold a variety of monetary, historical, and cultural values.

The sheer breadth of the enterprise is perhaps one reason for the particular cultural role held by the Smithsonian. All national museums are seen as important arbiters of national knowledge and narrative. However, whether for reasons particular to America or to itself, the Smithsonian is the holder of a particularly accepted "truth" and legitimacy for the American public.[63] The Smithsonian Institution is considered to have unimpeachable authority on the subject of America and American history and culture. Smithsonian officials acknowledge the sometimes-problematic nature of those expectations:

> Like Webster or Oxford, dictionaries par excellence, the definitions contained in the world of the Smithsonian are always taken as "the last word," the labels on the exhibits beyond question, the epitome of veracity. . . . This is a weighty responsibility. Are we really as correct and as profoundly so as we sound? I do not know, suspecting only as a scientific skeptic that the ultimate truth on almost any subject will always remain elusive, slipping between the sentences, intriguing us with the very *exceptions* which can never be explained by footnotes alone.[64]

These expectations have, to some extent, been created by the institution itself, and especially by the NMAH. Items usually found in the collections of the NMAH were the majority of the objects breathlessly noted by previews and reviews of the *Treasures from the Smithsonian Institution* in Edinburgh. It is almost as if the NMAH functioned as a kind of copyright library of American culture—receiving, as the Library of Congress does, one copy of everything important published in the country.

Whereas the original establishment of the Smithsonian Institution called for the immediate transfer of any objects of interest that were already in Washington, DC, the modern Smithsonian Institution is the recipient of anything of cultural interest from anywhere in the United States. This includes items from popular culture, such as props from television shows and items associated with iconic places or people. A large example of this was the acquisition of the entire kitchen belonging to Julia Child, a famous food writer and television host. They did not want just any kitchen—they wanted this very specific one.[65] So, a team of curators went to the Child family house in November 2001, documented everything, took the kitchen apart, transported it to the museum, and then reconstructed it.[66] The Smithsonian approach to telling stories about the past is linked to the individualism of the American experience and the narrative role of the iconic object. The question of how to present this type of museum artifact and experience to a new audience in another nation was one of the major questions hovering around the design process for the Scottish exhibition.

Treasures from the Smithsonian

In a pre-exhibition memo about the prospective form of the exhibition, the director of SITES called for a general approach. He wanted to showcase the breadth of Smithsonian Institution collections and act as a public relations exercise for the institution, as well as an exhibition of American history and culture.[67] This idea of using the Edinburgh exhibition to celebrate the whole scope of the Smithsonian as an institution was also echoed by other strong voices early in the design process. The curator of the Castle building, the heart of the Smithsonian, James Goode, also recommended this approach. In addition, he also added a second possible theme: "To show Scottish and English connections with American cultural development . . . the effort to focus on beautiful objects which reflect the close ties between American culture and the British should be very popular at the Edinburgh Festival."[68] In the end it was decided that general themes of this kind were the best way to present the whole of the Smithsonian in a miniature form and in a very different context than its objects normally have. To emphasize these ideas of scope and size, two special display cases were created, one for the entry to the exhibition and one for the end.

A complex interplay between space and objects shapes the process of designing a permanent museum. The same issues arise in a temporary exhibition. It is generally accepted that museum objects are multivocal—they can say more than one thing at a time. Yet, when an object is put on display, one of its stories is always privileged above others. Here, the specific issue to consider is how the meaning of the object—the story that it is allowed to tell—is influenced by the context in which it is displayed. Like words in a sentence, objects are put into display cases, and while each individual object says something on its own, it also has a meaning as a component of the whole. The designers of *Treasures from the Smithsonian* were aware of the ways that they could manipulate objects and space to create certain moods and ideas in their audiences. The key way they did this was by the assembly of those two important book-ending cases, which were called "Diversity I" and "Diversity II."

The "Diversity" cases were meant to encapsulate the themes of the exhibition, setting up the viewer for what they were going to encounter, and serving as front and end pieces for the ideas they saw on their journey. The assistant director of the exhibition, Mary Dillon, said that "Planning 'Diversity I' was like writing a good lead sentence to a novel. . . . It puts one right in the thick of the show. It says 'We have all these incredible objects. Watch out!'"[69] Startling juxtapositions and intentional blurring of the usual lines among art, ethnography, and historical artifact were consciously manipulated in the Diversity cases in order to create a sense of awe in the visitors before they encountered the majority of the show.

Although this approach has been used by museums more and more since the advent of the "new museology" in the 1990s, it was novel at the time of the 1984 Scottish exhibition.[70] The contents of "Diversity I" included a banjo from the NMAH, a portrait of Benjamin Franklin from the Portrait Gallery, a satellite from the Air and Space Museum, and an intricately carved box from the Museum of African Art.[71] These two display cases contained in miniature all that visitors were about to see in the exhibition, which itself was a miniaturized version of a much larger museum complex. In essence, this is what temporary exhibitions can do—bring the heart of one nation's material culture to another location and context. Because of the concentration of scope involved, the narratives layered on each particular object get both more complicated, as they try to convey more information, and also simpler, as they are divorced from the cultural expectations audiences in their own national context bring with them to the museum.

Franklin's and Washington's Walking Stick

Most of the contents of *Treasures from the Smithsonian* clearly and easily told stories about the breadth of artifacts in the collections of the Smithsonian, and through that, of the scope of American history and culture. However, some stories did not transfer to Edinburgh in the same straightforward way as others.

Benjamin Franklin is one of the first people that an American child learns about in history class—or perhaps in science class, via the iconic "kite flying in a thunderstorm" method of discovering electricity. In many ways Franklin is the iconic American. He came from an undistinguished background and yet was able to become an important figure in the fields of science, publishing, government service, and many others. One of the icons in the *Treasures from the Smithsonian* show was his walking stick, given to him in the 1780s when he was serving as minister to France. He used it frequently as he was increasingly hobbled by the vicissitudes of old age and a good life, and in his will he passed it on to a particular acquaintance. He wrote that "my fine crabtree walking stick with a gold head curiously wrought in the form of a cap of liberty I give to my friend and the friend of mankind, General Washington. If it were a Scepter, he has merited it, and would become it."[72] General Washington is, of course, George Washington, to whom the former colonists' victory in the War of Independence was attributed and who turned down offers to become the king of the new United States of America. Instead he became the first president, stepping down after two four-year terms, and thus setting a precedent that is still used today.

Exhibition texts in the NMAH tell the visitor this story, using Franklin's words. The labels also say that by the time of his will, the walking stick was already seen as a symbol of the "Revolution and its ideals."[73] These associations are related not only to the specific details of this cane but to the ideas linked with canes in general. Gentlemen's canes developed from pilgrim's staffs and swords.[74] As it became unacceptable to carry a sword with you inside, men began including ornate canes with them as part of their formal dress. Because of this, they were symbolically valuable as signs of masculinity, power, and class. These deeper meanings meant that the gift of the walking stick to Franklin, and his later gift of it to Washington, was freighted with significance about their public personas as men of virtue and knowledge.

The particular decoration of this specific stick, imbued with neoclassical references, further heightened this effect. The "liberty cap" that crowns the cane is a symbol of freedom that was used in the French Revolution and also in antislavery and other sorts of radical political movements, though it has its antecedents in classical Roman society.[75] A proposal was made in 1855 to have the female statue at the top of the U.S. Capitol's imposing dome be a symbol of "Freedom," complete with liberty cap, but the secretary of war, Jefferson Davis, objected to this gesture as lending support to abolition; it was replaced instead with the crested war helmet she still wears today.[76] All this meaningful decorative detail contributes to a rich and symbolic history intertwined with that of the country and the ideals enshrined there.

Because of these multiple strata of meaning, the walking stick was exactly the type of object that the exhibition designers had wanted for *Treasures from the Smithsonian*. Donald McClelland had said that he wanted to display "George Washington–icon sorts of thing[s], but also objects in storage that hadn't been seen for some time."[77] While the stick had been on public display, it had not often been put forward as a treasure of the nation. Its worth had instead been directly tied to Washington as former president and father of the country.

The walking stick first became national property in 1843, when Washington's grandnephew donated it to the U.S. government in an elaborate ceremony. It was displayed in public for the first time in 1880, when the Patent Office put it in their library along with a sword that had also belonged to Washington. Then, in 1922, the State Department transferred all government historical collections to the Smithsonian, where the cane sat in a Hall of Presidents in the Natural History Museum before the opening of the NMAH. It had been in the *Treasures of the Smithsonian Institution* book in 1983 and then came to Edinburgh for the later show.

The walking stick is an icon in the most secular and old-fashioned sense, as a small item that connects to larger ideas of culture and history. It also has relic value, as it links the viewer to two iconic personages—people without whom there would be no nation of which to tell stories. Tracing which person this walking stick has been associated with most strongly at various times and in various spaces is an interesting exercise in the manipulation of meaning. Almost without fail it is, and has been, called "George Washington's walking stick." Only one of the many newspaper articles about the exhibition in Scotland even mentioned its early connection to Franklin, though that writer did believe that "the walking stick Franklin bequeathed to Washington must be the best piece of memorabilia" in the show.[78] Following the cane's life through other exhibitions though, we find that in its most recent incarnation—a small exhibition held at the National Air and Space Museum in 2008 called *Treasures of American History*—the walking stick was presented as a symbol of Benjamin Franklin, with only a passing mention of "his friend and fellow revolutionary George Washington."[79] The rest of the text is concerned with Franklin's role in American history and culture. This change is perhaps insignificant, but it is intriguing. While the focus could be attributed to the exhibition's location in a science-based museum, the placement of the show was coincidental, rather than causal. *Treasures of American History* was organized entirely by staff from the NMAH to serve as a small glimpse into their collections while the rest of the museum was closed for renovation. As a self-contained package, the show could have been displayed in any of the museums that circle the Mall. The National Air and Space Museum venue was chosen after the exhibition had been designed, as an ongoing reorganization of their collections meant that there was enough free floor space for visiting artifacts. Today, it could be that the scientist is considered a better representative of American-ness. But in

Scotland in 1984, it was more important to portray American history as belonging to the statesmen and politicians.

In its time in Scotland, the walking stick appears to have mystified many observers. While it was mentioned in the press releases (written largely by Smithsonian staff) and thus was highly visible in early preview articles, it seems not to have struck a chord with many visitors or reviews, as it is largely absent from later reports.[80] This may have been because of the explicit focus on treasures in the exhibition. "Treasures" are iconic objects in their purest form. They need no connection to anything else in order to be understood. They merely *exist*, and in existing, attract attention because of their power to draw the visitor in. Many of the other iconic objects that are used in museums to create certain ideas of identity, narrative, and nation are icons of this type. The problem lies in when they are removed from the context in which that sort of wordless connection works. Within the national public consciousness of the United States, a label such as the one given to the walking stick would be enough to enhance and bring attention to the iconic value of the object. In Scotland, in the space of another nation's museum and narrative, and divorced from this public consciousness, the aura around the walking stick did not work in the same way.

Smithsonian officials were aware that this would be a problem. The exhibition labeler, Karen Fort, admitted as much when she said that "if something is a treasure it is explicitly so, and you shouldn't have to explain why. That works for many things in the show, but there are a number, like the walking stick Ben Franklin bequeathed to George Washington, that need more interpretation."[81] The interpretation that was given, however, did not go far enough. It gave it a stronger narrative than other objects, but it did not step outside the assumed information of American nationness, and so was unable to connect as strongly with an audience coming from outside that space. In order to be understood as more than its shape, the walking stick needed to be surrounded by context-giving knowledge about American history and its personalities. Without that assumed information in the audience, creating a recognizable narrative around the object was difficult and perhaps rendered the icon incomprehensible. The net of signifiers of "banal nationalism" that theorists such as Michael Billig have identified provides the sort of mass public consciousness of the nation and its mythical history that these more complicated icons require in order to operate at their highest narrative potential.[82] When outside of its reach and embedded in the space of another nation, the larger connections are lost, so that what could be a powerful statement of history and culture becomes merely an interesting curiosity.

Judy Garland's ruby slippers and Benjamin Franklin's walking stick both illustrate several of the roles and tensions of the iconic object in the temporary exhibit context. Some recognizable icons can be completely stripped of the supporting information that they would have in their home space. This reliance on wonder works better in the temporary exhibition, as the visitor is more apt to be looking for entertainment than for information, and they recognize and even expect a lack of context. The temporary exhibition is a pilgrimage to rare sights, rather than the trip into a history book that is often expected of a museum. Conversely, other, less celebrated objects need more context than they would normally have in order to be understood in the temporary space. It is debatable which of the two objects said more about "America" and its nationness to international audiences. Even their treasure value was subject to interpretation. There is only one iconic walking stick, and the museum placed a million-dollar price tag on it for insurance estimates.[83] In contrast, there are several pairs of ruby slippers from the original film of *The Wizard of Oz*, each slightly different and all worn by Garland. In terms of rarity, then, the walking stick would be the most "treasured." However, the ruby slippers have come to take a place in popular culture that is unlikely to be matched by the walking stick, however avid aficionados of Franklin, Washington, or walking sticks in general become. The slippers have become an icon both within and without the museum, whereas the walking stick needs the museum's academic legitimacy and narrative support in order to be understood as an icon of American history and culture.[84]

Exhibitionary Outcomes

These objects and hundreds of other Smithsonian artifacts took over the main iconic space of the Royal Scottish Museum—the vast and soaring Great Hall, with its allusions to London's 1851 Crystal Palace and other Great Exhibitions. It was also the main and, at that time, only entryway into the museum. This combination of circumstances set up a situation where visitors entering the Royal *Scottish* Museum were first encountering *American* national objects. This is one of the multiplicities of meaning that a temporary exhibition can impose on museum space. By being located and "read" in a nominally Scottish space, the American artifacts were not as purely American as they would be if seen in the space of their nation. By the same token, being exposed to those from outside that national context would have changed the Scottishness of the Scottish objects.

In 1984 the RSM was not yet truly a Scottish national museum, as it did not set out to tell the story of the nation in the same way that the National Museum of Antiquities of Scotland did. For the purpose of this exhibition the RSM was framed both as a representative institution of Scottishness and as an international and European venue, through the influence of the International Festival. Even though the RSM's objects were mostly concerned with things either from other cultures that had been brought back to Scotland or from the technology of modern life, by being framed as Scottish in relation to the Smithsonian's Americanness, the objects within took on a stronger Scottish narrative. The explicit narratives imposed by the visiting artifacts changed the meanings of the permanent displays as well. Temporary exhibitions often have this effect of reframing the meaning of the host institution's icons, just as the loan icons are changed by being seen in different space.

Like many issues around iconic objects, these changes cannot be measured quantifiably. However, there are many outcomes of the temporary exhibition that can. *Treasures from the Smithsonian Institution* was free to the public, as the Smithsonian and other donors paid all costs. This meant that, unlike many other traveling or temporary exhibitions, the RSM as host did not have to pay anything to host the show. However, they also did not profit as much as they would have done otherwise. Deals were worked out prior to opening that saw 90 percent of all profits on Smithsonian-sponsored events and merchandise sales returned to America.[85] Not all benefits of the exhibition were monetary though. Because of the scale of the show, the RSM got press coverage that it would not have normally, especially in London-based newspapers. The staff at the RSM was also able to leverage the huge infrastructure of the Smithsonian to expand the show beyond Edinburgh, by asking them to create a series of text panels with information and pictures of the objects that toured rural communities and schools in Scotland before the opening of the larger exhibition.[86] These were then reused when they traveled to other non-museum public spaces in the United States.[87] *Treasures from the Smithsonian Institution* was very popular. Attendance numbers were double those of the previous year's festival show, and "at several points during the second weekend, the museum was obligated to close its doors due to overcrowding."[88]

This had many causes, including the fact that internationally known objects were on display, the large amount of media coverage, and the "wow" factor of American objects being suddenly accessible. To some extent temporary exhibitions always attract more attention than their more staid permanent equivalents. The attraction can be heightened if the exhibition is framed in order to draw attention to the rarity and celebrity value of the objects featured and if attention is purposely attracted to the exhibition and its artifacts as something out of the ordinary. *Treasures from the Smithsonian at the Royal Scottish Museum* did this very well. But is this only possible when the objects on show are foreign in some way, and thus stand out more sharply in their new, temporary surroundings?

2
Scotland, for Scotland
1989

Temporary exhibitions, of course, are not always about unfamiliar objects from foreign lands being displayed to new and unusual audiences. Sometimes they are spaces for the temporary reframing of well-known objects and the creation of narratives relevant to a particular moment in time. Inspired by the large scale of the temporary exhibition *Treasures from the Smithsonian Institution at the Royal Scottish Museum*—particularly its focus on creating a narrative of American identity through the national museums' objects—museum officials in Scotland created a similarly inspired temporary exhibition in the Royal Scottish Museum (RSM) on Chambers Street during the Edinburgh International Festival of 1989. Like the American blockbuster five years previously, this new show significantly shaped the eventual form and narratival contents of the permanent National Museum of Scotland (NMS) and affected the way in which material culture was presented and understood as part of a national Scottish heritage. It occupied the same space as the American exhibition, aimed to attract the same audiences, and thus hoped to place Scotland on the same plane as the United States—as a major nation with an important historical and cultural collection that deserved recognition.

This was all taking place in a context of political change within Scotland as well. A few months after *Treasures from the Smithsonian* closed, the new National Heritage (Scotland) Act passed, which made several major changes, though their impact was mostly on paper for years to come. The first of the changes was the formation of a new Board of the National Museums of Scotland, which would have responsibility for the collections and management of the RSM and the National Museum of Antiquities of Scotland.[1] The two formerly separate institutions would now be linked by their shared board, and, at least on paper, by this top-level institutional name, the National Museums of Scotland. On the ground, no funding changed, and no staff reported feeling a change at this point.[2]

The act additionally allowed for the creation of a new Museum of Scotland that would pull objects from the collections of the existing RSM and National Museum of Antiquities, as well as establish its own collections.[3] The act did not mandate the creation of this new institution, and it did not, crucially, allocate any funding for it. Thus, this also was a change on paper more than anything. But it was an important piece of paper, and it signaled that important things could be coming. However, some in Scotland were impatient with what they saw as a slow pace of change and as merely cosmetic shifts, rather than real solutions to problems that people had been talking about since the eighteenth century.

Object-ifying the Political

Many, if not all, museum exhibitions have a political undertone. They are designed and presented in a specific way because of the context of the society in which they are developed—and that context includes the political mood of the time. Still, this political narrative is usually tacit. To find it one must delve behind the scenes, as was the case with the Smithsonian exhibition. Yet an exhibit entitled *The Wealth of a Nation in the National Museums of Scotland* wove certain political goals into the very center of its name and public storyline. The name alludes to the famous Scottish economist Adam Smith's 1776 foundational study that forms the intellectual basis of modern capitalism—*The Wealth of Nations*. Smith was one of the major figures of the Scottish

Enlightenment, where Scottish universities, and the intellectuals that they produced made the small nation the center of European thought and innovation.[4]

By calling on this heritage in the exhibition's name, the museum, which stood on a street where Smith and many of his colleagues had once walked, reminded visitors of the deep roots of Scottish history. The exhibition was meant to show the rich and large collections of Scottish artifacts held by the museum and — most importantly — demonstrate how facilities for the display of these collections were lacking due to the absence of a true national history museum.

Where the mission of the previous blockbuster exhibition had been only to showcase the grandeur of America through its material culture and, through the popular appeal of the show, open the International Festival to a wider audience, the missions of the new temporary exhibition had even more political and cultural import. In 1989 the summer blockbuster was to have a longer run than the Smithsonian show (opening on June 9, 1989, and closing on December 31) but also a larger remit. It was meant from the very beginning to be the impetus for the creation of a new museum, and in doing so, hoped to force public and governmental recognition of Scottish nationness.

This had been an ongoing conversation. By 1989 it was not enough to say that there "may be" a new Museum of Scotland but not fund it, give it a space, or move it forward in any way. The decision to demonstrate the physical need for a new space by placing many supposedly neglected "treasures" on display was just a new tactic in an old fight. However, the approach embraced by the temporary exhibition made the case in a subtle yet effective way. Part of this success was due to the framing of the exhibition, some to the objects selected, and some to the design of the exhibition space. The outcomes of the exhibition were also tinged with the influence of less quantifiable factors such as timing and the larger political climate. Without any one of these components, *The Wealth of a Nation* might not have had the cultural and physical repercussions that it had.

The grand success of the *Treasures from the Smithsonian* show had demonstrated that putting on a blockbuster temporary exhibition at the RSM during the Edinburgh International Festival was a way to guarantee substantial attendance figures and national media coverage. Both of these things were important for *The Wealth of a Nation,* given its overt political agenda. Publicity was key to the missions of the exhibition, as was the public pressure that might be mounted if enough people were aware of its goals. In the stridently toned foreword in the catalogue that accompanied the exhibition, Magnus Magnusson, a well-known journalist and personality, claimed,

> In order to house and conserve and display the Wealth of the Nation as it deserves, we need a new Museum of Scotland building to give it the setting it deserves. At no time in our history have we had an adequate home in which to display our wonderfully rich cultural heritage to its best advantage and to the best advantage of the nation. At no time have we had a great national building in which to tell the story of Scotland's people and show all of her most treasured possessions.... Only a new and visionary Museum of Scotland will do full justice to the collections that make up the real Wealth of a Nation.[5]

The media echoed this message, reviewing and previewing the show as, for example, "an exhibition celebrating a great heritage and at the same time lamenting the lack of place where it can be adequately displayed."[6] The objects in the show were selected not only because of their beauty or rarity but also to make the point that without a new museum, they would never be shown at their best. The exhibition was put together mindfully to create and solidify those ideas. So too was the accompanying book, in itself much more solid than the usual temporary exhibition catalogue, which acted as a portable and less-constrained version of the show.

Framing *The Wealth of a Nation*

Over five hundred objects were selected by curators to make up *The Wealth of a Nation.* Some of those were taken from their regular display cases in exhibits at the National Museum of Antiquities of Scotland, but most came out of storage or conservation labs so they could be shown publicly for the first time. This is part of the appeal and power of temporary exhibitions as a whole. The mystique inherent in the notion of a limited time offer and the sense of superiority that comes with being given access to a privileged glimpse of things normally hidden in the depths enhance the appeal of the objects on display.[7]

A temporary exhibition, being a space apart within the larger space of the museum, can also reinforce the ideas of exclusion or distinction set up first by the larger space. Even the titles of our two temporary exhibitions—*Treasures from the Smithsonian Institution* and *The Wealth of a Nation*—make clear the idea that the contents are in some way valuable and worthy of adulation or at least highly focused attention. These naming conventions, the use of a clearly defined space apart from that of the "regular" exhibits, and the limited time and rare contents of a temporary exhibition are all ways in which the aura of the objects can be enhanced. Although the two titles echo one another, they also reflect the particular circumstances, contexts, and goals of each show. *Treasures from the Smithsonian* was meant to be popular, wide-ranging, and intriguing, and to draw attention to its international pedigree. The concept of "treasures" was ideally suited to those goals. *The Wealth of a Nation*, while similar in approach, was able to imbue its title with added layers of significance. "Wealth" implies an investment in the future and its bounty, not just the past, which is connoted in "treasure." This invocation of the future and its potential was critical in the context of the exhibition's political aims. Also important, given the exhibition's location at the RSM, was the mimicking of Adam Smith's seminal Enlightenment text *The Wealth of Nations*. The title of the show was constructed to further particular narratives, just as the objects within it were.[8]

The organizers of *The Wealth of a Nation* wanted the objects on display to have as much aura as possible. Aura-filled, or iconic, objects draw the viewer in, connecting them to a larger narrative than that of their specific history. They have enough power to stand alone, devoid of interpretation, and yet still manage to create a story. The other strength of an iconic object is that many stories can be mapped onto it, given slight changes in placement or context. Thus, museum icons function in the same way as words or narrative images within a language.

The need for and place of icons in the museum exhibition becomes especially clear when looking at temporary exhibitions, such as *The Wealth of a Nation,* which are created with a specific mission in mind. The iconic value of the object is heightened not only because of the factors already addressed—the defined space and time frame as well as the display of objects not normally seen—but because everything must contribute to the overall narrative of the endeavor. The extent to which there is an overarching storyline differs in each exhibition. The *Treasures of the Smithsonian* was meant to be an aesthetic experience that triggered certain ideas of America without hewing to a coherently linear path. *The Wealth of a Nation* echoed these general principles, as it also aspired to a much more specific outcome, as we saw earlier. How exactly certain iconic objects were selected and used in the exhibition illustrates how that outcome was manipulated throughout the narrative of the display.

The Icons of a Nation

The Wealth of a Nation exhibition was an exercise in envisioning and imagining a new Museum of Scotland, and how that museum might present the objects of Scottish material culture. It was a first chance to set these icons up on their own and see what they could be made to say about Scottish history. Some of the display strategies first seen in *The Wealth of a Nation* would be repeated in the museum when it finally opened almost a decade later, and some, though altered slightly because of demands of space and architecture, remained the same in spirit. Icons were born over the course of *The Wealth of a Nation* that then lived on to speak throughout the process of creating the museum and beyond.

Chief among these icons was the small artifact known as the Monymusk Reliquary. It is a small Celtic house shrine, circa 700 AD, and is thought to be associated with a number of important Scottish historical figures. William I, the Lion, supposedly gave

The Monymusk Reliquary, a Celtic house shrine made of bronze, silver, yew wood, glass, and enamel. It is small—just 4.4 inches wide, 3.5 inches tall, and 2 inches deep—but has a powerful and conflicted history. © National Museums Scotland.

the reliquary to the abbey at Arbroath as a relic of Saint Columba, Scotland's first patron saint. Later in its life it may have been at the famous Battle of Bannockburn in 1314 where the Scots king and his forces defeated an invading English army. This is quite a pile of connections to important Scottish national moments, people, and symbols for one small object to have.[9]

Today it is the first object that a visitor to Museum of Scotland encounters, right in the entrance to the gallery known as the *Kingdom of the Scots,* which covers the time period between 1100 and 1707. That gallery addresses three main ideas about the time period: Scotland was European, Scotland was independent, and Scotland was Celtic.[10] One of the first proposed narratives for the permanent gallery space suggested that "visitors should be encouraged to feel that they are stepping not just into medieval Scotland but into a treasure house of Scotland's recorded past. The first objects they see must convey that message."[11] The Monymusk Reliquary was able to fulfill that role in the permanent museum because of the narrative power it had been given in *The Wealth of a Nation*. A preview of the exhibition perhaps said it best:

> Malcolm Rifkind [the secretary of state for Scotland] will find the Monymusk Reliquary waiting for him when he arrives on Friday at the Royal Museum of Scotland to open an exhibition called "The Wealth of a Nation." ... The trustees of the National Museums of Scotland seem to be confident that it will do the trick again and bring them victory in their long campaign to secure a home for Scotland's national collection of historical treasures. One of the most precious possessions of the nation, this little travelling shrine is being placed at the entrance of the exhibition.[12]

This passage shows that in 1989 the reliquary was iconic enough to encompass all the hopes layered on to the *Wealth of a Nation* exhibition. But how did it get to that point?

The reliquary, like any icon, is both an object and an idea. In 1859 an empty silver, wood, and enamel hinged box, discovered in a corner of an old attic in a castle belonging to the Grant family of Monymusk, was shown to a group of scholars in Aberdeen. Then in 1880 it was displayed for the Society of Antiquaries of Scotland. After that meeting Joseph Anderson, keeper of the society's museum, wrote up a notice positing that the box was in fact a long-lost unidentified object, listed in medieval documents as the *brecbennoch* of Saint Columba.[13] This was the beginning of the story that created the national icon put on show.

Brecbennoch is a Scottish Gaelic term that has a few potential translations, but the most agreed upon seems to be "little speckled peaked one."[14] In wanting the Monymusk Reliquary to be the lost *brecbennoch*, curators and researchers mentioned over and over how the enameling that covered it made it speckled, and how its traditional house-shrine shape is small and peaked. Adding another layer of complication onto this, the *brecbennoch* was mentioned from the 1200s as a *vexillum*. *Vexillum* technically means "banner," but scholars such as Joseph Anderson believed, even prior to the discovery of the Monymusk example, that *vexillum* could be a more general term used to refer to things that were carried in front of armies to ensure success on the battlefield. Using that description, the reliquary could be the mysterious *vexillum*. Anderson was uncertain about the reliquary's exact provenance, other than the fact that it had been in the possession of the Grant family at Monymusk for a long time, but he desperately wanted it to be the *brecbennoch*. Doubts did slip in but were quickly brushed aside: "If this reliquary, which is still preserved at Monymusk, be not the missing *Breccbennoch* . . . it can at least be said of it that its form is that of a *vexillum*. . . . It is, moreover, the only example of its class now remaining in Scotland, and the beauty and specially Celtic character of its ornamentation invest it with an interest of no ordinary kind, independent of all such questions of historical association."[15] Whatever Anderson's desires for the story, at this point he also recognized it as an important object in its own right.

This idea faded away as Anderson and others became increasingly sure that the reliquary was also the *brecbennoch*. Its importance as a highly decorative and ancient shrine object became secondary to finding proof that it was the *brecbennoch*. Nearly twenty years later Anderson again wrote about the Monymusk Reliquary. There he acknowledged that "the Monymusk shrine has no known history. It is unquestionably a reliquary of the Celtic Church, which enshrined an unknown relic of the very first order of importance . . . but absolutely nothing is known about it to account for its presence and preservation at Monymusk."[16]

After this revelation, which would appear to have been the death-knell of reports of the *brecbennoch*, Anderson restated the connections he longed to make twenty years earlier, linking the reliquary with "one of the most famous of the Scottish enshrined relics of Saint Columba." He did not clarify his statements but instead expounded on the tenuous links he was aiming for. He claimed special status for this Columba relic, "a relic which, though its nature is unspecified, bore a name which implies that it was enshrined in such a shrine as this."[17] An uncertain statement, surely, but it served as a next step in creating a national icon.

After a period of silence, the object came up for sale in 1933. The negotiation was fraught, but the National Museum of Antiquities of Scotland acquired the reliquary. Notes on the acquisition ignored all previous doubt and said that "it is manifestly impossible to question the identification of the reliquary . . . with the *Brecbennoch* of these medieval documents."[18] The connection between the actual object and the idea of the object had been established solidly, from its beginnings as wishful thinking to a truth that was "manifestly impossible" to deny.

It remained thus for many decades to follow. The Monymusk Reliquary was accepted as the *brecbennoch* of Saint Columba, and as such it was invaluable to the museum. It was the object that had rallied the troops at Bannockburn—the triumphant battle of the Wars of Scottish Independence—and also the finest emblem of Scottish identity from a time where there barely was a Scotland with which to identify. The Monymusk Reliquary was an art piece valued for its ornamentation and unique enameling techniques. However, the reliquary—as *brecbennoch*—was historically valuable and associated with certain important people and events, and thus even more important.[19]

This, then, was the first object that visitors to *The Wealth of a Nation* encountered. It had been placed at the entrance to make a point—but the idea in the Monymusk Reliquary was not the same as in the rest of the exhibition. The director of the NMS at the time of the exhibition, Robert Anderson, described the content and context of the show: "The emphasis in *The Wealth of a Nation* will *not* be on static, individual objects to be looked at for their own sakes. The exhibits are intended to reflect the beliefs and achievements of the land, as well as daily life, commerce, religion, and technological change. We also want to show how these objects can be used."[20] While the multitude of other artifacts on display may have reached this objective, it is clear that the Monymusk Reliquary and several other objects were of value to the exhibition precisely because they were not placed in deep levels of cultural context. The reliquary had a label laying out its story and connections to Saint Columba and Bannockburn, but it was not linked explicitly to "the beliefs and achievements of the land" nor did the text demonstrate how such an object would be used. It stood on its own, allowing visitors to read the story of all the famous events and people associated with it and come to their own conclusions.

This difference in treatment served not only as an introduction to the larger space but also as a link to the yet-to-be-imagined space of the Museum of Scotland. In *The Wealth of a Nation* only those objects at the beginning—the reliquary and the object it was positioned with, a twelfth-century wooden statue of Saint Andrew—had any amount of empty space around them. The rest of the objects, for reasons that are discussed later, were crowded close to one another. The more space that separates an object from other artifacts, the greater its iconic power or aura.[21] By setting these two objects apart from the rest they were given the scope to say more than their neighbors, and it is clear that they were meant to be the icons that drew visitors into the rest of the exhibition.

Prior to its central role in *The Wealth of a Nation*, the Monymusk Reliquary had been in a case at the National Museum of Antiquities with other objects, clearly just one more artifact among many in the collections. It was hard to see or assign any particular importance to the little box on the lower tier of a large display case. Over the years, as its prominence increased, so did the amount of empty, reverential space framing it. Thus in *The Wealth of a Nation* it shared a case set aside at the beginning with one other iconic object. The statue of Saint Andrew, current patron saint of Scotland and potent national symbol, was taken out of storage for this exhibition. It was also used as the figurehead of another campaign for a new museum at the time, when it appeared on the cover of a pamphlet entitled *St. Andrew: Will He Ever See the Light?*[22]

A wooden statue of Saint Andrew, the patron saint of Scotland, with his saltire cross, circa 1500. It was in storage in the old National Museum of Antiquities of Scotland before being used to help advocate for a new National Museum of Scotland. Now he sits just behind the Monymusk Reliquary, under a spotlight, at the entrance to the Scottish section of the NMS. © National Museums Scotland.

In this campaign the statue acted as a symbol of the hundreds of Scottish cultural artifacts languishing in storage because of lack of dedicated display space. In a wider context, it served to represent the Scottish Office administration based in St. Andrew's House and their refusal to "see the light" and fund a Museum of Scotland. Thus there was a symbolic double importance to putting the Monymusk Reliquary and the Saint Andrew statue together in the temporary exhibition. Later on, the iconic value of both objects was increased when they were installed in the Museum of Scotland. Today both are found at the start of the *Kingdom of the Scots* exhibitions, but each sits nobly ensconced in a separate glass case, located several feet apart, though still in the same line of sight. This placement shows the increase in aura and iconic value that both the reliquary and the statue have experienced as they moved from mere antiquities in a historical museum, to star representatives of a temporary exhibition, to symbols of a nation, installed at the forefront of a museum devoted to that nation. It is also a concrete conclusion to the campaign for the Museum of Scotland, as Saint Andrew is situated directly beneath a spotlight, bringing full circle the question asked in *Will He Ever See the Light?* Thus a narrative is created, as Saint Columba's Monymusk Reliquary leads directly on to Saint Andrew, now firmly "seeing" the light in their joint permanent museum home.

The lack of established links to the rest of the narrative of *The Wealth of a Nation* demonstrated by the Monymusk Reliquary and Saint Andrew statue would have heightened what author Stephen Greenblatt terms the "resonance and wonder" of the objects contained within. Artifacts can have qualities of resonance, which is the power of the object to reach out to viewers and draw them into a larger story. They can also be full of wonder, which is for Greenblatt "the power of the displayed object to stop the viewer in his or her tracks."[23] Usually modern permanent exhibitions rely more on resonance, and temporary exhibitions call more on wonder.

This was obviously the case with the *Treasures from the Smithsonian Institution* temporary exhibition. Because those objects were so far from their normal national context—America—and because of the motive and concerns that prompted that exhibition, the objects could just show themselves and be admired for how different and wondrous they were. They did not need to evoke larger ideas in the minds of their viewers. However, such was not necessarily the case with the later *Wealth of a Nation*. Because this was a nation being displayed within its own space, the objects would have a certain amount of resonance for the audience already. The particular political narratives and motives of the exhibition only heightened this. For these reasons the resonance of the chosen iconic objects had to create not only an idea of what these objects were and why they were important but also that they deserved their own space of permanent display. Greenblatt might be echoing the desires of the exhibition designers when he writes that "a resonant exhibition often pulls the viewer away from the celebration of isolated objects and towards a sense of implied, only half visible relationships and questions."[24] These questions, in the case of *The Wealth of a Nation*, were about the place of material history in the culture of a nation, and of the need for designated space to house such. The exhibition created this response in its viewers by manipulating the relationship between object and space within the temporary exhibition area, in such a way as to make thoughts about space and object persist after the visit was over.

The Space of the Nation

This account of the evolution in display strategy used for the Monymusk Reliquary and the statue of Saint Andrew over time helps to illustrate the power of space in determining the story that objects can tell. Space was used in *The Wealth of a Nation*, as in almost all museum exhibitions, to help heighten the messages of the curatorial narrative. Given the political missions of the exhibitions, it is understandable that the exhibit designers would use every possible tool to create the right atmosphere in the exhibition.

The emphasis in the campaign for a new museum—from the *St. Andrew: Will He Ever See the Light?* pamphlet through *The Wealth of a Nation*—was on the sheer numbers of artifacts important to a full understanding of Scottish history and culture that were not being displayed effectively, safely, or at all in the existing National Museum of Antiquities of Scotland. Again and again artifacts were linked to national identity and care of artifacts to care of the nation. The exhibition catalogue began with this impassioned commentary: "For the real resources of a nation are its people; and the story of that people is uttered through what they have left of themselves to posterity, the material of their culture, to be unearthed by the archaeologist, cherished by the antiquarian and illuminated by the scholar. It's not artifacts that make a nation; but it is the artifacts made by people and for people that speak most clearly of the quality of people and provide tangible expressions of the qualities that have made Scotland the nation she is."[25] The subtext here is that without the artifacts, the objects of history, it would be impossible to tell what Scotland is or was as a nation. Through this rhetoric the importance of the objects to the nation was established.

Next on the agenda was to foreground the idea of the sheer number of crucial objects that there were in the collections. This was done deftly by saying that "the National Museums of Scotland have the finest and most extensive collections of Scottish material in existence. These collections form a marvelous treasury of Scotland's past, held in trust for the nation. The function of a great national museum is to preserve and elucidate and present to the world that heritage of the land, that patrimony of the intellect; for these collections form the landscapes of the past that it is the business of the museum to map."[26] Through these two sections of catalogue text it is easy to see how the exhibition curators created a climate in which issues of nation, artifact, and space could and would be discussed. However, space played a role that was not merely confined to theoretical discussions. Space was very consciously engineered to create certain feelings and impressions within the exhibition hall and the text of the exhibition narrative.

The curators of *The Wealth of a Nation*—David Bryden, David Caldwell, and Geoff Swinney—and their designers used space, or the lack thereof, to their advantage. They sought to create an illusion of an overflowing abundance of objects with little or no space between them. One case, called the "Cornucopia," held a treasure chest overflowing with silver and gemstones, along with a stuffed magpie with a gem in its beak. The intended message was that while the museum possessed a large number of treasures, it was not merely a magpie collecting glittering goods. Rather, the case was meant to create a view of the museum as a place where treasure was collected and framed as of importance to the nation—changing treasure into wealth.[27] This aesthetic and message suited the purpose of the exhibition, showing as it did that these objects needed more space so that they could be displayed better. The head designer of the exhibition, James Simpson, deliberately crowded cases with objects and restricted the ease of travel through the area in order to heighten the visitor's consciousness of the amount of objects and lack of space.[28] This is completely different to how things are displayed in most modern exhibitions, but in this context the use of space added another layer of meaning onto the experience.[29] It led the viewer through the stunning myriads of objects held by the NMS, while asking them to think widely about the role of museums and their collections within the nation, rather than about the specific details of particular artifacts.

Treasures from the Smithsonian Institution had also taken this approach, though the motives were different. Both shows were aiming to tell not just one story about their nation or their collections but rather to showcase just how many stories could be told by the collected artifacts. Using inspiration from the Smithsonian show before, cases at the center of the *Wealth of a Nation* exhibition space focused directly on this multiplicity. They displayed artifacts alongside the material used by curators to prepare them for display and some of the academic papers that had come out of research into the natural history sections of the collections. The idea was to balance the glittery wealth of the nation shown in the Cornucopia display with the more understated, but no less important, role that national collections could hold in international scholarly networks.[30]

NMS director Robert G. W. Anderson stressed the profound and thoughtful nature of attending an exhibition, with statements to the press that framed the exhibition as an intellectual exercise: "Exhibitions like *The Wealth of a Nation* can be used to illustrate national history, to tell a story. But we must be careful not to trivialize what museums are. They are serious places with serious things which can teach the public about the past."[31] However, he also emphasized more casual learning, saying that the exhibition "offers the visitor an opportunity to look with fresh eyes at the vitality and creativity of human societies, past and present."[32] While this statement avoids any mention of what society it is that the exhibition sought to present, at other times the director consciously framed the show as integral to Scotland. When he claimed that "We [the curators at NMS] want to stimulate thought about the national collections as an invaluable resource for Scotland and see how different objects can be said to reflect the nation's wealth," he could have been quoting from *Treasures from the Smithsonian Institution*.[33] Thus, despite the differences in the two exhibitions, there were obvious similarities between them, with implications for national museums, artifacts, and identity.

Temporary Nations

What does it mean for a nation to be represented in miniature during a temporary exhibition? How is it that objects can come to hold the meaning of something much larger? About 260 artifacts were present during *Treasures from the Smithsonian*. Over 500 made it into *The Wealth of a Nation*. Do the sheer numbers of objects tell us anything about the nations involved? The smaller amount of items in the earlier exhibition had been made to speak about a much larger nation, although they did not attempt to create the same type of exhaustive narrative that would cover the whole of the nation and its history. Objects are naturally multivocalic. They have many potential stories they can hold at once. Material culture history differs from textual history in this way, simply because the historical object can tell more than one story.

Texts can of course be interpreted in varying ways depending on the viewpoint of their reader and the context in which they are deconstructed. However, they are more limited—the casual viewer takes the text as fixed and static but is more open to seeing multiple stories in the objects. Although one story will be privileged because of its placement on an artifact label, visitors may or may not choose to read the text and instead see in the object the story that they prefer. We have seen how curators and exhibition designers can use the actual multivocality of objects in order to create various narratives with the same objects in different contexts. The public, though, also use the multivocality of objects. Exhibitions are read by visitors, and each visitor and each time period creates different visions of the object on display.[34] The objects selected and the museum professionals who put them on display produce the knowledge in the exhibition space, but it is consumed by the viewer—and the knowledge produced does not exactly mirror the kinds of knowledge consumed.[35] This process of production and consumption is prevalent throughout museum and gallery spaces and forms a critical part of the theoretical literature on the subject.[36]

The process becomes more noticeable, and more fraught, however, in the space of the temporary exhibition. Because of the limited number of objects available for display and the limited time in which the exhibit will be available to visitors, as well as the weight of expectations and narratives placed on these items, issues of how the objects are presented and how the experience is framed for the audience become even more critical. While in permanent exhibits iconic objects can be interspersed with smaller objects that serve more to reinforce points already made than to speak loudly on their own, temporary exhibitions need only the clearest of icons in order to support the narratives presented. Just as the Smithsonian Institution exhibition designers selected each object primarily because of its place in American history and culture, so that it could best help them create a limited version of their nation, the *Wealth of a Nation* curators had to comb through the collections to choose things that spoke of Scotland the nation and of the wealth of its material history.[37] These missions and the nature of the display space meant that the iconic value of the objects used was heightened.

However, it was not only the exhibition itself that created narratives around *The Wealth of a Nation*. There were other forms of narration and storytelling being presented to the public in tandem with the show, and each of those presents another aspect of the exhibition, its social and temporal context, and the tensions it had to navigate. While one primary focus of the exhibition was to show the scope and importance of the collections in Scotland to an audience in an aesthetically pleasing way, the exhibit also had to be seen to fail at this mission. To be too successful would have negated its political aims of exerting pressure for a new museum. This central dilemma between display and politics colored many of the exhibition's forms and contents.[38] After all, the new institution, this Museum of Scotland, existed now on paper but had no funding, no space, no building, nothing more than the promises that had always been given to those who asked for a home for the Scottish collections.

The Narratives of the Nation

Spatial and contextual manipulation of objects allows curators to create an artifactual narrative within exhibition space. This type of narrative exists both in temporary and permanent exhibitions, though it is perhaps more noticeable in the limited space and time of the temporary show. These narratives do not just spring into being of their own accord but rather are constructed purposely by exhibition designers and curators. These professionals create a story much as writers do, but in place of words and paragraphs, museum narratives are built out of objects, display cases, and explanatory panels. A handbook on how to create temporary exhibitions tells curators that "preparing an exhibition is a lot more than simply gathering together several objects and placing them in a pleasing arrangement. When selecting your own things, ask the question: *What do I wish to accomplish?*"[39] Even once the objects are selected there is a great deal of manipulation that takes place to create the correct feelings, storylines, and spaces: "Designing museums exhibitions is the art and science of arranging the visual, spatial, and material elements of an environment into a composition that visitors move through. This is done to accomplish pre-established goals. The presentation of exhibitions in museums should never be haphazard or left to chance."[40] Usually, though, visitors are unaware of the exact, constructed nature of the three-dimensional text in a museum, as they have been socially conditioned to see museums as the holders of "truth" and to think of objects as silent testaments to the things that they have seen over their material lives.[41]

Visitors, too, as we have seen, create their own narratives in the museum. Even in a very regimented space it is impossible to completely dictate what a visitor will look at, in what order, and how they will choose to interpret what they see. This is as true with the mass of objects in an exhibition as it is with the individual solitary artifact. Thus, there are any number of individual narratives coming out of the exhibition space to complement or challenge the curatorial one.[42]

Nonetheless, object- and space-based narratives that rely on the arrangement of artifacts in a particular space are not the only ones to circulate around a temporary exhibition. The exhibition catalogue is a critical and usually omnipresent component of any exhibition. Historically, exhibition catalogues took the place of object labels and were carried though the museum by visitors so that they could refer to them for more information as they gazed at particular objects.[43] Now, though, they are more important as a commodity than as a useful guide. The books serve as a source of income for a museum, allowing it to profit from what can often be the expensive undertaking of creating and mounting an exhibition, and also take on iconic value of their own as status objects that can represent the owner's sophistication or cultural value.

What a catalogue does most clearly is provide a different sort of narrative take on the exhibition.[44] Transferring the exhibition experience to text produces a distorted version of the experience, allowing both clarification and obscuring of the information presented there as it moves into a new, two-dimensional form. The multivocality of objects—their ability to tell more than one story at a time, depending on how they are framed and presented or read—is necessarily flattened in a written text. Only one interpretation is available to the reader of a catalogue, whereas individual visitors to an exhibition can construct their own personal visions of the object and its story outside of the narrative given in the space.

However, while narrowing the scopes of narrative, temporary exhibitions also widen their path. There is more focus on individual objects in temporary exhibition catalogues than is usual in other forms of museum literature. The catalogue is one of the few places in which specific objects are given as much attention as the history of the whole institution. The objects are the focus of a temporary exhibition, instead of merely being an ancillary feature—which is how they are often treated in guidebooks, press releases, or histories of a museum. Furthermore, there are two ways in which objects can be presented in catalogues. Catalogues can use objects to either illustrate a story or to star in one of their own. The American exhibition chose to use the objects pictured in that catalogue as attractive additions to the story of the United States being laid out in the text. The *Wealth of a Nation* catalogue, conversely, had few narrative essays, and fewer still that dealt with the history of the nation. Instead, the bulk of the book was made up of short essays on the state of material culture and museums in Scotland and then an indexed list of all the objects featured in the exhibition, arranged by type and with scientific and catalogue data included.[45]

In this way the catalogue was more an encyclopedia of Scottish material culture than a history of Scotland. In the particular case of *The Wealth of a Nation*, the design of the catalogue reflected the missions of the exhibition itself—to showcase the objects of Scottish significance in all their multitude to an audience made up largely of those who already knew the bigger contextual history or who did not care. The objects in the exhibition, as in the catalogue, were meant to be important as and for themselves, without any need for explanation.

Some objects, however, can gain a considerable amount of aura and importance when they are explained and situated in context.

This was the case of the Monymusk Reliquary, where its story was entirely changed depending on the context in which it was seen. It is not always such a noticeable re-situation of aura that comes with contextualization, but rather a subtle enhancement of something that is independent of aesthetic or historical value. When given their correct framing and history these objects can become even more important for the temporary exhibition and for the museum in which they reside permanently. This can be seen in the story of another "star" iconic object from *The Wealth of a Nation*. In this case, the historical research that proved the object's provenance managed to tie it both to an iconic individual and to past incarnations of Scotland the Nation, which heightened the object's presence and story in the more modern time of the temporary exhibition.

Proving the National

Stories about the identity of objects and their provenance can be complex. On one hand they enhance the aura of the artifact by providing the solid veneer of authenticity. However, as in the case of the Monymusk Reliquary, they are sometimes hard to prove, even when they have persisted for decades and centuries. In the 1960s it came to the attention of both the National Museum of Antiquities and the RSM that a silver canteen set supposedly connected to the Stewart dynasty was about to go to auction. Christie's, the international auction house, sold the set on March 20, 1963, for £7,200. At the time of the sale, the canteen set was framed and presented in tandem with a story about the canteen and who and what it had witnessed in its life. This story, while intriguing and embedded within historical detail, was not accepted as a true and authentic provenance by museum officials at the time.

The action house's unofficial narrative claimed that in 1740 a Scottish Jacobite family had commissioned the Edinburgh Jacobite silversmith Ebenezer Oliphant to make a gift for the twenty-first birthday of Prince Charles Edward Stewart. Oliphant made a canteen picnic set, intended to be used when traveling or

The ornate silver picnic set made by Scottish supporters for the twenty-first birthday of Prince Charles Edward Stewart in 1740–41. Inside are a drinking cup, cutlery, a wine opener, and a nutmeg grinder, among other necessities. Outside on the richly chased exterior are a plethora of Jacobite symbols, from the three feathers in the crown, showing the Stewart's right to rule, to the ring of thistles showing never-ending Scottish support. © National Museums Scotland.

hunting. It included two beakers, two sets of cutlery, a combined corkscrew and nutmeg grinder for the preparation of spiced wine, a teaspoon that doubled as a scoop for bone marrow, and a little container for various condiments. All of this could fit into the highly decorated outer case, with a small dram cup that attached to the lid. Oliphant probably only made the outer case and beakers, and then fitted in other premade objects into the green velvet–covered organizer. When the canteen was completed in 1741 it was sent to Rome with one of the many nobles and messengers that frequently traveled back and forth between the courts at the time. The narrative goes on to say that the prince was very pleased with his gift, and he brought it with him when he landed in Scotland in 1745 to stake his claim to the throne.

The Jacobite cause did well at first, only to be pushed back and suffer a massive defeat on the fields of Culloden in April 1746. The prince managed to escape the carnage of the battle and its aftermath but had to flee Scotland without any of his baggage to avoid being captured. Opposing Hanoverian troops ransacked the carriages that had been left behind afterward, finding the canteen and passing it along to the commander of the loyalist forces, the Duke of Cumberland. Cumberland gave it to George Keppel, Lord Bury, his aide-de-camp, as a payment for loyal service both during the battle and after, when he was sent to London to spread the word of victory.[46]

This was the story with which the object was presented for sale in 1963. There were some documentable elements of the narrative. Lord Bury later became the Third Earl of Albemarle, and the canteen remained a family heirloom for many years. It was mentioned in the will of George Thomas, Sixth Earl of Albemarle, on May 17, 1888, as "the silver bowl and cover and travelling case of Prince Charles Stuart the Pretender, found in his tent at Culloden and given immediately after the battle by his royal highness the Duke of Cumberland to his aide-de-camp George Viscount Bury, afterwards 3rd Earl of Albemarle."[47] The canteen continued in the hands of the Albemarle family for two centuries, occasionally being loaned out for exhibits but mostly remaining a family object, albeit one with a celebrated history.[48] In 1963 it was exhibited at Christie's as part of their "Royal Gifts" sale. The trustees of the National Museum of Antiquities tried then to acquire it but failed due to lack of funds. Instead, it went to a Scottish collector and then continued to bounce between other collectors for some years, largely staying in Scotland.[49]

With its removal from the Albemarle family, though, the canteen seems to have lost some of its history as well, at least briefly. In 1967 the RSM organized an exhibit titled *Treasures from Scottish Houses* for the twenty-first Edinburgh International Festival. In the catalogue the canteen, on loan from Honorable Alan Mackay of Enterkine, was described as nothing more than "Camp Canteen, Scottish (Edinburgh), 1740–1741."[50] The detailed specification of the appearance and contents of the canteen made clear that it was the one formerly belonging to the Albemarles, but absolutely no mention was made of any links, supposed or actual, with the Stewarts, Culloden, or even the Albemarle family. The presence of the object had taken over any larger stories that it might have been held to tell, though Christie's had been very willing to use those stories to push a Scottish sale, and others had long shared these tales in order to ground themselves in where they were and what they had done historically.

This case highlights the ambiguities of provenance, its necessity, and its institutional use. In the modern museum context, objects are expected to have provable and authentic provenances. Having these gives the artifact the legitimacy it needs to be worthy of a place in the museum. This was not always the case. Earlier collectors such as William Hamilton, John Soane, and Walter Scott bestowed authority on their objects merely by having them. The presence of the object in the collections of these great men was proof enough that they were what they said they were.[51] Authenticity, then, is not a static truth but rather something that changes over time.[52]

Provenance, which now has to be "proven" with documentation and scientific tests, used to be a matter of word of mouth. Cultural theorist Dean MacCannell believes that the establishment of proven authenticity is one of the ways in which the modern world enshrines its objects and thus sets them apart from the life of the ordinary. This has to happen prior to what he calls the "naming phase" of the socialization process. Before an object can be sacralized, or given the legitimacy to be placed in a museum, it must be authenticated.[53]

The object that fails these tests—that is deemed inauthentic—is immediately considered less valuable, if it is worth anything at all. If a museum is "caught" displaying an inauthentic piece then some of its own credibility and legitimacy as an institution of history is tarnished. Because museums are expected to preserve and display the authentic, the presence of the inauthentic damages the mission of the whole.[54] However, overtly commercial enterprises such as the auction house are not seen as this same type of mediator for truth. Thus, Christie's could frame the canteen set using the story from the Albemarle family, even though it was not authenticated through the normal processes of provenance, which at that time would have focused mostly on a paper trail of documentation through the centuries. Four years later, though, the museum context in which the canteen was displayed had to opt for a more cautious framing and strict view of authentication, to avoid any criticism. What was authentic in the auction was not so in the space of a temporary exhibition.

But the familial narrative that linked Ebenezer Oliphant, the canteen, Prince Charles Edward Stewart, and the Earl of Albemarle would not disappear forever. It would return, and be better documented, but simultaneously raise new questions, this time about the one part of the story that seemed never to have been doubted—the essential Scottishness of the artifact. The canteen was put up for sale again in 1984, this time by a dealer who wanted to export it to a collector in America. He approached the museum before finalizing the deal, however, to give them the opportunity to match the offer he had and thus to secure the canteen for display in Scotland. Museum resources were immediately mobilized to prevent the canteen from leaving the country. They quickly applied for funding from the Heritage Lottery Fund and other sources.

By this time, though, doubts had emerged about the provenance of the artifact. If it was not what it claimed to be, was it really worth "saving" for the nation? Skeptics had even begun to doubt that the canteen could possibly have been made in Scotland. They pointed primarily to the decoration on the exterior cover of the canteen. It is lushly "chased" in the rococo style, covered with engravings of thistles, a medal of Saint Andrew, the Prince of Wales feathers, and other iconography. Supporters of the canteen-as-Jacobite-relic story saw these designs as proof of the connection with the Stewart dynasty. The decoration and symbolism was a sign of who Charles Edward was thought to be. The Collar of the Thistle was bestowed on him when he was young, as was the designation Prince of Wales and the Saint Andrew medal that denoted the Order of the Thistle. The decoration of the canteen was not meant just to look attractive but also to send a message of identity and belonging, telegraphing both what the giver of the gift valued and what the recipient was meant to embody.⁵⁵

To those on the other side, however, it was this very decoration that proved that the canteen could not be authentic, either as a piece of Jacobite history or as a noted example of Scottish silver making. The rococo art of chasing was not believed to be well known or well developed in Scotland at the time the canteen was made, and conventional wisdom in the 1980s held that the style, while long practiced in France, did not become truly widespread in Britain until the Victorian period.⁵⁶ Its presence on the canteen meant to many that it could not truly be a Scottish object of the 1740s, and therefore could not have any links with Prince Charles Edward Stewart and was not worth a campaign to raise the £145,000 necessary to procure it for the museum. Even the public got into the debate, as can be witnessed in the letters section of the London *Times*. On November 1, 1984, the newspaper ran a letter from a Judith Bannister, who wrote, "I do not believe that any silver chaser of 1740, either in Edinburgh or in London, would have treated the decoration in so typical a Victorian manner." She then continued, theorizing that a more obvious course of reasoning would be that it was "being later decorated in retrospective and nostalgic honor of the Young Pretender."⁵⁷

This appeared to be the general consensus. When the NMS appealed to the National Heritage Memorial Fund for help raising the purchase price, the fund responded with a list of detailed reservations about the authentication. Could a Scottish craftsman really have made something that was so unlike that which was being produced by English silversmiths at the same time?

Research into the nature of silversmith training in the eighteenth century, links between Jacobite networks in Scotland and France, and detailed examination of the object in question were all undertaken in an effort to prove the authenticity of the icon. In the end the Heritage Lottery Fund was presented with a letter of rebuttal by curators, former curators, and the director of the museum, as well as experts from the Victoria and Albert Museum. These experts said that new research had proven that

Edinburgh silversmiths were often in receipt of training from France that exposed them to skills and styles England did not see until much later. Ebenezer Oliphant, being a known sympathizer with the Jacobite cause, was likely to have had these connections, given the Stewart dynasty's relationship with France.

This research, along with documentary evidence from the Albemarle family and other chroniclers of Culloden, made it increasingly probable that the canteen had an authentic provenance as a relic of the Bonnie Prince. With this proof and the support it brought from the lottery fund, the National Museum of Antiquities of Scotland was able to appeal for the withholding of an export license, stopping the sale of the canteen abroad, giving them time to launch a successful public campaign to "save it [the canteen] for the Scottish people."[58] Finally it was purchased, and its first major public viewing was in *The Wealth of a Nation*, where it was presented both as an important relic of the Jacobites and as a detailed example of Edinburgh silver manufacture.[59] It was especially suited for display in the temporary exhibition, as the campaign for its purchase had already drawn attention to issues such as the dispersal of "Scottish treasures" outside the nation and the need to preserve these important objects for the public. All these ideas were central to the narratives of *The Wealth of a Nation*, and the way in which they could be "read" in the canteen strengthened their potency and added a veneer of immediacy to the project.

The canteen is now displayed as the centerpiece of the museum's exhibit on the Jacobites and Culloden and considered the most important of all the relics and personal possessions of Prince Charlie.[60] Potential narratives about the artifact as an important piece of Edinburgh silver, or as proof of artistic and trade links between Scotland and France, have to be left to other, more specific, temporary exhibitions. In the permanent galleries of the Museum of Scotland it is part of the story of the Scottish nation as a whole, thus its Jacobite narrative is foregrounded.

The Monymusk Reliquary, statue of Saint Andrew, and canteen set can all be easily understood as "treasures" of the nation. They are all old, rare, and associated with important and heroic figures from the Scottish past. Many of the other objects in *The Wealth of a Nation* were less obviously tied to the nation, even as curatorial staff included them in the narratives of the show. Modern objects, such as a specially commissioned outfit of tweed made in 1985, were displayed, as were selections of twentieth-century glassware.[61] Paintings and historic photographs shared space with art tapestries, fossils, and semiprecious stones. While discussing the objects grouped together into the "Transport Collection," which included a boat, a steam engine, and a car, the exhibition catalogue made a statement that could apply more widely to the whole show: that "the bulk of the material has a Scottish provenance although manufactured elsewhere."[62] What defined the majority of the objects in *The Wealth of a Nation* was a less-definable "Scottish provenance" than that which was seen in the iconic objects profiled above. However, the important idea for the narrative of the show was about the spread and scope of objects held by the NMS from which the individual Scottishness of each artifact could be assumed. Because of this expansive nature the catalogue from *The Wealth of a Nation* is still often cited as a comprehensive look at the national collections, giving the book a life above and beyond that of most more ephemeral temporary exhibition catalogues.

Temporary exhibitions are usually mounted to attract new and diverse audiences to a museum.[63] They also can serve to cast permanent exhibitions in new light and to give new narratives a chance to be explored. *The Wealth of a Nation* did all this and also much more. Because of its political and social mission to change the way that the material culture history of Scotland from ancient times to the present was displayed and thought of, it took on a more significant role than other temporary exhibitions. It further succeeded in its mission to convince the British government to at last commit the funding needed for a new, purpose-built National Museum of Scotland to replace the National Museum of Antiquities of Scotland and tell the story of Scottish history through the artifacts that had been collected since 1780. The next step would be to start the planning and get the museum built.

3
Creating a National Narrative
1998

In 1985, the National Heritage (Scotland) Act made the decision, at least on paper, to create an entity called the "National Museums of Scotland." Other than the new board, though, nothing changed with the existing museums. A small bit of wording in part 4 of the act, however, changed everything:

> (1) The Board may form a "Museum of Scotland" and may include in that museum any or all of the objects which:
> (a) are presently in the collections of the Royal Scottish Museum or the National Museum of Antiquities of Scotland; or
> (b) may become vested in the Board in the future.[1]

Finally there was a remit to create a museum officially of Scotland and Scottish history. It would take over a decade to do so.

In that time, several competing ideas emerged of what a Museum of Scotland should be. It could be a repository for an iconic collection, whose objects then speak for themselves, without the need for interpretive narrative history, or it could be an iconic architectural space that told of the importance and weight of the Scottish past through its strikingly modern presence. These were overlapping but also conflicting, visions. If the building made too large a statement, the objects would be lost within it. If the objects were foregrounded, there would be the danger of

The Newcomen engine in place in the gallery of the National Museum of Scotland. At 26 feet tall and 27.5 tons, it had to be cemented into the very fabric of the building. It was first installed in Caprington Colliery in Ayrshire in 1811. © National Museums Scotland.

creating a nondescript box of a building to house them. Battle lines were drawn throughout the long process of planning the museum in the 1990s. In the physical reality of the Museum of Scotland building as it was eventually realized, however, the division between the two sides is less obvious. The places where building and object intersect have only increased the iconic value of both. By their placement in the space, the objects' stories are strengthened, and the building takes on the nature of the stories that are being told within it. This point is best illustrated by the final positioning of one of the most striking objects in the museum.

The Newcomen Engine

As visitors enter the *Scotland Transformed* exhibits on the second floor of the Museum of Scotland, their attention is doubtless drawn to the soaring bulk of the metal and stone Newcomen engine. It reaches more than three stories high and is in operation at least twice a day. It would be grand and awe-inspiring no matter where it was displayed, but in the context of the Museum of Scotland building, it has extra resonance. The engine is iconic—it is used in the museum to tell stories that are larger than just its own. The museum houses many different iconic objects, but together all of these help the museum showcase different and overlapping narratives within its space. The stories of the Newcomen engine reflect the narratives of tension between collection and building, thus saying much more than it would were it displayed anywhere else. At the same time a visitor does not need to consciously know the story of the building of the Museum of Scotland to understand the engine. This is the beauty of the iconic object—it can be at once particular and universal. Uncovering the singular story of the artifact can bring to light much larger ideas.

The particular engine that is displayed in the museum is not unique in and of itself. It was made at the Carron Ironworks in Falkirk around 1781, following a type invented by Thomas Newcomen in 1712. It was installed at the Caprington Colliery near Kilmarnock in Ayrshire in 1811, and it worked pumping water out of the mines there until 1901.[2] There were hundreds of these engines produced and put to work in Scotland at the time, and they graced the vistas of the industrial central belt, coming to seem like any other natural feature in their ubiquity. Indeed, both the ironworks where the engine was made and its later industrial home became tourist sites in the eighteenth and nineteenth centuries, attracting hardy travelers looking for scenes of the "awesome" and "sublime." Thomas Pennant, one of the first travelers to note down his experiences in Scotland, wrote approvingly of his time observing the ironworks and the great modernity of its products, which were helping to improve Scotland.[3] The engine was considered as impressive and attractive a sight as the Highland waterfalls and craggy forbidding mountains also on an early tourist itinerary.

However, the engine was not just a static object of observation. This type of atmospheric engine, along with its descendant, James Watt's steam engine, were the first large-scale mechanisms for moving power and energy from one place to another. Without this capability, mines would have been abandoned before their stores were exhausted, and the industrial revolution would have faltered. The Carron Ironworks and engines like the Caprington Newcomen fulfilled a particular and urgent need that shaped modern Scotland in innumerable ways. Unlike some museum pieces, this engine was a vitally important working object, not a beautiful or special object created primarily for display. It did act as a type of muse for tourists, allowing them to envision the new prosperity that industrialization would bring to Scotland, but the workers in the foundry where the engine first came to life would doubtless have scoffed at the idea of preserving the engine inside, away from any useful work, just to be seen by tourists.

The transition from machine to artifact began when technological advances made its original purpose redundant. Although there were many Newcomen engines made in the eighteenth and nineteenth centuries, not many of them survived into the twentieth century. Most were removed from service and disposed of, either allowed to rust away or melted down to serve other purposes. The example at the Museum of Scotland is now one of a very few authentic engines on display. It was gifted to the Corporation of Kilmarnock for the Dick Institute Museum when the mine closed in 1903.[4] At the time it was presented in a series of boxes, rather than as a complete engine. The Dick Institute later gave it to the Royal Scottish Museum (RSM) in hopes they had space to display it. In 1958 the Newcomen Society in London congratulated the RSM for "preserving the last of the race in Scotland," even though there was no plan to display it at that point.[5]

It did not go on display until the new Museum of Scotland opened in 1998. Its large size, which had prevented it from being exhibited before, strengthened the artifact's case for display in the new space. "Wonder cabinets" of the Renaissance and later, which were often organized around principles of contrast, are usually considered the precursors to the modern museum. The smallest exemplar of something would be placed next to an abnormally large example of the same thing, in order to create a sense of awe in the viewer.[6] Although museum organization practices have moved beyond this in the modern era, visitors still expect a certain amount of awe in their museum experience. The sheer size of the large and overwhelming Newcomen engine, as well as the bonus of being able to watch it function, provides that sense of wonder, and perhaps persuades visitors to stay longer than they otherwise might. As the centerpiece in a large exhibition space, the engine tells its own story but also has a role to play in attracting visitors and pulling them through the gallery.

Appropriately, the Newcomen engine is the center of the "Power" subsection, surrounded by weaving machines and other detritus of mechanical Scotland. Whereas some iconic objects gain more power from being solitary, the great bulk of machines around the engine serve to reinforce its formidable presence. The display is tangible proof that the museum has given industry in Scotland a significant role, and by soaring above the masses, the Newcomen is the star. The same stories about industrial Scotland, the coal economy, and its ultimate downfall could have been articulated around other, smaller objects in the collections. Other objects may also have had a more explicitly Scottish story, as Thomas Newcomen was from Devon and lived there his whole life.[7] However, the Newcomen engine is big and unusual. Both of these factors helped it become a central part of the narrative in this part of the museum. Its connection to Caprington and the "Scottishness" of the individual engine received precedence over any larger story about the engine's inventor and use across Britain.

The engine had a starring role in the exhibit space even before there was a physical museum building. Entrants in the architectural competition to design the new museum were given a list of iconic objects around which to focus their design plans. The engine was the largest of these, and all conceptual drawings from the beginning of the project included this object.[8] The line between artifact and architecture was blurred throughout the museum, but here the one was literally built around the other. The engine, still in pieces, was lowered into position by a huge crane almost as soon as the foundations of the museum were dry. The walls and floors of the emerging structure were built around the engine's imposing bulk. This resulted in some very iconic publicity images for the Museum of Scotland, as the sight of the huge engine dangling off a crane on its way to be installed in the scaffolding-shrouded building site illustrated many a news story about the construction process. Through the new museum undertaking of the 1990s, it became a symbol of how Scottish history was going to be portrayed in fresh and exciting ways in the museum. Of course, it is also now a fixed part of the building. This is no temporary exhibition.

As part of the original brief, the Newcomen engine was also built into the concept of the building as a whole. The architects Benson + Forsyth developed an idea of "serendipitous discovery" where there would be no fixed route through the exhibits; rather visitors would be free to choose their own paths, catching glimpses of what was ahead or behind from everywhere they chose to go.[9] This postmodern narrative structure allowed flexibility of interpretation within a broader chronological structure and gave the artifacts the ability to direct storylines, depending on how they were viewed. Thus, peering through an architectural and ahistorical "arrow slit" in the walls of the Victorian section, one is confronted with the behemoth of industrialization that the chronological structure should have left behind. This interconnectivity helps reinforce the point made by the engine in the first place—that the coal industry and the revolution that it helped to fuel, as well as its tragic downfall, both mirror and foretell many later episodes of Scottish history. The positioning of the object within the built space of the museum helps both object and space tell new stories. Neither would be the same without the other.

The eighteenth-century tourists who saw the ironworks and their impressive engines were interested in the overwhelming technology and modernity of a new industrial process and the implications for how Scotland would change, as well as in the awesome spectacle of industrialization. Now, though, the engine says something quite different. As a museum artifact, it became a metonym. It was impossible for the entirety of the ironworks and the colliery to be placed in an exhibit, so the engine was, and is, expected to stand in, with its imposing presence, for a much larger set of places and ideas. The *Scotland Transformed* galleries were designed to cover everything from the 1707 Act of Union through the Jacobite rebellions to the burgeoning textile industry and the decline of crofting in the nineteenth century. They chart a path from growing victory to utter defeat with the Jacobites, and then back through the cycle a century later—from expanding and thriving industrialization to the failure of the coal industry and the concomitant loss of economic and social power. The Newcomen engine stands today, as it did at the opening of the museum, as a large, visible statement to pull the attention of visitors to all these narratives.

A visitor standing in front of the Newcomen engine likely knows nothing of the years of debate between curators and architects about whose idea of the museum would triumph. There are some who feel that large objects should not have been given such precedence and that the needs of the collections should have come before the creation of an artistically envisioned space.[10] The very situating of the engine has made the flexibility that the curators were hoping for largely impossible. Now, though, everything looks so permanent that the casual visitor accepts things as they are, free of debate.

The draw of the historical museum is the presence of the "real thing." In glass cases and behind explanatory labels is the authentic, the relic of history. There is a legitimacy to the space of the museum, where people are willing to suspend normal processes of doubt and believe they are seeing truth. Merely by being removed from the ordinary contexts of commerce and function, the object in the museum becomes an "artifact" or an "exhibit." Once placed in the museum and in the context of the narratives of Scottish history told there, objects such as the Newcomen engine take on richer layers of significance. People see them as things worthy of veneration and ascribe to them near mystical qualities, expecting to be told something about what they are and where they came from. Even ordinarily powerful objects become something more in the museum. The interaction of interesting object and powerful space creates a multifaceted experience that itself also reflects the iconic nature of the nation in which it is located and of which it is representative.

Nation and Museum

From its very inception the Museum of Scotland was an iconic place, distinct from the objects it held. The years of campaigning for a museum and then the years that followed, filled with committee meetings and gargantuan piles of exhibition briefs, allowed many opportunities for the retelling of the story of the Society of Antiquaries and its quest for a museum. Successive speeches and fundraising campaigns recounted how "almost alone Scotland . . . had failed to provide an adequate home for the collections."[11] This became an almost ritual invocation of a right to possess high culture and history. By recounting how Scotland had initially failed to have a museum then finally succeeded over and over, the Museum of Scotland took on the force of a natural and inevitable *telos* to three centuries of almost mythical questing by the "Scottish people." The tale was complete with requisite amounts of adversity, colorful characters, attractive props, and now a satisfyingly substantial conclusion in stone and concrete. The story became a part of public culture—it formed part of "a system of ideas and signs and associations and ways of behaving and communicating"—where those included in the group could root themselves.[12] The finished museum was the public and legitimate representation of this culture.

These ideas of the importance and weight of a national museum were intensified when in May 1997 a Labour government took power in Westminster. The new government immediately began implementing plans for a promised Scottish devolution referendum. A "yes" vote on this would implement something close to a federal system in Britain, where the Scottish Parliament, closed since 1707, would be reopened and given power for some issues that concern Scotland. Meanwhile, the Westminster Parliament would continue to control larger British affairs and international relations. Thus, power would be somewhat "devolved" from London.

The referendum, held on September 11, 1997, passed with a 74 percent majority, which meant that a Scottish Parliament would be convened for the first time since the Act of Union. This focused a new level of scrutiny on the Museum of Scotland project, less than a year away from opening. Suddenly the museum was to be "the first public building in both the 'new Scotland' and in Scotland's renewed capital city."[13] It was inevitable that new expectations would be imposed on this building, given the weight that history, and the public articulation of it, has always had in national rhetoric. According to David Clarke, keeper of archaeology and longtime museum employee, this museum "legitimizes things like the Parliament. There's no question that the national history in that sense has a role in legitimating the present political structures. It says it's okay for Scotland to have a parliament because, you know, Scotland is really a nation.... I think the Museum of Scotland is more important as a symbol of nationhood than as an informer of the nation's past.... All nations somehow have their national museums."[14] In other words, the very process of creating a national museum is a political act. Public display of collections, of objects from history, necessarily makes some assumptions that then support a sense of nation-ness. The presence of historical artifacts imbues the nation with an authentic past, which then helps to strengthen the case for an independent future. A national museum therefore assumes the presence of a recognizable nation.

Different players in Scotland had been making this case since 1780—first David Erskine, the Earl of Buchan, and the Society of Antiquaries of Scotland with their ongoing collecting and organizing activities in different spaces, then the Edinburgh International Festival and the RSM bringing in big international institutions to tell their national stories in Scottish space, then the staff of the National Museum of Antiquities of Scotland using their collections to demonstrate how much of the material culture of Scotland was going unseen. At the end of this, a national museum for Scotland was created on paper in 1985. But it took until the end of the 1990s, an era that also saw Scotland decide to reevaluate its national identity in other ways, for the proposed national museum to become a physical one. Because of this timing, the symbolic and performative role of the national museum became especially important.

So it was that a museum first and explicitly designed to give primacy to surviving pieces of material culture became something more. It became an entity on its own, part of the greater context of its location and timing. In this role of "museum as location of identity" it made perfect sense for George Dalgleish, one of the coordinating curators for the Museum of Scotland project, to comment that "I don't know whether it worked out this way, but I certainly always thought that I would have liked to have seen the museum as one of the legs upon which the new Scotland stood on; the museum—the national museum—the Parliament, and all the other great pillars of Scottish society."[15] Such sentiments would have resonated strongly with David Stewart Erskine and his compatriots at the founding of the Society of Antiquaries in the 1780s, as well as with the later generations of Walter Scott, who wrote the historical fictions of the Scottish past and brought King George IV to Edinburgh, or influential curators Daniel Wilson and Joseph Anderson. For all of these men, merely having the objects and artifacts of Scottish history was not really enough. Even at the very beginning of the society's long history, when the collections were largely undocumented and haphazard, there were efforts made to display them to as many members of the public as possible in order to tell the story of Scotland. It seems that there were multiple layers of importance here. Possessing the collections was significant, but there was always a belief that the objects deserved a building, and that being able to produce a recognized public display space was crucial to the whole undertaking.

A museum is a public space—one that has specific connotations of history and group identity enclosed within it. The museum has "become a place where people feel they ought to come to, and certainly ought to bring their children to . . . even though most of them couldn't actually define why."[16] Ernest Gellner thought that in the modern era this pervasive national culture took the place of earlier forms of authority. For him, "the cultures now seem to be the natural repositories of political legitimacy."[17] The museum has become the natural repository of much of that culture in its material form. However, because of the prevalence of culture and cultural rhetoric in our society today, museums are no longer just houses for historical objects. They are expected to say something on their own, even at the risk of overpowering the stories of the collections contained within them.

This idea of a museum as standing for something larger than merely a building or nice collection of stuff can be seen quite clearly in the process of creating the Museum of Scotland. It was there in the name itself. Changing context and differing design philosophies made the Museum of Scotland into more than just a home for the collection of Scottish material culture stored in the vaults of the National Museums of Scotland (NMS). It became seen as a stage, or a location, for the performance of a particular view of national identity. It became an icon itself, more voluble than those objects for which it ostensibly existed. It spoke of a nation on the brink of large-scale change, of the history and environment that had made it so, and the grand hopes for the future of a culture that was increasingly public and politicized.

When David Erskine first began the Society of Antiquaries of Scotland in 1780, his vision was possible because enough time had passed to transform the Scottish past from something that threatened British life by riling up Jacobites to a nostalgic tourist attraction. By the time the Museum of Scotland opened more than two centuries later, the past was again powerful political currency. The historical distinctiveness of Scotland had served to loosen some of the bonds between Edinburgh and London formed in 1707. The form of history that was to be presented in the new, highly symbolic Museum of Scotland was, by opening day 1998, seen as reflecting the vision of a modern Scottish nation with a newly independent future. The museum became the iconic heart of a new national landscape that was being created for and by Scotland.

The planning for the museum started with a vision of creating a home for the iconic objects of Scotland's material past. The artifacts were going to tell the stories that they could, and a larger connective narrative not supported by objects was going to be mainly left to the imagination. This idea was central from the very beginning of the planning process for the museum. On October 16, 1990, ten months after *The Wealth of a Nation* closed, a symposium was held in the RSM. Participants found themselves next door to the proposed site of the Museum of Scotland to discuss ideas for the new museum. The symposium was convened by the head of the NMS, Robert G. W. Anderson, and it covered topics including the feasibility of putting the museum where it had been planned, the potential role of the building itself in the vision of the new museum, how it would compare to other major national museums in the world, and finally how it would serve the people of Scotland and beyond. This served as an important first step in moving the museum from a political and social dream to a recognizable concept. Over the course of this symposium it was decided that, in keeping with the ideas of Daniel Wilson, David Erskine, and other early supporters of the Society of Antiquaries of Scotland, the new Museum of Scotland should endeavor to focus on the objects and tell the story of Scotland that emerged from them. In Anderson's words,

"The objects should tell the story, not that we should present a story illustrated by objects. This would mean, of course, that we would not be presenting a history, as written in textbooks, with objects as three-dimensional illustrations. The objects should speak for themselves, and should occupy the primary role in all displays."[18] With this statement he and the other conference participants envisioned the new Museum of Scotland as an unabashedly object-centered project.

There have emerged two general categories of history museums. One is narrative-based, where a complete history is told with authentic objects used primarily to illustrate the story throughout the museum.[19] Diorama-based museums largely do this type of display. The other style, with which the planners of the Museum of Scotland were aligning themselves, tells only the parts of the historical narrative for which there are surviving authentic artifacts. This approach leaves some necessary gaps in the historical narrative, preferring instead to focus on what the objects in their collections can say about the time that they witnessed. In the imagined Museum of Scotland the narrative was to be one of the surviving material culture history of Scotland and what that had to say about the past. The collections were central, and only the stories to which they led would be showcased.

When the Exhibition Review Committee and the Museum of Scotland Project members assembled the Museum of Scotland Exhibition Brief in December 1991, these ideas about the centrality of the artifact still held pride of place. The introduction to this seminal document—a first envisioning of what the museum would grow to look like and what ideas it would embody—embraced a narrative primarily based on objects rather than explanatory text: "It became clear very quickly that it would be neither possible nor desirable to fashion this material into a comprehensive 'History of Scotland.' The unique nature of the Scottish collections suggested different approaches, based on particular kinds of evidence . . . which allow many of Scotland's stories to be told. Assembling this evidence allows us to present aspects of Scotland, her history and her culture."[20] Objects and artifacts were going to be crucial because of the long and deep history of the collections as a precursor to the Museum of Scotland. The objects had been collected long before there was a public and national space in which to display them, and so their history was also the history of the nation itself.

The exhibition brief also acknowledged that any story told this way was not going to be complete: "The collections of Scottish material held by the NMS are the result of centuries of discovery and preservation. They are also the result of changing interests and priorities. . . . Changing perceptions of the stories to be told have influenced collection, and serendipity has also played a part."[21]

This brief was compiled by the Exhibition Review Committee, which had been convened for the first time earlier in 1991. There were many other committees and focus groups around the creation of the museum, all under the wider umbrella of the Museum of Scotland Project, but this one was focused solely on the internal design and messages of the new space. On the committee were the architects who had been chosen to design the museum—Gordon Benson and Alan Forsyth—as well as the director of the museum, the curatorial head of the project, and several specialized outside consultants. It had already been decided to structure the museum around a roughly chronological spine.[22] By the end of 1991, the committee proposed further divisions. The narrative of the museum was to be divided into three major sections: Beginnings, Early Peoples, and Scotland in History. "Beginnings" was to be focused mostly on the natural environment and geological makeup of the Scottish landscape. The "Early Peoples" section would cover prehistory and the archaeological collections, roughly until 1100. "Scotland in History" was to be the largest and most wide-ranging section, covering from around 1100 until the present day, or as close to the present as is possible in a static building. The analytic focus of this book is largely with this last, and largest, section of the museum.

These three divisions framed some of the first conceptual stories that the building would contain. Each section had its own group of materials and approaches to the story of Scotland, as well as a distinct type and number of artifacts. They were each assigned their own groups of curatorial staff, with Scotland in History further subdivided. All of the curatorial coordinators for the prehistoric and historic sections had been working for museums in Scotland prior to the Museum of Scotland Project. They moved into their roles as visionaries of a new museum while still continuing to work at the National Museum of Antiquities of Scotland, the institution to be replaced. This meant that the staff members who had been dealing with the objects in their antiquarian context now had to shift perspective and imagine these same artifacts in a very different space and narrative.

Although many of the same objects were going to be on display, the guiding thoughts behind the exhibits were arranged, even at a very early stage, to be quite different. As has been mentioned above, the Museum of Antiquities was the space in which Daniel Wilson worked out his theories of comparative societies, and its style of display was reflective of this, as well as being problematically influenced by the neo-Gothic space it occupied. University of Edinburgh professor Michael Lynch, one of the historical consultants involved in the planning of the new exhibits, said of the National Museum of Antiquities, "I liked bits of it. Other bits reminded me of an elderly aunt's sitting room, with junk, usually dusty junk, all about. It had the mark on it of being a kind of timepiece . . . what that period [the early twentieth century] thought was important in Scottish history. It had some good objects, but they were not displayed properly because the building made it impossible."[23]

The design of museum exhibits and display cases go through fashions, as new ideas of how material knowledge should be displayed come to the cultural forefront. This has been documented in art galleries, with their various types of "hangs."[24] The same is true in object- and history-based museums. Nineteenth-century aesthetics had called for the museum to present as much as possible to the eye of the visitor, whether those objects were displayed for beauty or to make anthropological and cultural statements.[25] At the time of the building of the new museum in Edinburgh, though, fashions had turned against that crowded look, preferring instead the modernist "white cube" vision that made individual objects, rather than their abundance, the goal.[26] This was the aesthetic to which the architects, if not all the curators, aspired. It was completely different than the desires and necessities of the earlier space and its time. The new Museum of Scotland represented a chance to remove objects from the constraints that had been placed upon them and let them tell new stories as part of a narrative of nationhood.

In the yet-to-be physically constructed Museum of Scotland the nation imagined was one seen through its surviving objects, rather than through repetition of the same historical stories that had always been told about it. This approach did not always meet with complete approval. Hugh Cheape, curator of Scottish history, remembers,

> There was a lot of criticism when we opened that there was an assumption that this was to be a new history of Scotland. And we said "oh, hey, hang about, it may be a new history of Scotland but it's actually the material culture history of Scotland, which we want to present to you." If you like, the history books are there. . . . There's no point in us pasting that up on the wall. But what those books lack are the real objects, and the real essentials of surviving material culture.[27]

The objects were, in the minds of the curators at least, imbued with a "truth," a story that was somehow more valid than those that have already been written. These real objects link the observer to the past in new and different ways, and were central to the project for all the curators I interviewed. They wanted to present the objects like the scene-setting tools of a radio broadcast. As one commented, "A museum display has to be about that imaginary exercise. . . . Your display has to provide people with the props."[28] The Museum of Scotland was to be for a long-imagined nation, and each person visiting it was going to imagine their own narrative, with the help of the iconic objects in front of them.

But this vision of an artifact-centered museum was not the only one under consideration as the plans were made. It could not, after all, be just a collection on display. The museum also had to be a location, a delineated space, and with that came new ideas of architecture and the national past.

Building Museum Space

Before the writing of exhibition briefs, before the granting of definitive government funding at the opening of the *Wealth of a Nation* blockbuster exhibition, there were a series of "advisory committee" reports on the feasibility and necessity of a new national museum for Scotland. This was just another tactic in the centuries-old conflict between Scottish cultural and political leaders and their counterparts in London. The Scots would petition for a museum, the British government would require more information on the need for it, a committee would be appointed, a report filed, nothing substantial done, and the pattern repeated years later.

The first major one of these was set up by the British government and the Scottish Office. Called the Committee for the National Museums and Galleries of Scotland, it ran from 1979 until 1981, under the chairmanship of Sir Alwyn Williams, a geologist who at the time of his appointment was principal of Glasgow University and chairman of trustees of the Natural History Museum in London, among other prestigious positions.[29] The committee was meant to examine the current provisions and status of museums and galleries in Scotland and report back to the government about what needed doing. The ensuing Williams Committee report, titled *A Heritage for Scotland*, was clear about its belief that heritage preservation and presentation in Scotland needed help.[30] The report recommended the reorganization of heritage institutions in Scotland to eliminate confusion about the varying remits of galleries, libraries, and museums, and it also formally suggested the creation of a new museum, which they wished to call the Museum of Scotland, that would finally address the national history of the country.

The report was scathing in its critique of the care that was being taken of the objects of material history that had first inspired the formation of the Society of Antiquaries of Scotland two centuries before. It said, "The greatest deficiencies we found were, paradoxically, in the exhibition, storage, and conservation of the very objects which reflect the uniqueness and genius of Scotland and confirm the importance of her contributions to western civilization." Given that, it was perhaps obvious that for the committee, the "most fundamental recommendation therefore is that the artifacts of Scottish Culture should be the concern of a new institution, the Museum of Scotland, at least comparable in space, staffing, and resources with the Royal Scottish Museum and wider in scope than the present National Museum of Antiquities of Scotland, which it is intended to replace."[31]

The Williams Committee called for the new museum to be "housed in a showplace for Scottish culture," asking that this showplace be put somewhere that was big enough and flexible enough to house the collections that were already in the National Museum of Antiquities as well as leaving space to expand.[32] They disliked the idea of placing the new building on the end of Chambers Street with the RSM. However, by the time the next committee report came out five years later, that plea had been rejected and plans were afoot to adapt the Chambers Street site to the needs of the nascent museum. This was a highly symbolic site in the eyes of several observers. The street is the heart of academic and intellectual Edinburgh, winding alongside the Robert Adam–designed heart of the University of Edinburgh, now called Old College. The committee waxed poetic about its connection to both Old and New Edinburgh, applauded its visibility, and expounded on the history of Chambers Street itself. Proponents thus began seeing the museum as a symbolic place of learning and importance before the first plan was even drawn up.

The Chambers Street site necessitated the construction of a new building. Building new fit neatly with the spirit of the Williams Committee, who acknowledged the antecedents to the museum but still aimed to "describe the Museum of Scotland as new in order to stress our belief that Scotland's heritage should be in the custody of a dynamic museum complex which is popular as well as respected."[33] To this end, a New Building Working Committee chose to hold an international competition to select an architect and design for the project.³⁴ The curators and committee members put together a substantial brief for the competition, with a list of objects to build around and general ideas about the material to be conveyed in the museum and through the collections. The trustees of the NMS also contributed a statement to the competition brief, saying that they were hoping for display of the collections in "a museum environment which will be enjoyable, readily accessible, and comprehensible to the public."³⁵ The competition was officially launched in January 1991.

Buildings make powerful statements, though we are used to walking by them daily without a second thought. They are subject to the same forces of objectification as the artifacts in the collections. Architecture takes space and makes it tangibly important, just as collections take things and make them historically important.³⁶ The architectural competition aimed to create an important space for Scotland. At a symposium prior to the opening of the competition, Sir Philip Dowson, a prominent architect and head of the competition judging committee, reflected on the task ahead: "Buildings are experienced in memory, so the new extension will have to be strong enough to stand adjacent to that great space. There is narrative quality in moving from one place to another place, providing the story of the whole. Whilst being strong and holding its symbolic place, it should seek to do so with humanity and in a way that is accessible and inviting."³⁷

Many levels of narrative and symbolism were expected of the new building, as the external counterpart to the relics inside. It was clear that the collection could no longer be housed in just a "black box"–type shell, empty of any story apart from that of its contents. The building of the Museum of Scotland was expected to say things about Scotland and history and nation before it was even designed, partly because of the weight of expectations being placed on the museum as a shrine for a nation, but also because of the larger fashion at the turn of the twentieth century for iconic Modernist and postmodernist architectural statements.

From hundreds of initial entries the competition field was winnowed down again and again. The Edinburgh- and London-based firm of Benson + Forsyth was eventually declared the winner, and their design of "a building to encapsulate national identity" was much praised for its links to the surrounding area and the larger "national" ideas. It was to be a postmodernist building of Clashach golden sandstone, with a form inspired by the towers of Scottish brochs or traditional roundhouse castles found only in Scotland, the standing stones of Callinish, and Dunstaffnage Castle, among other references.[38] Interior spaces were made to evoke ship hulls and Glasgow's and Clydeside's industrial history of red steel, and to move from the dark spaces of medieval homes to the lighter, airier feeling of modern factories as a visitor moves through the chronological timeline of the museum. Much has been made of these links to a Scottish history and of the local materials used. All through the design process Benson + Forsyth proved themselves adept at creating an idea of the museum building as a type of *ethnoscape,* a specially produced space that, according to nationalism theorist Anthony Smith, creates certain ideas in the mind of people who experience that space. The ethnoscape is a place that is "no longer merely a natural setting. It is felt to influence events and contribute to the experience and the collective memories that molded the community."[39] The museum building was not a natural setting. It was created with certain thoughts and ideas in mind, ostensibly to set the stage for the "treasures" contained inside. However, it took on a role even bigger than this and became an icon representative of larger ideas about Scotland and nationness as well.

The new building was not merely to be the home for a particular collection of objects. In order to truly symbolize all of Scottish culture, not just hold it, the building needed to do more. Some of the competition assessors saw the design as "synoptic of Scottish culture and its artifacts."[40] This implied that the building was doing exactly what participants at the 1990 symposium had wanted it to do: "Buildings occupy, articulate, and enclose public spaces. . . . Above all, however, buildings are located necessarily in the dimensions of space and time—that is, context."[41] With its echoes of crumbling castles, rounded protective brochs, and rich local stone, the building was articulating an explicitly Scottish public space. This was not just any building but one steeped in Scottish

A detail of the entrance to the Museum of Scotland building. It was designed to evoke traditional Scottish brochs or round castle towers. Visitors would hopefully feel as if they were entering somewhere fortified, where treasures were stored. Local golden clashach stone was used for the cladding. © National Museums Scotland.

materials, Scottish history, and Scottish references. Context and connection of outside and inside were central to the design philosophy of the architects, who saw their role as more than simply the creators of a stage for the objects. They wanted their design to encourage visitors to wander, "composing their own journey not only through the building, but through Scotland's history, informing their own unique view."[42] Thus, "the narrative of the museum would enhance the narrative of the object."[43]

Where the museum used to be based solely on a centuries-old collection bereft of a permanent home, it now seemed to be in danger of being overcome by its space. The Museum of Scotland was, with name and building, taking on different stories than those purely based on the collections. It was becoming more of a symbolic place than an object-driven historical exercise. This set up a series of largely inevitable tensions between the two approaches. As curator David Caldwell later recalled, "The architects believed that they had been given a remit to come up with a building which would be a work of art, that would be a striking landmark, and that the objects in it were subsidiary, would support their architectural vision. . . . Whereas we as curators had started from the viewpoint that we wanted an empty space in which we could develop exhibitions about Scotland's past. And the two sets of aspirations were not a good match with each other, it's fair to say."[44] The architects were protective of their vision for the museum and sometimes unwilling to let objects or labels intrude onto the surface of their design plan. This meant that "there definitely was a tension between the building as a building, a work of art, and the building as a functional museum" developing in the minds of the curators.[45] This situation was dealt with in a variety of ways, from the archaeology section that effectively withdrew from the overarching design plan to the historical galleries that submerged curatorial ambitions to design imperatives. In general, the architectural vision often won over the curatorial one, as the museum was progressively being seen more from the outside as a whole, rather than as a collection of objects.

Since the building was completed, this architectural agenda has been constantly reiterated both inside the building in tour group monologues and expository labels, and outside the space in press coverage and public opinion polls. The building and the symbolism of the architecture is routinely mentioned well before the exhibits are discussed.[46] Indeed, the objects are secondary to people's impressions of the space. One of the earliest reviews of the new museum recognized this, noting, "The essence of the city and of Scottish history has been distilled into one supremely symbolic, semi-abstract object. The collection it houses seems a bit thin, but that hardly matters anymore; new museums attract people through their architecture, not their contents."[47] Because of its impressive new home, the museum said something that it had not before. Purely through architectural mass and gravitas, the objects within were imbued with a new sort of public legitimacy. One of its curators said that the architectural form meant that the museum became well known through being housed in "a building that says this is an important place."[48] The shape of the building also echoed other, older visions of the role of museums, namely as a storehouse where treasures are kept locked away.[49] The architectural images embedded in the building, like the aforementioned ones of castles and protective brochs, give the objects inside more importance by sequestering them away from the gaze of the casual passerby.

So, a museum is objects, and a museum is a building, but it is also more than that. It is a whole institution—one used by people. And as the Museum of Scotland opened and settled into itself, the curatorial team involved most heavily in the planning for the new institution recognized this fusion. Reflecting on the good and bad parts of the museum since it opened, Hugh Cheape spoke about expectations—particularly around the Scottish symbols of tartan and bagpipes:

> I think that if we are not prepared to recognize the expectations of our public, and the expectation of visitors coming from abroad and deal with those enquiries and that expectation and curiosity in a learned way because our collections are very very good in tartan and in bagpipes . . . I'm bemused as to why we are so shy about it. So that's something I would do differently. I would be more upfront with these things, they're colorful, they're sound, they speak, and they . . . tell stories of elements of European or world culture such as in music, such as in dress, where Scotland has produced something amazingly distinctive.[50]

Where during the planning stages the team was keen to keep the stories in the museum to the more academic, once the project was live, they realized that from a visitor standpoint it seemed a bit lacking. They began to see that, as George Dalgleish put it,

> We have a national museum. We have a museum of the nation of Scotland. It's not the national museum in Scotland. It's the national museum of Scotland. A large percentage of our collections relates entirely and directly to the development of Scotland as a nation, whether in the union, out of union, whatever, or before it was a nation. The land of the nation we now call Scotland. It's a national museum, and it says something about national identity. It's part of who we are, and to a certain extent I think that's true of any sort of history museum. It says something about the groups you see yourself as part of. And I do feel very strongly personally that Scotland does have a distinct, unique, national identity. For good or bad. So, I see it very much as a statement about national identity, created by a group of people who encompassed all kinds of parts of Scotland's makeup. It wasn't created entirely by Scots, whatever being a Scot means. But it was created by people who at the time were part of Scotland.[51]

Once the hard work of crafting new exhibition plans and commissioning a new building was done from 1990 to 1998, then the team could sit back and really consider the larger impact of what they had accomplished. Scotland finally had a national museum. They may not have been entirely pleased with the building or the layout or the signage. They may not have thought visitors would completely understand what they intended to do by telling only the stories of Scottish history that had surviving authentic objects. But there was now a national museum where before there had been none.

4
Objects Connecting Nations
2005–2006

The 1984 *Treasures of the Smithsonian* and the 1989 *Wealth of a Nation* exhibitions paved the way for the 1997 creation of the Museum of Scotland, which then allowed for the establishment of a new object-centered narrative of Scottish history. This focus on the home nation did not mean, however, that museums in Scotland became introspective. Museums have always been embedded in a worldwide network of fellow institutions that allows for sharing of knowledge and trading of exhibitions. In Scotland this has, of course, dated back to at least the nineteenth century, when curator Daniel Wilson closely collaborated with his Scandinavian counterparts to organize and exhibit both of their collections.[1]

This tradition of curators forging international connections in order to better understand their own Scottish collections remained, particularly during the summer international festival season. This was a time for the National Museums of Scotland (NMS) to emphasize its connections with other large institutions and to host exhibitions that framed its permanent collections in new ways. Earlier shows had relied on the unilateral narratives of one institution, even as these nations' objects were displayed in a new space. However, more collaborative temporary exhibitions allowed new storylines to emerge that were not native to either of the partner museums. These would not exist without the moment in time when the new display was created. It was this sort of narrative, produced in partnership with a new type of museum, that came to the NMS in 2005 and 2006. These two summers marked the start of a collaboration with the State Hermitage Museum in Russia and featured two exhibitions—first *Nicholas and Alexandra: The Last Tsar and Tsarina* and then *Beyond the Palace Walls: Islamic Art from the State Hermitage Museum*—which were both distinct from the types of temporary exhibitions that had come before them.

The institutions that had first generated temporary exhibitions in Scotland were explicitly national museums—ones whose guiding narratives were of the history of the nation and its objects. But this approach is not the only possible format for a large museum. There is also the type that some scholars of museum studies have termed "universal survey" institutions, such as the Louvre and the British Museum.[2] Their collections hold representative samples of art and objects from across the world and signal national identity through displays of power, rather than displays of national events or personages. Treasures of acknowledged universal importance stand to represent the relative power of the displaying nation and make statements on their taste and sense of civilization. The iconic objects held in these institutions differ from the ones already profiled, as they do not attempt to represent a story of national history. Instead, their aura is all about the power of the icon to transgress national boundaries and speak to all of human history. The universal survey museum holds collections of these universal icons of culture, which are expected to resonate with audiences regardless of their particular nationality.

Universal or not, museums are all national in location, as they are all situated in a particular state, and in many cases were established with significant government help. The boundaries of "state" and "nation" are often far from congruent.[3] Nonetheless, state institutions such as museums are expected to represent the nation in the public consciousness. By their very presence, national museums elide the difference between nation and state, creating as they do so a unitary identity, where a perhaps-conflicted identity can be clarified and set into the very stones of the buildings.[4]

So far in this analysis, I have given most attention to Scotland as the home of a national museum. However, the Royal Museum of Scotland (RMS), though connected physically and institutionally to the new Museum of Scotland and falling under the larger umbrella of the NMS, is closer to a universal survey museum than an explicitly national one. As was discussed earlier, the history of the two institutions is a complicated one, changing and evolving over time. In 2005, they were physically connected buildings, with the RMS meant to show "the world the Scotland" and the Museum of Scotland meant to show "Scotland to the world," both under the institutional control of the NMS board.

It was in the space of the RMS that most temporary exhibitions were held, but it is the story of the particular nations involved that have been the central focus of the book so far. The pair of temporary exhibitions in 2005 and 2006 that came to Scotland were from the State Hermitage Museum, St. Petersburg, an institution that has similar tensions between the national and universal. The collaboration created new storylines for both host and loan museum that called on their dual identities and allowed interesting new narrative features to emerge that spoke not only of the two nations involved but of more universal themes as well.

Establishing links with large museums such as the Hermitage can be extremely beneficial for smaller partner institutions. However, it can also be beneficial to the larger museum, providing a way for it to reinterpret itself and break out of old stereotypes and an opportunity to reevaluate collections and narratives. Because of the level of expectations placed on them, the large iconic institutions often have less scope to change their exhibitions, reinterpret their collections, or try something new. The visitor to this type of institution expects certain things, and to see them in a certain context. The British Museum could not just place the Elgin Marbles in any ordinary exhibit room, interspersed with other objects of antiquity. The public expects them to be special, and so they must be framed as such. They also have to be easily accessible to the audience, not demanding too much self-direction from the majority of the visitors that are going to see them.[5]

At points in their history certain institutions become associated with particular iconic objects. The museum can then heighten the implicit aura of these objects by framing them differently for the larger expected audience. Within this sacred and delineated space, then, the aura and power of the iconic object grows merely because it has been set apart from the "regular" museum artifacts. Thus a cycle of iconicity is created from which it is nearly impossible to break, especially in the current climate of the heritage sector, where "audience response" seems to be the guiding principle. If visitors demand it, the museum must to some extent give into those expectations.[6] Temporary exhibitions can reinforce these expectations in crowd-pleasing shows, such as that of the Chinese terra cotta army at the British Museum, but exhibits can also challenge them, providing an opportunity to try out new narratives, with new icons, to new audiences.[7] A partnership with Russia provided an opportunity for this in Scotland.

Making Contact, Building Bridges

Russia and Scotland would not at first glance seem to be the most obvious partners for a joint venture. Whereas the United States is a country of immigrants (many of whom claim and celebrate Scottish roots), Russia does not have that history. Nonetheless, there have been many historic and cultural connections between Scotland and Russia. At the height of the Romantic era the poetry of Robert Burns and the novels of Walter Scott became fashionable in Russia, creating a strata of the Russian elite who glamorized the wild, awesome landscapes of the Scottish Highlands.[8] Many ties developed between the Russian ruling families and their counterparts in Britain, along with the myriad travelers, missionaries, soldiers, and teachers from Scotland and Britain who lived and worked in Russia. The catalogue and advertising material for both of the temporary exhibitions examined here highlighted these themes.[9] What were less well explained were the larger contemporaneous global and societal contexts that shaped the connections between the two nations and their museums.

Although the court of the tsars was internationally focused, and succeeding monarchs prided themselves on their familial and cultural ties to Western Europe, after 1917 isolationism took hold with the rise of the Bolsheviks. This inward vision intensified and persisted throughout the Soviet era. But with the fall of the communist state in the 1990s, bridges to the West were recreated. In decades where the political and economic structure of Russia was struggling to find stability, cultural outreach focused international attention on the rich history of the country, rather than on the more difficult current situations. Given all this, as well as the detailed themes of the two exhibitions to be mounted, the connection between the Hermitage and the museum in Scotland come to seem clearer. It was a way to reestablish and reemphasize ties between two cultures that were formerly close and to do it in a way that would benefit two separate museums. For the NMS it was a way to raise its profile both within and outside of the United Kingdom and to attract new visitors.[10] For the Hermitage it was a way to reframe parts of the collections while exposing itself to an audience outside Russia.

The State Hermitage Museum has been open to the public in some form since 1714, though most sources date it only from Empress Catherine II's purchase of its first substantial collection in 1764.[11] It existed in many different locations and forms over the centuries, and now takes up the entirety of the Winter Palace in St. Petersburg, formerly one of the homes of the tsars.[12] The Hermitage is of the same universal spread and international caliber as the Louvre. Like the Louvre it also contains historical objects, but in both cases the art triumphs in the public's view.

Nevertheless, in 2004 several curators and members of the staff at the RMS approached their colleagues at the Hermitage about mounting a series of exhibitions in Edinburgh that would highlight some of these lesser-known parts of the State Hermitage collections, and thus would expose the depths of the Hermitage's collections beyond iconic pieces of art. These exhibitions would take advantage of the summer festival season in Edinburgh, and the added publicity gained by an international spectacle of rarely seen objects would hopefully be a blockbuster, of benefit to both associated institutions.[13]

The "blockbuster" exhibition relies on a near-perfect convergence of subject matter, style of presentation, and timing, as well as a smattering of luck.¹⁴ The work put into creating excitement around the exhibition is always important, and the Edinburgh International Festival provides more than enough media and public relations coverage to create a certain level of excitement and capture audience attention. While a museum can never be entirely sure of creating a blockbuster, there are certain things that can be done to make the outcome more likely.

Primary among these is the selection of subject. Something that fires the imagination with grand sweeping narratives and that is also well-established in public consciousness is a good starting point. If it can possibly include the universally titillating themes of opulence, death, and mystery, it is likely to succeed. Like a novel or a film, museum visitors often see an exhibition as an escape from the reality of their lives. The extraordinary and fantastic, the luxurious or shocking are always attractive because they appeal to the emotions as well as the mind. This has been the case from the earliest proto-public museums, the cabinets of curiosity, to the first "blockbuster exhibition," that of the treasures of King Tut.¹⁵ The recipe seems to ask for a representation of ubiquitous human values added to the basic factors that create and emphasize the aura of museums and their objects at any time. In this way, a blockbuster can be seen as the distilled essence of what museums should strive to do more generally.

Nicholas and Alexandra

The first exhibition in the NMS-Hermitage collaboration, *Nicholas and Alexandra: The Last Tsar and Tsarina,* had in its very nature all the ingredients for a blockbuster. While the Russian state and Soviet government largely put tsarist history behind them for decades, the Western world remained fascinated with tales of tragic royalty, ill-fated opulence, and mysterious death, all of which were contained in the story of Russia's doomed final rulers. The imperial families of Russia were famously acquisitive and employed large numbers of craftspeople to create treasures for them, as well as inspiring others. The public has long been intrigued to see these sort of goods, especially if they were previously hidden away in royal coffers. One has only to witness the lines at the crown jewel rooms of both the Tower of London and Edinburgh Castle to see that interest in the shiny artifacts of ruling families is driven by urges more universal than just the tragic story of the doomed tsars of Russia.

To some extent this desire is why museums exist. In a time when very few can entertain like a Russian tsar, all can at least see the luxury that once surrounded the royal family. Treasure, riches, rarity—all are words of great power and mystique, as well as ones repeated over and over in the published catalogues and other publicity for temporary exhibitions. The close association of these types of descriptors with royal families, especially that of Russia, can help to explain why the tsars are perennial favorites for various temporary exhibitions. Some are historically focused, such as *Nicholas and Alexandra,* and some are design-centered, such as *Magnificence of the Tsars,* a 2008–9 exhibition of imperial costume at the Victoria and Albert Museum.[16] However, the central storyline of these shows, no matter what discipline they are framed within, is that of the opulence and essential foreignness of the tsars and their lifestyle.

The Russian imperial court realized quite early on that accumulating luxurious and historically valued goods would increase the esteem in which they were held by their Western neighbors. Empress Catherine II, also known as Catherine the Great, was the doyenne of this sort of thinking, and she had no qualms about opening the imperial coffers for symbolic purchases, like a 1,222-piece dining set bought in 1773 from famous potter Josiah Wedgwood, each with different hand-painted views of Britain, including a special hidden frog.[17] This huge commission was displayed in London prior to being sent from the factory, and some pieces were also displayed in 1909, before returning for a major Wedgwood show at the Victoria and Albert Museum.[18]

Being able to make such a large purchase from Britain's preeminent designer, especially of items decorated with quintessentially British scenes, was important to Catherine, as she wanted to both impress other heads of state and also make her own courtiers hew closer to the British style.[19] In addition to the Frog

Service, as the china was known, and several other Wedgwood commissions, Catherine amassed a huge collection of European art. The first purchase of paintings was the collection of Johann Ernst Gotzkowsky, a Prussian trader faced with bankruptcy. His collection included 317 paintings by Flemish and Dutch masters including thirteen Rembrandts, eleven Rubens, and a Titian. In her lifetime she acquired 4,000 paintings, 38,000 books, 10,000 engraved gems, 10,000 drawings, 16,000 coins and medals, and a sizeable natural history collection.[20]

The original Hermitage was inspired by Peter the Great's trip to France, where he was much taken with Versailles and in particular the small house that Louis IV called his "hermitage." When Peter returned to Russia he built for himself the Peterhof, a model of Versailles complete with small "hermitage" outbuilding.[21] His descendant, the Empress Elizabeth, designed her palace, Tsarskoe Selo, after his designs and also included a "hermitage" — in this case a large baroque dining room for private meals with her confidants and beautiful pictures on the wall.[22] Following the tradition, when Catherine II had her own palace, the Winter Palace, she had a small addition put onto it that she too called "her hermitage."[23] This was both a place to put treasures that were overflowing the rest of the Winter Palace and, interestingly, a guesthouse for famous French writer and playwright Voltaire, one of Catherine's frequent correspondents, if he ever came to Russia.[24] Another major expansion, called the Old Hermitage, was built in 1770. By creating these treasure houses, Catherine — herself an iconic personality who was well aware of the importance of creating a public persona — was helping to form the first strands of ornate mythology that would grow to encompass her ill-fated successor Nicholas II.

Nicholas II, the great-great-great-grandson of Catherine II, thus grew up in an environment full of the very best objects from across Europe and naturally became accustomed to having gilded treasures all around him. It was these treasures of his reign, as well as his eventual tragic demise, that led to the positive reception that the exhibition received in Scotland.[25] Bolshevik revolutionaries shot Nicholas; his wife, Alexandra; their four daughters;

and one young son in 1918—though these facts remained a mystery for many decades afterward.[26] The opulence and luxury that surrounded the last Romanov family and their death, as well as the many Hollywood films that the story inspired, made the story of Nicholas and Alexandra an exciting concept for the designers and marketers of a temporary exhibition.[27] Its popularity as a narrative and exhibition helped to explain why the planning for *Nicholas and Alexandra: The Last Tsar and Tsarina* in Edinburgh could be completed much more quickly than is usual for a major temporary exhibition. Ordinarily, an exhibition of this size and scope would have been three years in the planning.[28] Instead, working together, NMS and State Hermitage Museum staff had everything constructed in twelve months.[29]

This speed was possible for a number of reasons. First, like the quickly assembled Smithsonian exhibition, the Edinburgh exhibition was preceded by a similar show organized by the Hermitage. From 1999 to 2001 an exhibition titled *Nicholas and Alexandra: The Last Imperial Family of Tsarist Russia* toured three sites in the United States. The exhibition was co-organized by the State Hermitage Museum and a company called Broughton International.[30] This company was one of a growing number of professional organizations that design, coordinate, and market self-contained exhibitions. They specialized in procuring internationally famous objects for smaller or lesser-known museums that wanted a boost of publicity and attendance.[31] By any measure, this first incarnation of the Nicholas and Alexandra exhibition was a roaring success. Its host museums in Wilmington, Delaware; Mobile, Alabama; and San Diego, California, all apparently had large numbers of visitors, an increase in entrance fees, and empty shelves in their gift shops.

The website and exhibition catalogue for this first incarnation says that "he exhibition was conceived as a way to show the human side of the well-known story of the last imperial family of Russia—the love story, their devotion to family, the unparalleled splendor of the Russian court, and the tragic fate which befell them." To do this, the exhibition was divided into five themes: "The Family," "The Church," "Wedding and Coronation," "The

Wardrobe," and "Court Life."[32] In contrast, the NMS exhibition "tells the story of the last imperial family of Russia. Through the very personal items connected to the family—including court costumes, uniforms, paintings, furniture, and toys—it is possible to gain an understanding of the relationships and events which eventually cost them their lives. At times it is a very moving and human story, set against the backdrop of a society in the midst of significant change."[33] There were more themes—ten major ones, each with affiliated subthemes—and the story follows a much more narrative arc. However, the similarities in rhetoric are obvious, and most of the objects from the American exhibition were also seen in Scotland. The changes were mostly additions of Scottish objects added into the narrative.

The American traveling exhibition about Nicholas and Alexandra meant that the collections of the Hermitage had already been assessed for objects that could help to tell their story. Some of the material culture narrative was already established and would have made the planning of any related narrative easier. That is not to say, though, that the processes were identical. The American incarnation was generic, meant to showcase treasures, tell a brief story, and act in precisely the same way in a variety of spaces. It was to stand completely alone and be consumed by the visitors with little need to access a deeper meaning than that of "treasure." The storyline about the individuals involved acted merely as a way into the life of the objects and all their glory, as well as providing the suitably tragic ending. The Scottish exhibition, on the other hand, was orchestrated by a designated team of NMS staff, in concert with their colleagues in St. Petersburg.[34] Not only was it to show the human side of historical personages; it also meant to highlight the longstanding links between Scotland and Russia. This was a major addition to the existing framework of previous Nicholas-and-Alexandra–based exhibits and books, as well as something that the Hermitage exhibition in Scotland had in common with its Smithsonian predecessor, *Treasures from the Smithsonian*.

The addition of personal story and national links to the narrative of the exhibition meant that the objects were treated differently than in the American incarnation of the exhibition. In a unique twist to the common construction of these temporary exhibitions, the NMS curatorial team was allowed to roam freely through the Hermitage collections and personally select the objects they wished to use. Only one object out of the hundreds on the wish list was refused—and this, a ceremonial throne, was on the grounds of conservation and condition, not because the Hermitage curators did not want it used in the exhibition.[35] The curators tried specifically to locate and display objects that highlighted the connections between imperial Russia and Britain, particularly Scotland.[36]

National Icons, but of Which Nation?

In the foreword to the *Nicholas and Alexandra* catalogue, the director of the NMS, Gordon Rintoul, posited that "he links between Scotland and Russia go back many centuries. Scots were instrumental in the formation of the Russian Navy.... Scots served as soldiers, physicians, and governesses to the Russian Imperial families and aristocracy. The architect Charles Cameron, another Scot, was responsible for some for the finest buildings commissioned by Catherine the Great. To this day there continues to be an enduring affinity between Scotland and Russia."[37] These connections, as well as the cultural ones mentioned earlier, were continually emphasized to legitimize the Hermitage's visit to Edinburgh—in much the same way as the story of James Smithson's trip to Scotland was used to underpin the Smithsonian's visit to the Royal Scottish Museum twenty years before. Rintoul then continued on this same theme even as he thanked the exhibition sponsor, Scottish & Newcastle (a major brewing company), lauding it by claiming that "the activities of the company in Russia today continue the long-established trade links between our two countries."[38] The director of the State Hermitage Museum provided a noneconomic rationale for the longstanding and growing connections between the two countries. When asked by a journalist about why the Hermitage agreed to help with the exhibition, he first gave generic explanations, such as increased publicity for his museum. He then veered from the normal bland path of public relations to say that "the character, the personality of the Scottish people is a little bit like the Russian people. They are very much different from the people in England."[39] This gives a bit of the flavor of the rhetoric that surrounded the connection between Scotland and Russia in the exhibition. Each of the objects in the show was framed in the catalogue and text to be highlight it emotional charge, especially ones that could be held to represent both nations in their provenance.

Whether these dual narratives of nation would have been noticeable without the particular constructed context of the exhibition is debatable. Constructivists such as Pierre Bourdieu would say that the object itself is inherently mute, and that all the meaning it has is a result of how it has been manipulated and framed. Objectivists, such as Bruno Latour, on the other hand, believe that the object, any object, speaks of and for itself, despite efforts to alter its voice.[40] Both of these viewpoints have their adherents and are useful intellectual angles from which to look at museums and their objects and exhibitions. But each artifact, each exhibit, each institution, calls on elements of each. The iconic object speaks for itself, regardless of context. At the same time, because of their multivocality, the stories told with and by objects can be changed by shifts in context and time—as previously discussed. A good exhibition takes the objects that naturally fit into a given narrative and then enhance that part of their story by creating the correct frame around them, so that the visitor to the exhibition sees the narrative that the curators choose to present at any given time. This is just what the curatorial team in charge of *Nicholas and Alexandra: The Last Tsar and Tsarina* did. They consciously chose objects that represented the links between Scotland and Russia, and then strengthened those narratives through the use of the other trappings of an exhibition, such as labeling, photographs, videos, and catalogue text.

Icons and Iconic Objects

One of the most interesting feats of the *Nicholas and Alexandra* exhibition was the display of a 394-foot-long painted panorama scene of Queen Victoria's Golden Jubilee celebrations, which showed the royal parades and events that occurred during the Jubilee. Paintings are liminal objects in the world of museums, belonging as they can both to museums of fine art and museums of history. Their meaning would necessarily change given which of these two contexts they were seen in, and the decision of where to place them is often a fraught one. However, they also very easily become iconic artifacts. Indeed, they were the first objects to be considered "iconic." Because they actually depict the people and often the ideas that they are trying to evoke, paintings are one step closer to a "pure" icon than objects—which rely more on the viewer to understand what they stand for. The viewer of the painting is not just seeing events as they unfolded but seeing something of the artist who is recording them. Also, the iconic object (or painting) does not only represent the people depicted within it. The iconic painting can transmit ideas about the nation that holds or displays it, and many other concepts as well.

When a painting is chosen for display in a history museum or exhibition, it becomes primarily an object of history, rather than an object of artistic value. The impact of crossing this line of interpretation can be seen by looking at the differing ways paintings are labeled and presented in portrait galleries versus galleries of art. National portrait galleries tell the history of the nation through portraits of those people who have impacted its history and formation. Labels on these paintings are mostly concerned with the subject of the portrait, rather than the artist. National galleries of art, conversely, treat the portraits that they display as examples of certain artists or artistic styles and put less emphasis on contextualizing the subjects.[41] When a painting is used in a temporary exhibition such as *Nicholas and Alexandra,* care has to be taken to contextualize it, not only for its contents but so that its place in the exhibition narrative is clear. Adding this contextual meaning onto the object is important even in the case of iconic paintings, if it is meant to say something that supports the larger exhibitionary storyline.

The panoramic painting of Queen Victoria's Jubilee was the largest object in the *Last Tsar and Tsarina* exhibition. Nicholas and Alexandra commissioned the panorama because they were unable to attend the festivities but wanted to witness them for themselves. Both the tsar and his wife were related to Victoria—Nicholas as first cousin to future king George V and by the marriage of his sister to Victoria's son Alfred in 1874. Alexandra was a granddaughter of the queen. They were also emotionally close to the matriarch, and she was one of the most fervent supporters of their marriage, unlike Nicholas's parents, who did not approve. In this way, Nicholas and his family were themselves representations of the many-faceted links among Britain, Scotland, and Russia. After this, young Nicholas spent considerable time with his relations in Britain and got along with Victoria so well that she routinely addressed letters to "dearest Nicky."[42] Alexandra was called Alice, or more commonly Alix, when she lived in England. The girl's mother had died when Alix was very young, and she rapidly became a firm favorite with the monarch. Alix spent large amounts of time on her grandmother's estate at Balmoral, and the pair went together to many social and state events, such as the Glasgow Exhibition of 1888. Close to both, Victoria was overjoyed when the engagement was announced, and it appears that she became even fonder of the pair thereafter.

Thus, Nicholas and Alexandra were disappointed not to be able to make the long trip from the Russian Empire to Britain, and they commissioned this in-depth look at the festivities in order to make up for their loss. The painter, Pavel Yakovlevich Piasetsky, came to Britain to make sketches of the country but also used magazines and other paintings for reference.[43] The panorama had long been in the possession of the Hermitage Museum but had not been on display. This was mostly due to lack of space, which also meant that the contents of the painting had never been fully investigated. When Maureen Barrie and Godfrey Evans, the two NMS curators on the *Nicholas and Alexandra* project, arrived in St. Petersburg, Hermitage curators pointed out that they believed there was some Scottish connection to the painted panorama. Barrie reminisced in an article on the exhibition about the moment of unveiling, when the pair and their colleagues at the Hermitage unrolled the panorama bit by bit, and their initial disappointment at not being able to identify anything as Scottish.⁴⁴ Finally, just at the end of the roll of canvas, there was a recognizable scene of Leith Harbor with Edinburgh in the background. This was possibly a reference to Nicholas and Alexandra's visit a year earlier to their "dear granny" at Balmoral. Jubilance reigned in the storerooms at this proof of the iconic and visible connections between Scotland and Russia.

After such a discovery, of course the panorama had to be a central part of the exhibition in Edinburgh. In order to avoid conflicts of space, the whole length of the panorama was filmed, and the film ran in a continuous loop throughout the exhibition. Not only was this the first time that the painting had been out of Russia; it was also its first time on public display anywhere. The video, as well as the placement of the object at the center of a Scottish exhibition, helped to give the painting a context of the familial relations to Britain and allowed it to embody the guiding narrative of the exhibition as a whole. The painting became representative not only of Russian-Scottish connections in the time of Nicholas II but also of the modern links between NMS and the Hermitage. Other video displays were used, showing scenes of Nicholas and Alexandra at Balmoral and of the state funeral that was held for the family in 1998, after the executed bodies were finally forensically identified. All of these further enhanced the story that the objects were already telling about the connections between this doomed royal family and the nation where their artifacts were displayed in 2005.

Nicholas II in Modernity

A completely different type of iconic object—one that is much closer to the original meaning of "icon"—was displayed for the first time and acted as a critical connection point in the narrative being woven between Scotland and Russia, though it was unconnected to the Hermitage and not a conventional museum artifact. A traditional Orthodox religious icon of Nicholas II, it joined several other religious icons and paintings in the museum hall, though it has a rather more complicated backstory and daily location than the storage halls of the Hermitage.

In 1894 Victoria appointed Nicholas a commander-in-chief of the Royal Scots Greys, one of the then-elite cavalry divisions of the British Army, as an engagement and wedding present. Nicholas was happy with the gift, repeatedly remarking on how honored he was to be connected to this illustrious division. He wrote to his "dearest Grandmama" that "words fail me to express my surprise and the pleasure I felt upon receiving the news that you had the kindness of appointing me Colonel-in Chief of the beautiful Royal Scots Greys, just the regiment I saw and admired so last summer at Aldershot. I shall be so happy and proud to appear one day before you in their uniform."[45] By the first of December of that year Nicholas had already received an official monthly account of the regiment from a Lieutenant-Colonel Welby, along with a letter of welcome. An official uniform was made for Nicholas at the request of Edward, Prince of Wales (who Nicholas referred to as "Uncle Bertie"), by the tailor to the officers, and it was brought to Russia in 1895 by an official delegation of Royal Scots Greys officers. They also presented their new commander with an official portrait of him leading the regiment. Unfortunately in the conversion of measurements between metric and imperial, something went awry and the uniform arrived slightly too small, but it was altered on the spot and quickly became a favorite with Nicholas.[46]

In 1896, four months after their coronation, Nicholas and Alexandra and their first baby, the grand-duchess Olga, traveled from Russia to visit Victoria. They sailed into the Firth of Forth, where a reception was held for them in the Port of Leith. They then took the train from Waverly Station in Edinburgh to Queen Victoria's Highland retreat, Balmoral, where an honor guard of Scots Greys was waiting to welcome their leader. Nicholas wore his uniform and appears to have spent a considerable portion of his two-week stay devoting himself to reading regimental accounts, greeting his officers, and bestowing honors on worthy soldiers.[47]

While he obviously could not directly lead a British Army unit while in Russia, Nicholas's interest in the Royal Scots Greys remained strong throughout his life. He received copies of all regimental reviews and battlefield citations, along with dispatches and reports of notable events and acts of heroism or tragedies. It seems there was always a sense that he was looking over the regiment from afar. This impression was hardened as he routinely singled out particularly laudable soldiers and sent them insignia of his other regiments from Russia. He also arranged to award medals for bravery to twenty soldiers in 1915.[48]

Nicholas and his family were executed as the Bolsheviks rose to power in 1918. The assassination heralded the start of communist rule in Russia and led to the formation of the Soviet Union. The tsars were expunged from Russia's official history. However, with the loosening of doctrine and boundaries in the later twentieth century, the country gradually reclaimed its imperial past. The burial site of most of the Romanovs was discovered in 1979 but not made public until 1989 and 1990.[49] The site was fully excavated in 1991, but definite identification took time. Many tests were run, including bringing the remains to the United Kingdom so that DNA testing could link them to current members of the British royal family.[50] Finally, on January 30, 1998, the bodies of Nicholas, Alexandra, and three of their five children were positively identified.[51] A huge state funeral was held in St. Catherine's Chapel in the Peter and Paul Cathedral in St. Petersburg on July 17, 1998, exactly eighty years after their death.[52] In August 2007 the enquiry into the death of the Romanovs was reopened, and additional remains were discovered to be those of the missing children, Maria and Alexei.[53]

In the eighty years before the state funeral, new commanders-in-chief were appointed for the regiment formerly known as the Royal Scots Greys. However, interest in its former leader, the doomed tsar, remained, and that interest was revitalized with the discovery of the bodies. Because of this, as well as Nicholas's evident love of the regiment, a delegation of officers from the new incarnation of the old Royal Scots Greys, now called the Royal Scots Dragoon Guards (Carabineers and Greys), was invited to take a major role in the funeral ceremonies. So, dressed in official ceremonial uniforms, regimental pipers from Scotland preceded the coffin of the erstwhile emperor of all Russia down the aisle.[54]

With religion and history increasingly out in the open in a new Russia, interest in the Romanovs remained strong after the funerals. Indeed, on August 14, 2000, the family was canonized as saints in the Russian Orthodox Church. Prayers were composed to the new saints, addressing them as "Holy Royal Martyrs," which were meant to aid anyone under suspicion wrongly or in need of protection.[55] Official icons were made, and the royal martyrs were enfolded in the center of the church. The Royal Scots Greys had evidently made an impression at the funeral, for they were presented with their own icon of Nicholas in 2001 by the Caledonian Society of Moscow on behalf of all the people of Russia, a gift that caused a symbolic reconnection between the regiment and its former leader. Barring its time as a museum artifact in the *Nicholas and Alexandra* blockbuster, the icon travels continuously with the regiment on training and deployment and is considered a good luck charm. It arrived at the exhibition a week late because it was with the troops training in Canada and could not be transferred until military maneuvers were safely finished.[56]

The exhibition showed many links between Nicholas and his Scottish regiment, exhibiting pictures and paintings of him in uniform, the dispatches he wrote, and the medals he gave to Scots soldiers. However, it is this modern object, the military-religious icon, that seemed to most effectively emerge from its display to become more than an artifact. An "iconic object" can take many forms, some of which are fairly insignificant in outside appearances. Not all iconic objects are recognizable from first glance, and some fade away in the company of their shinier, but not as theoretically meaningful, counterparts. However, here is a case where an icon is iconic, where the gilded object has an importance as bright as its coloring. It embodied the spirit of the exhibition and also shows how wide a gulf there was between this Scottish *Nicholas and Alexandra* and its sanitized American ancestor. This icon would not have had much meaning if it had been displayed in Mobile, Alabama, or San Diego, California. It would have been reduced by those contexts and spaces to just another one of the many lavishly decorated religious icons at the heart of Russian Orthodoxy. It might have said something about the death and afterlife of Nicholas and the regaining of his central role in Russian national mythology. However, the emotional and historical tug of the icon seen in Edinburgh has to do with more than that. This is an object that connects to the people who were seeing it, and to the particular time in which it was displayed. That is the power of an iconic object, whether or not it is a traditional religious icon itself.

Blockbuster Icons

Highlighting links among Nicholas, Alexandra, and Scotland that had previously been largely ignored did not mean that traditional images of death and riches were absent from the exhibition. The two objects most frequently mentioned by visitors and media reports were blockbuster icons of the commonly accepted sort. Although blockbuster rhetoric often employs terms such as "glittering" profligately, the *Nicholas and Alexandra* show was full of objects studded with gems that, under the spotlights in their display cases, did actually glitter. The most extreme example was a miniature replica of the imperial regalia made by the famous craftsmen at the Fabergé Company in 1900 for the International Exhibition in Paris, and later purchased by the Romanovs and kept in the Gallery of Treasures in the Winter Palace. Many of the reviews published in the media mentioned the regalia, most with an associated picture and descriptions such as "opulent" and "glittering."[57] Most also chose to quote both the object label and the catalogue in their precise reporting that the regalia was made of "gold, silver, platinum, diamonds, spinel, pearls, sapphires, rose quartzite, wood, and velvet."[58]

This is an impressive object in spite of—or because of—being only 2.8 x 2 x 6.2 inches at its largest points.[59] Visitors have long been attracted to miniaturized objects.[60] However, the bigger reason the regalia garnered so much attention is that it matched the public idea of what an exhibition on imperial Russia should contain. The iconic notion of Russian culture at the time of the tsars has been constructed as a narrative about luxurious overindulgence, which then led to rebellion and the overthrow of the greedy elite. This cultural trope was prevalent in media reports about the exhibition. For instance, one review noted that the regalia "provides perhaps the most jaw-dropping moment. . . . It is awe-inspiring, but it is also a poignant reminder of the self-indulgence that eventually ushered in the revolution."[61] Along with article titles such as "Why the Russian Revolution Had to Happen," it is easy to spot the biases about the role of Russian opulence in its eventual downfall.[62] The Fabergé objects worked as icons for the exhibition because they served as uncomplicated symbols of a story everyone already knew.

Narratives like this are common to exhibitions where a particular national identity is displayed in the space of another nation. Certain types of objects serve as cultural shorthand for specific national identities. The artifacts acquire their representative generic iconicity in a variety of ways—through the influence of the media and popular culture, or as a consequence of their ubiquity in one area and rarity in others, or in some particular and indefinable quirk of fate. Once established, the connections between object and nation are hard to eradicate. In the American case, moon rockets and cowboy hats from popular television shows reinforce ideas of American identity with its connections to scientific and cultural hegemony. It was these sort of objects that best represented the national goals of the exhibition, and they were highlighted. Even though *Nicholas and Alexandra* came from a universal survey museum, it was still attempting to say something specific about national history, and so its narratives did not differ greatly from those in earlier shows. Nominally the story of monarchy, the exhibition became a story of the nation, because of the deep connections between the nation and the imperial leader. Objects that represented the idea of "monarchy" helped to tell this story.

The Tsarevich's Shirt

Beyond glitter, the other common idea of Russia in the age of imperialism, and especially in the age of Nicholas and Alexandra, is the specter of death and tragedy. The second most popular object in the exhibition was meant to evoke these other feelings in the viewer. This was a bloodstained shirt worn by the young Nicholas, not yet a tsar, on a visit to Japan where an attempt was made on his life. The catalogue tells the story this way: "During a visit to the town of Otsu on 29 April 1891, a Japanese policemen hit Nicholas over the head with a sabre. The man was overpowered and Nicholas was not seriously injured. The Japanese Emperor came to see him and remained in Kyoto until he [Nicholas] had recovered. Alexander III [the tsar] ordered his son to return home. The Japanese Emperor accompanied the Tsarevich to the docks at Kobe, where he boarded the *Pamiat Azov* and set sail for Vladivostock." Interestingly, though the title of the object is "The Shirt Nicholas II Was Wearing during the Assassination Attempt on Him in Japan in 1891," the description puts little weight on the bloodstain itself and focuses on the political outcome of the event, rather than the macabre reminders of it.[63] By contrast, it was the blood that made this object a favorite of the press. The interest in this particular artifact was not hidden away either. "Bloody Shirt the Tsar Attraction at City Show" was one of the first articles to be written about the exhibition, and it claimed that "the most grisly exhibit will be the bloodstained shirt worn by the future Tsar when he survived an assassination attempt as a young child."[64]

Like the miniature Fabergé regalia set, the shirt would probably have been an interesting and intriguing object in any context. If any important person, especially one of royal blood, had survived an assassination attempt and the bloodstained clothing worn at the time were displayed some years later, people would experience a type of resonance at seeing it. However, it is hard not to believe that this particular shirt is more powerful because of the ultimate fate of its owner. Much of the conjecture and conspiracy theories surrounding the deaths and lives of the Romanov family was either ignored or glossed over in both the exhibition and the surrounding media and printed materials. Most visitors, however, likely would have come in contact with many of the basic facts about the last of the Romanovs before their visit. Dark and mysterious stories like this are common cultural capital and would have created expectations in visitors' minds. The narrative of exhibitions read by visitors is shaped by these preexisting expectations and could have altered the way objects were encountered by the audience. Thus, a shirt that, to curatorial staff, speaks of a superficial injury inflicted in the name of politics can also prompt thinking about a much more vicious attack conducted in the name of revolution. Again we see the power of iconic objects to create the framework of narrative for an exhibition.

The combination of commonly recognized artifacts from the State Hermitage Museum, objects usually held in storage there, and items gathered from sources such as the queen's private collection at Balmoral and the Scottish Army led *Nicholas and Alexandra: The Last Tsar and Tsarina* to be one of the most successful exhibitions in the history of the NMS. It attracted 71,000 visitors over its relatively short time at the museum. It is routinely considered a "summer blockbuster" and was a triumph for both museums involved.[65] It did what was wanted—it raised the profile of the NMS internationally, attracted new audiences, and earned money for the institution. In that way, it was much the same as both the *Treasures from the Smithsonian Institution* and the *Wealth of a Nation* exhibitions from decades earlier. However, some temporary exhibitions fail to meet their expectations.

Beyond the Palace Walls

The summer after *Nicholas and Alexandra,* the NMS hosted another temporary exhibition that had been developed in concert with the Hermitage Museum. This one was a very different experience, though, with different goals, a different target audience, and a different type of artifactual narrative. *Beyond the Palace Walls: Islamic Art from the Hermitage Museum* ran in the same exhibition space as *Nicholas and Alexandra* at the NMS from July 14 to November 5, 2006. Again, it was a new exhibition designed by the teams at two museums, based on several temporary exhibitions that had gone before, including a similar undertaking in Amsterdam in 2004. However, as with *Nicholas and Alexandra,* the design and use of Scottish space in *Beyond the Palace Walls* made it unique.

The exhibit was created to display the wealth of a collection rather than tell a story. Objects were arranged thematically, based on form and origin, rather than chronology or in a way that would evoke visions of personages from the past. It echoed the American exhibition *Treasures from the Smithsonian Institution* far more than it did its Hermitage predecessor. The objects were the stars, more than in any other exhibition discussed so far. They were powerful because they were being displayed solely for themselves—their shape, craftsmanship, life stories, and so on—not for what they could say about anything else.[66]

At least, this is how the catalogue sought to frame the exhibition. Usually, even when the object is central to the story and when it is meant to be speaking for itself rather than illustrating an existing narrative, the artifact is often overlaid, or even obscured, by the expectations it bears. Here, the only story given was about the objects, how they came to be in the museum, and what they had been discovered to mean for, and by, scholars of the field. In fact, it was a deliberate choice to cut the possible narratives down to one that centered just on the artifacts. Islamic culture was in 2006 an intensely fraught social and political issue. Terrorist attacks, most particularly the bombings in London underground trains and busses on July 7, 2005, had made many issues around Islam and its objects difficult to address. Keeping the focus on the artifacts, their construction, and their beauty, allowed the museum to avoid other potentially troublesome stories about religion, culture, or history.

As different as this exhibition was from its other Russian predecessor, some common themes emerged in Gordon Rintoul's foreword to the latter catalogue, even as the paths diverged. He wrote,

> The latest exhibition, *Beyond the Palace Walls: Islamic Art from the State Hermitage Museum,* has been built on the foundations of mutual respect and friendship forged during last summer's highly successful exhibition *Nicholas and Alexandra*. It examines the beauty and diversity to be found in the networks of Islamic cultures and

demonstrates its willingness to adopt and adapt the traditions and craftsmanship of other cultures into a myriad of art forms. The exhibition is rich in costume, textiles, and paintings, and features breathtaking works of art wrought in precious metals often studded with precious stones.[67]

It seems museum staff were themselves acknowledging that this exhibition used the collections of the two museums for very different reasons than the earlier collaboration. *Beyond the Palace Walls* had the treasures and international cachet that are present in most blockbusters but lacked the strong, recognizable central identity or narrative that pulls in large crowds. There was no iconic image, person, or idea for the theme of "Islamic Art." The show, in attempting to avoid potentially controversial statements about identity and culture, instead reduced the weight and span of Islamic culture to an appreciation of the aesthetic and provided little context or extra information. In a way such a one-dimensional subject was perfect for exploration in a temporary exhibition, as people come in to learn something new and the educational mission of the institution and its artifacts can shine. However, without a preformed expectation many visitors hesitate to enter an exhibition—especially one that includes the payment of an entrance fee in a usually free museum.

This mix of factors meant that *Beyond the Palace Walls* was bound to attract a different type and scope of audience than *Nicholas and Alexandra,* including more specialists with a particular interest in Islamic art, who were glad of an opportunity to see a group of objects not normally on easy public display.[68] In this way the 2006 exhibition was an anomaly. It had more in common with the earliest ages of museums and their functions than with the current cult of continually increasing access, visitor numbers, and marketing. Because of their temporary nature these exhibitions create an impetus to visit. In everyday life the museum is present and perceived as never changing. It does not matter if you visit one day or the next or the next year. It will still be there. But the temporary exhibition comes in a blaze of hype and only stays for a clearly delineated and limited amount of time, creating an immediate need to visit and increasing visitor numbers.[69]

It has not always been so, however. For most of the nineteenth century, museums, even when nominally "public," were for the use of educated men who wished to consult the collections for the benefit of their scholarly work. Exhibits were laid out and categorized by their contents, rather than any sort of larger narrative or aesthetic concerns. Artifacts were largely unlabeled, as curators assumed that anyone looking at the cases would have enough intrinsic understanding of the subject to know what it was they were looking at. This was a crucial way in which the museum differentiated itself from other public institutions, as a visitor had to meet a certain threshold of civilization in order to enter.[70]

Of course, all the objects in *Beyond the Palace Walls* were expertly labeled, and anyone could have entered and enjoyed the exhibition. However, more context was needed in order for it to be understood. In a February 2007 interview, Jane Carmichael, the director of collections for the NMS, said that it was "a pretty arcane subject. It was very interesting to those people with an interest in that area, but it's not something with a hugely wide appeal. And if you take that out of context it needs a lot of interpretation to an audience that's unfamiliar with it." She continued by clarifying the other reasons why the two exhibitions from the Hermitage were received so differently when they came to Edinburgh. It had to do with the nature of the story that was being told in each: "It's very hard, I think, to simply display beauty and culture. For the general public to really get interested you need a name that they recognize and you need a really good personal history as well. And then there is drama."[71]

This statement highlights the differences between art exhibitions and history exhibitions. *Beyond the Palace Walls* was closer to an art show, where objects are displayed for their aesthetic qualities, than to a historical one where the artifacts on display evoke a defined narrative. One of the reasons that *Beyond the Palace Walls* seemed weaker in execution and audience response than *Nicholas and Alexandra* was because of the separation between its artistic nature and the national historical space in which it was displayed. Visitors to the NMS expect artifacts that will tell them something about the nation, or at least something that will have the type of narrative expected for a history museum. By not having this type of narrative, *Beyond the Palace Walls* challenged visitor expectations and understandings.

The divergence between the two sister exhibitions was visible in the catalogue. Where *Nicholas and Alexandra* and *Treasures from the Smithsonian Institution* had historical essays that only tangentially involved the objects, *Beyond the Palace Walls* used the objects in the catalogue to illustrate essays about workmanship, style, and evolution of design. Again we see that in this exhibition the artifacts were the central draw, rather than any romantic narrative or big idea of national identity. Instead of telling a story, the catalogue acted as a space for the objects to speak more freely and make connections that would not be possible within the actual exhibition space. In that way, this catalogue provided a more accurate vision of the exhibition than do most. The images of the objects were interspersed throughout the text as they would be approached in the exhibition space, and the associated text was in the style of what an educated observer would already know about the objects, rather than something completely new and outside the artifacts.[72]

There were four sections in the text—"Early Islamic Art until the Mongol Invasion," "Islamic Art and China," "Islamic Art and Europe," and "Diplomacy, Warfare, and Trade: The Muslim World and Russia"—each following the same format with a brief introductory essay and descriptions and images of each object from that particular theme. Dimensions, material, and provenance were all laid out, as were details of any previous references to the object in exhibitions or printed material.

There was also an appendix listing all the objects from the collections of the NMS that were included in the exhibition.[73] This points to another interesting detail that makes *Beyond the Palace Walls* different from most other temporary exhibitions. Whether or not creating the exhibition is a collaborative effort between institutions, usually the contents are in the form of what is called a "capsule exhibition."[74] This means that all the objects included in the temporary exhibition come from the lending institution and live within their own little bubble inside the hosting institution's space. While visitors are encouraged to cross the liminal space between the "regular" and "temporary" exhibitions, artifacts are not. In this situation, objects from the two museums were placed next to each other within the space of the temporary exhibition. Because of the unusual feeling of the exhibition, the proximity of these objects from different contexts did not necessarily change the narrative of the whole exhibition at all, but this was mostly because there was little narrative of identity to be had in the beginning.

Exhibitions such as this, which lack a central "story," are challenging for visitors and for analysts. It is considerably easier to reflect on the role of objects in an exhibition narrative if there is a narrative apart from the objects. This is reflected somewhat in the numbers of visitors who came to see *Beyond the Palace Walls*. The 2006 exhibition had twenty thousand visitors, a huge decrease from the numbers seen at *Nicholas and Alexandra* the year before.[75] It is simpler to see the representative power of iconic artifacts when there is already an idea of the story they are meant to represent. This is not to say that there were no iconic objects in the *Beyond the Palace Walls* exhibition. Rather, they were iconic in a way that is distinct from anything we have already seen, and one that is harder to articulate in the normal frameworks. They served as icons of commercialism or of institutional triumphs, rather than of grander ideas of nation, identity, modernity, or any other elite theoretical concept. Although displayed in a national museum, the exhibit was not a "national" exhibition, and its narratives proved much more difficult to present through the artifacts displayed.

Rarities, Commodities, and Icons

The object highlighted most in reviews and the catalogue for *Beyond the Palace Walls* was an "eighteenth century Ottoman tent, which has never before been on display."[76] The rest of the exhibition was abstractly and physically arranged around this imposing object. Visitors actually walked through the tent in order to access the rest of the objects. It became a symbol for all the exhibition was doing to extract forgotten treasures of Islamic art from dusty store cupboards and put them on public display. On labels and in the press, attention was paid to the amount of conservation time used to make the tent ready for display and also to the fact that it was the most complete representation of this type of object known to exist. This rhetoric plays on a theme common to all the temporary exhibitions that we have investigated so far—that the particular objects involved can only be seen during a particular limited time in a specific space in Edinburgh. As had been observed especially with the American objects in *Treasures from the Smithsonian Institution,* the power of the artifact increases if the objects involved are not normally on display in their home spaces. There is a feeling of entitlement or object lust that comes with being able to see something that you are told is important and that other people do not get to see.[77] The scholar Walter Benjamin believed that an object is more sacred the fewer the number of eyes that have profaned it. Thus, some religious icons are brought out of their secret, sacred spaces only for special holy days.[78] The museum, as keeper of the sacred relics of the nation, acts in much the same way as earlier holy spaces.

If the rare and hidden object is iconic, so too is its exact opposite. This is, of course, the object that everyone can see and own. Each temporary exhibition brings with it its own selection of contents for the obligatory gift shop. In the case of *Beyond the Palace Walls,* the bestselling objects in the specialized gift shop during the time of the exhibition were replicas of Turkish and other Islamic tiles, modified for use as coasters and decorated with the stylized images of flowers and flowing script often seen in illuminated manuscripts and other Islamic objects.[79] There were several authentic tiles of this sort in the actual exhibition. However, none of the replicas that were for sale were exact copies of the ones seen in the noncommercial space of the museum. In fact, the saleable replicas were not even unique to this particular exhibition. The exact same ones could be bought at gift shops at the British Museum, the Victoria and Albert Museum, and the Royal Botanical Gardens at Kew, and most likely also at a number of other heritage and museum sites.[80] Thus, these ceramic tiles were not so much a piece of a specific exhibition but a symbolic icon of the idea of the exhibition. They were attractive decorative objects that whispered "Islamic art" rather than NMS Museums of Scotland.

Tiles are perfect museum commodities. They are inexpensive, portable, inviting, and a way to have at the same time something specific—a replica of objects seen at a particular exhibition—and something much more general—a cultural artifact that hints at the idea of "Islamic art." The type of artwork on these tiles represents "Islam" in the cultural collective unconscious. The use of Arabic script, the particular color schemes, and the kinds of images reproduced combine to create something that symbolizes a particular part of the world and a unique style of artwork, while also being aesthetically pleasing and "exotic" when displayed in a home setting. Just as the purchase of an exhibition catalogue can imply that a consumer is cultured and knowledgeable, regardless of whether anyone actually reads it, the purchase of an item such as the Islamic tile can speak more about the owner of the object than the exhibition at which it was purchased.

These two exhibitions—*Nicholas and Alexandra* and *Beyond the Palace Walls*—were both collaborations between the same two teams of curators and same two publishing units, and yet they produced two very different types of catalogues. Exhibition catalogues, it appears to me, can be divided into two major types. The ones made for the two Hermitage exhibitions each fall into a different category, where they can be joined by the catalogues already discussed in earlier chapters. The first type is the novel catalogue. In this incarnation, the catalogue is meant primarily to tell a story. That story follows the theme of the exhibition, whether that theme is obviously articulated within the exhibition or not. *Nicholas and Alexandra* and *Treasures from the Smithsonian* are both examples of this catalogue style. In both shows, the exhibition used objects in order to highlight aspects of national identity, whether that was historic nationness (as in the case of *Nicholas and Alexandra*) or a more contemporary and all-encompassing identity (as in *Treasures from the Smithsonian*). The catalogues expanded on this theme of the nation and its history by presenting a number of narrative essays that delved into particular events or personages who had helped to shape the identity of the nation involved. In the main body of the novel catalogue, museums and the particular exhibition are mentioned only fleetingly. Images of displayed objects are used in the margins and sidebars only to add color and decorative flourish to a story already in progress.[81] Although often written by experts in the particular nation and their museums, the text makes obvious concessions to the nonexpert reader, providing timelines and genealogies for the nations concerned. To read through the central section of a novel catalogue is strikingly similar to reading a basic history book about the nation, with the addition of colorful anecdotes and pictures of objects. It gives no sense of how the exhibition itself was laid out or what the experience of walking through it would have been like. Only in an attached appendix are objects made the focus of study, and these object appendices read like an afterthought for the experts, rather than an integral part of the whole catalogue.

Another type of approach is the scientific catalogue. More like a classic commercial sale catalogue than a lavishly illustrated art book, the scientific type of catalogue is primarily concerned with allowing readers to continue engaging with the objects after they have left the exhibition. *Beyond the Palace Walls* and *The Wealth of a Nation* both did this, though they may have done it for quite different reasons. Both exhibitions based themselves on the centrality of the tangible object. *The Wealth of a Nation* had a political reason for making the objects as obvious in their physicality as possible, whereas *Beyond the Palace Walls* had a more academic slant. However, both based the central premise of their catalogues on the objects, which helped each continue to accomplish the goals first elucidated in the context of a temporary exhibition. The clear object focus of this approach creates a situation where the objects are leading the text, rather than the other way around. The only bit of text not directly related to a pictured artifact tends to be setting the context for a group of similar objects.[82] The objects are thoroughly indexed, and the information given about them goes beyond the basic data found in the novel catalogue. The scientific catalogue is at heart a reference document; as such it tells its readers where to find more related information and provides a sense of how each object relates to others and to the exhibition ideas as a whole. *Beyond the Palace Walls* took this visual reference idea to an even higher level by including a large number of objects in the catalogue that were not actually in the exhibition. In this way, the catalogue is sometimes a record of the curators' *ideal* exhibition, rather than the one that actually took place. Catalogues are a sanitized version of the exhibition, free of the crowds that obscure carefully designed sets, the misreading of object labels, and the flexibilities of space that could allow a backward approach to the exhibition narrative. The catalogue is thus clearer and easier to "read" but is also necessarily more fixed, one-dimensional, and devoid of context. It cannot incorporate all the layers of meaning that can be found in the interplay of object, narrative, and space in the exhibition, but rather attempts to provide something that people often feel is lacking in exhibitions—a strong dose of narrative and background history, as well as more detail on the objects concerned.

Both the novel catalogue and the scientific catalogue tend to sell well, though perhaps to different audiences. The *Wealth of a Nation* catalogue topped the list of Scottish bestsellers when it was released.[83] More so than any other souvenir or replica in an exhibition gift shop, the catalogue gives the buyer a way to bring the exhibition home as a commodity. Visitors consume the temporary exhibition as an experience, but it is an ephemeral one. The catalogue, conversely, is tangible and recognizable. It is both object and narrative, and as such is the perfect souvenir of an artifact-filled experience like the temporary exhibition. Museums try to increase the commodity value of the catalogue by making them bigger, with more full-color pictures and more lavish production values. The *Nicholas and Alexandra* catalogue was originally meant to be 192 pages, but was increased to 224 pages "as publishing staff found themselves entranced by an icon, costume, or family photograph." Using rhetoric common to most all catalogues, *Nicholas and Alexandra* is "lavishly illustrated" and "truly a timeless memento of a stunning exhibition."[84] News reports about *Treasures from the Smithsonian* noted that "a richly illustrated catalogue has been prepared specially for the occasion," although official Smithsonian reports commented that sales were slow in the first fortnight of the exhibition.[85] The use of words like "lavish" and "rich" to describe catalogues helps to show how they are framed similarly to the objects they profile. Increasingly, the exhibition catalogue—especially one that falls into the category of novel catalogue—is just as much of an aura-filled iconic object as the artifacts it exists to record.

To some extent this has always been true. Catalogues in early museums were used for the information they contained but also for their presentation value.[86] However, most catalogues in modern institutions were more like guidebooks, designed to alert people to the space they were in and its connection to the nation, rather than create any specific storyline with the objects.[87] With the birth of the "blockbuster," however, came the lavish catalogue—permanent reminders for groups of people who had seen the show, those who had missed it, and the curators whose project it had been. It is one of the few ways for curators and other expert museum staff to receive lasting recognition for the fleeting narratives they create with their objects, and can also show that a visitor was culturally aware enough to have gone to the museum during the exhibition's short stay. While temporary exhibition catalogues have become increasingly ornate and popular, an older form of catalogue, that which lists the whole permanent collection of an institution with little contextual information, has become less common. Instead there are catalogues of sections of a permanent collection, modeled after those of temporary exhibitions.[88] These provide ways for the experience of the museum to be consumed outside of museum space, engaging audiences in the museum's artifactual dialogue in a different way.

Collaborative Outcomes

In the summers of 2005 and 2006 two exhibitions designed by the same two institutions, showcasing the same nations, were shown in the same spaces, within largely the same contexts. However, as we have seen, they had radically different approaches to the nature of narrative and object in the exhibition, and quite distinct audiences received them very differently. One was a huge show that the museum continues to hold out as an example of how good it can be. The other came mostly under the public radar, even after getting positive reviews from critics. Between the two they covered a wide scope of museum exhibition style and pointed the way to a more internationally recognized NMS, which, though not present in 2005 or 2006, would bring together the universal museum and the national museum to create yet other new narratives in the future.

In the summer of 2012, a year on from the gala reopening of the now reenvisioned and renovated NMS, a third Hermitage exhibition opened. This one, *Catherine the Great: An Enlightened Empress*, was a return to the more traditional blockbuster style of *Nicholas and Alexandra*.[89] Like the earlier show, it too highlighted specific instances where Scotland and Russia came into contact, both throughout the narrative and in a special section titled "Scots in Catherine's Court." There, Catherine's preferences for surrounding herself and her family with Scottish doctors, architects, soldiers, and governesses was given as yet more evidence for her "enlightened" status.

The Hermitage exhibitions were the first large international collaborations taken on since the creation of the Museum of Scotland and the amalgamation of the RMS into the National Museum of Scotland. Being able to attract and produce big temporary exhibitions like these showed the increasing stability of the institution after a series of major overhauls to its identity and role. These hybrid Scottish-global narratives also previewed how the completed NMS would seek to present Scottish identity—as that of a small nation with an outsize impact on the world.

However, that identity as the museum of a nation still finding itself after political devolution was not, of course, completely solidified merely by hosting a series of exhibitions from another national museum. Sometimes the NMS had to look within itself for a sense of identity. The next big show at the NMS was jointly assembled by all of the national cultural institutions of Scotland. This exhibition again engaged with ideas of narrative and nation as seen through objects, and it opened a window into how the NMS was, and is, involved in producing images of the nation and its history.

5
Objects Unifying the Nation
2007

The questions "what," "where," and "who" are a nation have long been at the heart of the nationalist and nationalism project. They are the things that must be defined for a national identity to be created. Part of creating or supporting an identity—national or otherwise—is identifying who belongs and who does not.

Most non-Scots think of Scotland as a unitary identity, identifiable by romantic landscapes, tartan, *Trainspotting*, and Mel Gibson in blue face paint. The problem lies in that some of that is Highland Scotland, some of that is Lowland Scotland, and a lot of it, of course, is Hollywood Scotland. There has always been a split between Highland and Lowland Scottish histories and identities, as was discussed in the introduction, especially with the Jacobite rebellions.

In the eighteenth century the Jacobites wanted to topple the government of the United Kingdom, while the opposing forces (made up in no small part of Lowland Scots) supported the British king. When the rebellion ended, many of the things we now think of as "Scottish" were banned, including tartan, the speaking of Scottish Gaelic, and traditional Scottish games now practiced at Highland games across the United States and the world—largely because of the large number of Highland Scots who emigrated after the Jacobite rebellions.[1]

Nearly a century later, Queen Victoria came to the throne and began to reclaim the Scottish Highlands for the United Kingdom.

She purchased Balmoral, her Scottish retreat in Aberdeenshire, and outfitted it with tartan everything—from carpet to curtains. This, of course, set a trend across the country and the world. The Highlands became fashionable. It also made Scotland into an identifiable symbol. It is hard to "picture" a country, other than its flag, and not many people outside Scotland know the blue Saltire of St. Andrew that stands for Scotland. But tartan and kilts and heather and all that is known as "biscuit-tin tartanry"?[2] That is easy to package and sell. Thus the Highlands came to stand in for the whole of Scotland over time.

The Scottish Government declared 2007 "The Year of Highland Culture," soon shortened to Highland 2007. This was, in part, a touristic and economic decision by the government. They advertised the Highlands as "the Gateway to Scotland" and attempted to show it as a good place to live and work.[3] However, more widely, the amorphous nature of the relationship between the Highlands and the "rest" of Scotland means that the identity needs to be continuously reexamined.

Highland 2007 was a way to continue the conversation without having to really engage with any of the deep questions about how or who the Highlands are or were. Just as objects in exhibitions can tell a variety of stories depending on which narrative is foregrounded by the context and labeling practices of the exhibition, so too can the Highlands as an object tell many stories. Depending on the time and context, the Highlands tell the story of savage nature, romantic defeat, depoliticized culture, emigrant diaspora, or new modern modes of life, among many other possibilities. In order to tell these multiple stories, Highland 2007 had a traveling exhibition of objects and art culled from all the Scottish cultural institutions as one of its central events. This was titled, in both Gaelic and English, *Fonn 's Duthchas: Land and Legacy*.

When particular nations go on display in exhibitions meant to highlight their culture and identities, they always become an object in the exhibition themselves. This can be seen in both the American Smithsonian and the Russian Hermitage exhibitions, as well as the constructed Scottishness of *The Wealth of a Nation*. However, it was in 2007's *Fonn 's Duthchas* that the pattern is clearest, perhaps because of the historical ambiguity of the Highlands, which left Scotland's identities more open to reinterpretation. It may also have been, however, because of when the exhibition was staged. By 2007 the political motives behind exhibitions and their styles were very different than they had been two decades previously. In 1989, at *The Wealth of a Nation,* there was little mention of any objects having "Highland" origins or identities. Much the same type of narrative was seen in the 1998 opening of the Museum of Scotland. In both 1989 and 1998 an overarching Scottish identity had not yet solidified or been politically realized. As a result, the "Highlandness" of material culture had to be subsumed into the larger narrative—"Scotland" was on show, and even if much of the symbolic value of that Scottishness was actually based on Highland motifs, the fact was not acknowledged. By 2007 "Scotland" was a recognized cultural and political identity, with associated civic institutions such as a parliament, so marginal cultures could begin to be reinstated. It is only when the cultural boundaries of the majority nation are congruent with the political boundaries of a state that that nation can allow other narratives to challenge its hegemony.

Highland 2007 and *Fonn 's Duthchas: Land and Legacy* were designed to tackle the questions of who and what the "Highlands" had been. Instead they led to a series of questions of who and what Scotland was, what role the Highlands had within it, and what stories objects can tell. It was quite a different exhibition from either *Treasures from the Smithsonian* or *The Wealth of a Nation.* The motives, structure, implementation, and narrative all vary, more than they echo other exhibitions. Exhibitions such as *The Wealth of a Nation* had a political edge. Others, such as *Beyond the Palace Walls,* addressed issues of identity within underrecognized subcommunities. *Fonn 's Duthchas* did all of this while also physically moving within a Scottish context that was more politicized than the pre-devolution 1989 *The Wealth of a Nation.*

Devolution

In September 1997 the Scots voted overwhelmingly to reopen their long-closed national parliament and begin "devolving" government powers back to Scotland from the British government. These were powers that solely related to Scottish local affairs, which mirrored those preserved in the original Act of Union of 1707. Education, law, and health, among other departments, were all now the business of members of Scottish parliament, under the leadership of the first minister of Scotland. At first the Labour Party led the Scottish government, just as it did the British government at the time.

The Scottish National Party (SNP) won a majority in the Scottish Parliament a decade later, in May 2007. This marked the first time since devolution that there was a non-Labour first minister. Obviously this was well after the start of Highland 2007, which began in January, and the project was planned several years before anyone would have predicted the success of a nationalist government. However, the presence of the SNP fighting for, and settling into, the seat of power did change the context for the Year of Highland Culture. The SNP always have been unabashed advocates for Scottish independence from the rest of Britain. Celebrating the historic and present identity of the Highlands — the area of Scotland that has always been most different from England — became in the hands of an SNP government an act of political propaganda greater than anyone would have expected.

One of the main premises of nationalism is what many theorists, including Tom Nairn, have identified as its inherent duality or paradox.[4] National feeling relies simultaneously on modernity and history. The technology of modernity — mechanized printing, vernacular education, and the rhetoric of global connectedness — is needed to spread the word of nationalism to the masses that make up the nation.[5] At the same time, these masses need to believe that they are only the latest incarnation of a timeless national past. Without the weight of history behind them the elites who serve as spokespeople for the new movement have no legitimacy.[6]

So, according to theorists of nation-creation, nations rely on the technology of modern life and on history for their self-creation. It is also a constant process. In contemporary national settings the creation and shoring up of national ideals is done much less self-consciously than previously, but the undertaking is the same.

Scotland, with its complicated relationship between nation and state identities, is even more susceptible to the constant reiteration of identity than other countries. Some of the ways in which this is done are quiet—the flags, signage, and other detritus of everyday life. Others are altogether different events, more specifically delineated as national and meant to focus attention on the nation. Highland 2007 was one of these national events, especially its associated exhibition *Fonn 's Duthchas*, which traveled to various sites around Scotland over the year. This exhibition smoothed over some of the many complications of Highland identity and was able to serve as the flagship event of Highland 2007. It also continued a long history of the Highlands standing in for a larger Scottish national identity, at home and abroad. It was a touring exhibition composed of objects and documents from the three major national culture institutions: the National Museums of Scotland (NMS), the National Galleries of Scotland, and the National Library of Scotland. The exhibition revealed the role of the Highlands in Scottish identity, how material culture is meant to represent prevailing political roles, and how history is put to the service of the present.

The Highlands and Modern Scotland: The Year of Highland Culture 2007

Even now, mapping exactly where "the Highlands" are can be difficult. Different people all have their own definitions. One of the most prevalent is the area covered by Highlands and Islands Enterprise (the Scottish Government's economic and community development agency, started in 1965) and the VisitHighlands tourist bureau, as well as the Highlands and Islands parliamentary district—the counties of Caithness, Sutherland, Ross and Cromarty, and Inverness, as well as most of Argyll, Bute, and Moray Counties and the council areas of Orkney, Shetland, and the Western Isles.[7]

Inverness has long been the center of Highland life, acting as a rival to the Glasgow-Edinburgh industrial and cultural belt of the south.[8] In the twenty-first century it has undergone a period of rapid expansion in both cultural and technological terms, becoming one of the growth areas of Scotland. Part of this expansion has been the development of a new cultural strategy for the area. Inverness was at the heart of the movement to establish the Highland 2007. It started when Inverness, and by association the Highland area, put forth a bid to be given an European City of Culture designation for the year of 2008. The City of Culture program was started by the European Union in 1985 to show "the diverse cultural wealth in Europe and the common threads that make us all European."[9] Cities compete vigorously for the honor and the associated leap in tourism and other funding it brings.[10] However, in October 2002 Inverness was cut off the shortlist, and the honor eventually went to Liverpool, official City of Culture 2008.[11]

Immediately after it was announced that InvernessHighland — as the bid had been titled — was off the shortlist, regional leaders made plans for an alternate role for the area. This was the beginning of the Highland 2007 planning, though the timing was not settled for much longer. At first the alternate celebration was to be in 2008, just as planned, then perhaps 2006, and finally 2007. In its very first incarnations, Highland 2007 was just a way to use all the effort put into the European City of Culture bid, without it going to waste because of bureaucratic decisions. Some sort of effort to showcase Highland culture was going to be made. The form was not certain, but the ideals were — show the Highlands as moving beyond tartan and heather and savagery, as being an integral part of modern Scottish culture.[12]

Funding and support came both from Scottish administration units, such as the Scottish Executive (renamed the Scottish Government in September 2007) and the Highlands and Islands Enterprise, and also from United Kingdom–wide bodies like the Heritage Lottery Fund and private companies and corporations, or community boards. Events were also a mix of governmental and local or personal. In addition to flagship events such as the launch party and touring exhibition, anyone could apply to have an event included in the master calendar of Highland 2007 activities. In this way, it became an amorphous amalgamation of both specially planned occasions and normal events that were reframed as particularly "Highland." But what does it mean to be branded "Highland"? Examining why and how this area of Scotland is considered unique gives a clearer view of how those ideas were fostered in 2007.

The Highlands Throughout History

The most common vision of the Highlands is the one that dates to the age of Queen Victoria and her reign of "Balmorality."[13] However, "Balmorality" itself comes from the earlier years of Walter Scott and George IV, and was honed into its packaged ideal by travel agent Thomas Cook and Hollywood. Thus, it is necessary to go both forward and back in time from the late nineteenth century in order to understand how the Highlands came to have the place they do in the Scottish psyche.

In April 1746 two armies were fighting on Culloden Moor, outside Inverness. On one side were Scottish Jacobites, supporters of the claim of the house of Stewart to the throne of the United Kingdom. On the other was a mix of English and Lowland Scottish troops, under the control of the Hanoverian Duke of Cumberland. Two parts of Scotland were fighting each other over the direction in which the government should go in the future. This is hardly the act of a strong, unified nation. After the defeat of the Jacobites at Culloden, the Lowland/English vision of Scotland prevailed, stripping the Highlands and their inhabitants of any ways of life or material goods that were visibly different from those practiced elsewhere. This was an attempt to eliminate the divides that had persisted in Scotland for centuries and had been made visible through the Jacobite risings of the eighteenth century.

The first substantial groups of travelers went to, and reported from, the Highlands soon after the Jacobite defeat in 1746. The area had been considered savage and was thus largely unknown to non-natives before, but due to the demoralizing effect of the final battles and the subsequent Proscription Acts, was deemed "safe" for the intrepid few, such as Thomas Pennant and James

Boswell.[14] These travelers and their accounts were among the first steps in integrating the Highlands into a new idea of Scotland. However, it took more time removed from the Jacobite conflict for the Highland-ness of Scotland to appeal to a mass audience. The propaganda for the Union prioritized visions of the past over the political discussions of the present, which helped to create a unified culture.[15]

In 1814 Walter Scott published his first novel. *Waverley* was subtitled *'Tis Sixty Years Since* and recast the final Jacobite struggle in heroic, romantic terms.[16] It was precisely the sixty years of the title that allowed this to be done. With the passage of time fact becomes memory and allows for the formation of nostalgia and myth. Myth can then be integrated into the story of the nation, the "romantic past" indispensable to the formation of national ideals.[17] *Waverley* and Scott's other historical novels became wildly popular outside Scotland—particularly among the elite classes of England and Germany.[18] This added to the fervor for a Scottishness flavored with Highlandism that the publications of James MacPherson's *Ossian* poems had started in the 1760s. A craze for all things culturally Scottish took over across Europe and the Americas. Because of the ways in which the Highlands came to stand in for Scotland as a whole, these Highland cultural symbols gradually overtook previous ideas of primitivism and backwardness.[19] Thus, by the mid-nineteenth century Europe and the rest of the world began to see the Highlands as a part of Scotland, whereas before it was all barbarity and wildness.

This view from outside is crucial to the formation of identity, national or otherwise. By the early nineteenth century there was a growing level of comfort with the idea of the Highlands within the rest of Scotland as well. In 1822 King George IV visited Edinburgh. Although monarchs had been nominally the heads of Scotland as well as the rest of the United Kingdom since the Union of the Crowns in 1603, this visit marked only the second time a reigning royal had come to Scotland. The visit was engineered and stage-managed by Walter Scott and included a large dose of so-called Highland iconography and pageantry. All the burghers of Edinburgh were instructed to order new tartan suits, and the king as well came head to toe in brilliant Royal Stewart tartan.[20] There were pipers and military demonstrations, folk singing and Gaelic poetry. It proved that the people of Scotland were truly loyal.[21] The royal visit gave an official seal of approval on the Highland vision of Scotland.[22] It was now safe for Scottish identity to include the Highlands, rather than marginalizing them, as had previously been the case.

Queen Victoria greatly expanded on what George IV and Walter Scott had started, inventing the Highland's role in the public image of Scotland. Victoria loved the Highlands and her new residence at Balmoral Castle in Aberdeenshire, which she purchased in 1852. This was the ultimate sign of approval for the Highlands. If the queen was willing to live there, it must be both acceptable and the height of fashion. Her reign is connected in the public imagination with romantic Highland views, stags in the mist, and tartan in all possible forms. This is an earlier version of what is now marketed to tourists as "Scotland." Many of the symbols that had traditionally been on the margins and "Highland" became, by the Victorian era, visual shorthand for "Scotland." In the nineteenth and early twentieth centuries Scotland politically and culturally became more comfortable in its union with the United Kingdom. However, as differences between actual cultures in the United Kingdom moderated, there was a desire to cling to a certain degree of identifiable "separateness" in Scotland, to emphasize the largely superficial separation from the more powerful England. The trappings of Highland culture were an easy, nonconfrontational way to do this: "The symbols, myths, and tartans of the Highlands were appropriated by Lowland Scots as evidence of their distinctive culture. The irony is that until then the Highlands had been reviled as barbaric, backwards, and savage."[23]

Material culture has long been important in constructions of the Highlands. Objects were the clearest way in which the Victorian Balmoralist Highlands were projected throughout Britain and Europe. In 1856 Queen Victoria ordered tartan curtains for the newly decorated Balmoral Castle, thus starting off a trend for tartan in all forms and styles.[24] The tartan object became a stand-in for Scottishness, where it used to be an overt statement of difference within Scotland.[25]

However, tartan was not the only Highland object that became materialized as a symbol of identity. In fact, this type of Highlandism is often commonly referred to as "biscuit-tin tartanry." Highland scenes were painted on all manner of consumer goods, from soap dishes to tea towels to the aforementioned biscuit tins. In this way a degree of Highland identity was embedded in products that otherwise would have had little connection to northern Scottish identity. In later years, after the initial appeal of Victoriana had faded, new material visions of the Highlands developed, focused around tourist goods such as whisky and shortbread, as well as the kilts and bagpipes of earlier years. These objects, which inhabit the liminal space between saleable commercial goods and tourist souvenirs, are ways in which the idea of the Highlands is made tangible.

In certain ways this materialization of tourist vision happens in any location that draws visitors. However, there are several reasons why the phenomenon in the Highlands is of more interest than similar processes in New York or Paris. First, as was mentioned above, "the Highlands" are not defined, or definable, in the same spatial and historic ways as other geographic spaces. Thus the material objects of Highlandism serve as signposts to identify an unmappable location. They also identify in their shapes the ideas that have been, and are, tied to the land. While a tourist in New York may return from there with a branded apple or a miniature yellow taxi, and a visitor to Paris can easily purchase a keychain version of the Eiffel Tower, these are icons of a different sort. They are iconic incarnations of a very specific place. Their near-universal recognition gives them the power to invoke those places to which they have been tied.[26] Highland objects, though, get their power from the exact opposite—the lack of specificity makes them much larger and more comprehensive. Meanings apart from the geographic or touristic can be mapped onto their material forms, to change according to contextual cues. In that way even though museum curators in Scotland have sought to move beyond the "tartan and bagpipes" vision of Scottish material culture, those very objects have, because of their cultural ubiquity, the same multivocality as more "traditional" museum artifacts that are never seen outside the display case.

Material culture has always been part of producing the varying images of Scotland throughout time, and as we have seen, the Highlands were given the largest role in creating those materials and their associated identities. The Victorian tartan image was slightly overtaken by the later Kailyard vision—the name given to the image of bucolic farming communities and the striving young lad portrayed in sentimental fiction of the late nineteenth century.[27] That in turn faded in favor of a return to the militaristic Scot picture during and after the world wars. However, all of those iconic images of Scottishness foreground a Highland identity in one way or another. Only the brief inroads of a Red Clydeside socialist worker persona (which is based instead in the shipyards of Glasgow) made any dent in the hegemony of a Highland-dominated public perception of Scottish identity. There has been a complete reversal from historically, when Scottish identity was in conflict with Highland identity, to now when it is subsumed within it.

Creating the Modern Highlands

Today the tourist industry is a major part of the Scottish economy, and a large portion of the images tourists carry with them when they come to Scotland are Highland ones. Because of the strength and staying power of this iconography, the Highlands, or at least a tourist-ready version of them, are vitally important to Scotland economically and politically. But in reality the Highlands, though now recovering from the economic and demographic collapse that followed the Jacobite defeat, have long been much less prosperous than the rest of the nation. Highland 2007 had to walk a fine line between showcasing the Highlands as they are and were, and the Highlands as the tourists imagine them to be.

The tourist image of the Highlands is influenced by Hollywood productions like *Brigadoon*, *Monarch of the Glen*, and *Braveheart*, and is largely still the aforementioned Victorian vision of tartan, heather, and mist. In this way it is removed from time, aloof from the influences of modernity and change.[28] This is common in touristic incarnations, and the rhetoric is present all through material promoting the Highlands. For example, one website observes, "The Highlands are still a special place and a place apart, enjoyed not only for their unspoilt environment but for their particular sense of the intertwining of past and present. In such atmospheric Highland settings, Neolithic folk, Bronze Age warriors, Picts, Vikings, and clansmen need only your imagination to come alive!"[29] This rendering presents an image of a place where the normal processes of time do not occur. Not only is the image removed from time; it is also removed from any particularly identifiable location. The Highlands of tourism are generic and unmappable. This makes them more easily accessible and elides any potentially confusing differences between types of Highland experience. The image that is left is one of a sanitized, generalized, and universalized tourist destination. Through these processes, the Highlands are presented more as an idea than as an actual place, which is common when an area is repackaged for tourism.[30]

The idea of the Highlands in the tourist presentations is also one of rural countryside. Despite claiming the relatively large city of Inverness as its center, the vision of the Highlands—both within and without the particular constraints of Highland 2007—is overwhelmingly nonurban. In a way this focus merely reflects the geographical realities of Highland Scotland, an area that encompasses a majority of rural space and is culturally and spatially removed from the urban central belt of the Edinburgh-Glasgow axis. However, the conflation of rural with Highland also has to do with the ways in which images of urban and rural have been constructed over time. We think of cities as spaces of modernity and movement, while rural areas tend to be conflated with nostalgia and the past. This effect was important for the packaging of Highland 2007: the Highland countryside as land of the past.[31]

Privileging the notion of the Highlands as a rural land in close proximity to the romantic and wild past helped present a more accessible scene for the audiences expected at Highland 2007. International tourists, a major audience for the Highland 2007 events, had to be given at least a taste of what they expected when coming to the Highlands. This meant that the vision projected at Highland 2007 events had to at least somewhat match those that dated back to the romanticism of Balmoral; they also avoided mentioning the place of the Highlands in the twenty-first century. Although some tourists seek authentic experiences, many look for inauthenticity, especially when it better matches their internal vision of what should be seen.[32] For many travelers, authenticity lies in how well the "reality" they are seeing matches what they expect to see.[33] These sorts of tourists do not want to be disillusioned by a version of the Highlands that deals with telecommuting, farm-to-table bed and breakfasts, wind farms, or any of the other realities that have supplanted Victorian romantic ideals.

While the place- and timelessness of the Highlands were being constructed by the tourist board and other agencies, those very attributes were increasing in relevance in the actual Highlands. Although the Highland area had experienced a resurgence in population, language, and culture in the last several decades, the growth was not uniformly spread throughout the massive region. A "Gaelic Renaissance" began in the 1960s outside the Highlands with members of the diaspora becoming interested in the area's distinctive language and culture. This led in the 1970s and 1980s to a series of more political movements and government policies directed at supporting the use of Gaelic in Highland communities. But this was just a different version of the same ignorance about time and place. These policies assumed that the language of "the Highlands" was, and always had been, Gaelic before the forced imposition of English.[34] This, in fact, had never been the case. Norse has had a strong influence on the area, as well as Scots, English, and French. The Hebrides, Orkney, and Shetland all have very different histories and identities than that which is considered stereotypically Highland as well. These islands off the northern coasts have historical and cultural links to Scandinavia as much or more than they do to Scotland.[35]

A Very National Exhibition

Fonn 's Duthchas: Land and Legacy was a nominally Highland exhibition that was actually national on many levels. It took objects from three national collections, toured them to several sites around a nation, and presented itself as an exhibition about a nation—or at least a region of a nation that was critical in the formation of the nation's identity. The exhibit also referred explicitly to the land—the physical territory—of the nation. The title, in English, is *Land and Legacy*. In Gaelic it is a bit more poetic and a bit more vague. *Fonn* can mean "mood" or "music" and "tune," and *Duthchas* is the land but often meaning the hereditary right to land. So the Gaelic title can be read as the "tune that calls everyone back to claim their hereditary rights to the land." Many who have Scots ancestry in North America and elsewhere are there because their ancestors were pushed out of the Highlands during the Highland Clearances. This hard-to-accurately-quantify historical period ebbed and flowed over a hundred years from about the 1760s through the 1850s, as areas of the Highlands were cleared of small subsistence farms to make way for more profitable economic options.[36]

The Smithsonian Institution exhibition and all the Russian exhibitions were temporary shows—they came to Edinburgh and stayed there. *Fonn 's Duthchas*, in contrast, was a traveling exhibition. And though temporary exhibitions and their traveling cousins have many features in common, it is useful to distinguish between the two, as their differences mean some large changes for the objects they feature. Both types bring together material from loan institutions, transport it to a different space, and display it for a limited time at a host institution. There are varying degrees of control for contents, narrative, and arrangement held by both loan and host museums. In this much, then, the two forms are equivalent. However, a temporary exhibition is a singular collaboration between the institutions involved. It is a unique show, created for a particular institution, for a given period of time, and will never be seen in that form again.[37]

Similar shows may have been produced, as was seen in *Treasures from the Smithsonian Institution* and *Nicholas and Alexandra*, but the particular exhibitions seen in Scotland were original and ephemeral. Traveling exhibitions, alternatively, are created by a loan institution and then travel out to several different hosting museums. It is these type of exhibitions that are most common in the modern era of museology, as the costs of creating a large exhibition can be mitigated by the fees paid by each hosting institution. Creating a traveling exhibition can also help large national museums abide by their mission to expose their collections to wider audiences. The Smithsonian is especially fond of building traveling exhibitions, having establishing the Smithsonian Institution Traveling Exhibition Service in 1951 and created over 1,500 separate exhibitions in the more than half-century of the division's existence, with about fifty shows out on the road in any given year.[38] The ubiquity of the traveling exhibition, then, adds an extra level of importance to the rarer temporary show. As we have seen, press reports and in-house publications were keen to stress the individual nature of the temporary exhibitions held in Edinburgh, as well as the fact that they could be seen nowhere else.

Traveling exhibitions perhaps miss that prestige of rarity. However, they bring with them their own levels of meaning for the objects that they showcase. Because they are seen over a span of time in a variety of spaces and contexts, the narratives and objects within the shows have an opportunity to change and be changed. The value and meaning of artifacts alter when they are moved. Each new space brings with it a new reading of the narrative and an alteration in interpretation.[39] The Highland objects presented in *Fonn 's Duthchas* were, by necessities of space and social context, read very differently in Edinburgh than in Inverness or any of the other spaces throughout Scotland to which the show traveled. The constant movement to which the exhibition was subjected meant that the narratives of identity and history contained within it were continuously subjected to reinterpretation and reevaluation. Too often the museum is seen as a holder of static history. This is not true even in the so-called permanent galleries, but it is even less tenable in relation to a traveling exhibition. We have seen how objects brought into a different space for a temporary exhibition change both themselves and the space in which they are shown. When this process of alteration is repeated over and over again for a year, as it was in Highland 2007, the objects and their meanings are in constant flux as they adapt to fit each of the spaces and contexts in which they are seen.

Quite apart from any theoretical meanings and uses of the traveling exhibition, though, this example had other uses in the particular context of Highland 2007. The Highlands region is often seen as being geographically and culturally apart from the capital in Edinburgh. This separation was one of the reasons why there is a history of conflict over where Highlands-identified objects should be displayed. Many of the objects that curators in Edinburgh list as the most interesting or aesthetically pleasing of the Celtic cultures are displayed at local museums in the Highlands, Perthshire, and other locations, rather than at the NMS.[40] This makes no one happy, it seems, because it keeps the national museum from having a "complete" collection, and yet the local museums still miss out on many artifacts that they feel deserve to be seen closer to their original geographic and social context. The traveling nature of *Fonn 's Duthchas* allowed this problem to be addressed, however momentarily. By moving the objects out of Edinburgh to a variety of locations, more audiences were engaged, objects were evaluated in relation to other remnants of Gaelic culture, and the perceived or actual cultural hegemony of the capital was dissolved briefly. It was also an overt statement of nationness. By going almost literally from one corner of the nation to another, the boundaries of the nation, of Scottishness, were reestablished, even if tacitly.

Originally *Fonn 's Duthchas* was to be "curatorially quite complex," with a central narrative about what the Highlands were and are in Scottish identity.[41] This was downscaled to be more of a celebration of Highland culture, illustrated with the material and visual objects from the collections of the three institutions. The exhibition intended also to "use language, music, poetry, and art to provide a unique insight into the Highlands and the people who live there."[42] This approach gets at some of vague nature of the exhibition goals — to bring Highland objects back to their people, in part to acknowledge complaints about a hoarding of culture in Edinburgh, and to attract new visitors to the Highlands, in some ways by treating the area itself as a museum piece.[43] Gordon Rintoul, director of the NMS, said, "We will work with contributors across the Highlands and Islands to bring the richness of Highland culture to the widest possible audiences. We strongly believe that the exhibition will promote international tourism, inspiring visitors to explore the Highlands of Scotland."[44] It was also a way to "showcase Highland culture past, present, and future, giving people across Scotland the opportunity to join in the Highland 2007 celebrations."[45] These multiple audiences—international and British tourists, and Scots both local and diasporic—as well as the many narratives that could be construed out of a group of supposedly Highland objects gave *Fonn 's Duthchas* its power.

A number of the differences between *Fonn 's Duthchas* and previous exhibitions are related to the different structure of the experience, not to the content. Temporary exhibitions, such as the Smithsonian and Hermitage cases, come from the collections of a loan institution, are assembled in a space at the host institution, and then stay there for a prearranged amount of time before being packed up and sent back. The objects are stripped of their normal context, but they are settled into a new context with other artifacts from their same home museums. In contrast, *Fonn 's Duthchas* was a traveling exhibition, and more than that, an amalgamating one. By moving to four different locations throughout its yearlong display—Inverness Museum and Art Gallery, Kelvingrove Art Gallery and Museum (Glasgow), the NMS (Edinburgh), and Museum Nan Eilean (Stornoway, Isle of Lewis)—the objects were subject to a constant alteration of context.[46] Each museum had a slightly different way of putting on the show and surrounded it with a different permanent collection. This, of course, changed the way in which the objects were seen. The Inverness and Stornoway museums are overtly "Highlands and Islands" focused, with Inverness asking visitors to "pop in and discover the *real* story of the Highlands," while Museum Nan Eilean "holds collections of objects, photographs, prints and paintings and archives illustrating the archaeology, social, domestic and economic history of the islands."[47] In contrast, the NMS devotes itself to telling the material culture history of all of Scotland, and Kelvingrove is a collection of both objects and art, with no overriding narrative thread winding through its collections.

In these four very different situations, it seems clear that the material would mean different things. Curators are very familiar with the impact of moving objects to new spaces. As Hugh Cheape notes, "The actual placing of a thing is absolutely vital, its context. So if you take things from the one building and move them into another people don't recognize them, they don't perhaps link them with their original placing.... People feel they've never seen the objects before. Which is actually quite encouraging. Take a thing out of its normal place and redisplay it in a new building and people will be pleasantly surprised."[48] The removal and recreation of narrative context is something that has been addressed, but it is worth a second look now, given the repeated nature of the movement around *Fonn 's Duthchas*. Everything critical about the design and implementation of temporary exhibitions is heightened if the objects are moving more than just from home to away.

The meaning and context of *Fonn 's Duthchas* was affected by the nature of its formation as well as the pattern of its movement. The exhibition contents were made up of objects that normally do not speak to each other—and are not even expected to share a common language. There is a large divide between objects of "art," objects of "history," and objects of "archives." The institutions involved in *Fonn 's Duthchas* all embody their separate spheres while also crossing the boundaries.

The National Library of Scotland is a copyright library; as such, it receives, or can request, a copy of each book published in Britain. It also holds a large proportion of global literature about Scotland.[49] It is used by academics, students, and the general public as a traditional research library space. In addition, it has collections of historically important documentary sources that it presents in temporary exhibitions separate from the research rooms. Many of the objects in the collections of the National Library could, in a different context, be seen as historical artifacts. The National Galleries similarly hold objects that could be seen either as art or history, depending on context. Opened in 1850, the galleries were charged with protecting the artistic heritage of Scotland.[50] They have displayed the nation's pictures in styles that echo changing trends in art display.[51] However, some of its collections are displayed in the Museum of Scotland as historic artifacts, as objects from the time in which they were made.

These definitions, as well as the breaking of them, are not unique to Scottish institutions. Rather, they are common to archives, libraries, and museums throughout the world. Each of these three categories of cultural institution has its own way of displaying, using, and understanding objects of all types, and the public expects different things from each. The dual naming of both Inverness and Kelvingrove—both "Art Gallery and Museum"—demonstrates the degree to which each identity has to be signaled separately, even when contained within the same collection space. Also, while both art and history are deemed things to be on public display, archive objects are usually removed from this—witness the naming of Museum Nan Eilean, though its collections are mostly what would be deemed archival. The art object is elite, the history object is populist, and the archive object is hidden.

How, then, can an exhibition function when it is made up of all three of these disparate elements? Eliminating the original plan for an overarching narrative helped somewhat, as it allowed the exhibition to become "a sort of celebration and a serendipitous taking of items that were significant from the respective displays of the National Library, ourselves [the NMS], and the National Galleries and putting them together with lots of graphics and so on."[52] If each object is just presented on its own merits, without the net of narrative, it becomes at once more and less significant. Context and the issues of changing meaning retract, as it is not meant to have any meaning, but it must be a stronger piece individually. The political imperatives of the exhibition also helped to gloss over what might have normally been major stumbling blocks to creating a coherent exhibition under the constraints of different contexts and collections. The exhibition was orchestrated to support and encourage the wider project of Highland

2007. Because of this, it had to be in line with the political message of the project, best elucidated by the then-first minister of Scotland, Jack McConnell, just as the celebrations began. He said,

> History has not been kind to the Highlands. The Clearances of the eighteenth century led to a decline and stagnation that threatened the region's language and its distinctive view of the world. Highland culture was in danger of disappearing. But all that has changed. The Highlands has experienced a revival which few believed possible. No one who visits from now on can deny this is a region firmly on the way up. Population decline has been reversed and the economy is going from strength to strength. And the renaissance in Highland culture has been dramatic. . . . The next twelve months will be a tremendous showcase for all that makes the culture of this area inspiring. . . . But the Year of Culture will be good for the whole of Scotland too. We can all learn from the region's cultural renaissance and how we can celebrate our identity by combining our rich heritage with all that is good about modern Scotland.[53]

Here again is the historical dichotomy where the Highlands are both not Scotland and all Scotland. For a devolved Scottish government only a decade old and still establishing itself, the Highlands were an important image to include in governmental policies, while the government itself was ensconced in Edinburgh.

With all these political concerns, it is not surprising that curators felt the exhibition to be more about politics than about any museum or curatorial strategies.[54] Beyond the aspects of celebration and national collaboration, the aims for the exhibition as designed by the government harkened back to historical ideas of the museum display and focused on ideals of "treasure" and "multitude." *Fonn 's Duthchas* was to show the treasures of the three national collections that had connections to the Highlands, and it was to show as many of them as possible.[55] This led to a muting of individual objects, except when they were especially powerful, either in visual scope, such as the iconic, large-scale paintings contributed by the National Galleries, or in historic resonance. Curators and visitors may have felt that there was no interesting narrative, but certain patterns can be traced now by looking at specific objects, how they were made part of the exhibition, and what they have to say about the Highlands and Scottish identity.

Some very small objects have large voices and are known in spirit even if they have never been seen in person.[56] The *Fonn's Duthchas* exhibition made use of these type of iconic objects because of the political pressures, the lack of contexts and narratives, and the audiences expected. Well-known icons largely retain the same power regardless of shifts to their message, and so are particularly well-suited to traveling exhibitions. All the objects included in *Fonn's Duthchas* can be considered icons of their various collections by definition of the exhibition's mission—to showcase the best Highland objects, whether documentary, artistic, or historic. The archives contributed objects such as copies of Walter Scott's *Waverley* and *The Lyon in Mourning* and a ten-volume history of the Jacobite cause with pasted-in mementos, such as a fragment from the dress of Flora MacDonald, the young Jacobite sympathizer who helped Bonnie Prince Charlie escape to France after the cause collapsed. These are typical objects for a library, but they also had material that is a bit more ambiguous, such as a portrait of prize Highland cattle. Iconic images such as Antonio David's portrait of Charles Edward Stewart—the Bonnie Prince himself—were furnished by the National Galleries, as well as lesser-known pieces such as a modern artistic installation by twentieth-century Highland-born artist Will Maclean.[57] This combination gave a sense of both historic and modern Highlands, but it is questionable whether the audience connected equally with all parts of it. Would an audience of non-Highlanders, which is what the organizers wanted as their primary target, understand equally the "Highlandness" of all of these objects?

The Lewis Chessmen—Highlands, Scotland, Britain

The NMS is full of iconic objects of all shapes, sizes, and meanings. However, out of all of those, the Lewis Chessmen are the key iconic object in the NMS—at least from a public recognition and marketing standpoint—and their history makes them integral to the Highland culture in the museum. These clever, carved ivory chessmen with intertwining Celtic motifs are one of the most lauded and marketed objects in the NMS today. This is our friend Erik from the introduction and his family. They were originally found in a cave on the Isle of Lewis in 1831, though the details of exactly where and how they were discovered are disputed. It may have been a "peasant of the area" who saw them in a sandbank.[58] Perhaps they were uncovered by the erosion of a beach and the gradual exposure of an underground cavern.[59] There is even mention of them being seen in something closer to a house structure.[60] Regardless of how they were discovered, the find took place sometime prior to April 11, 1831.

It was then that the collection or hoard of chessmen were exhibited to a meeting of the Society of Antiquaries of Scotland. They were brought to Edinburgh by "Mr. Roderick Ririe, a merchant in Stornoway," and the antiquaries were suitably impressed with the ninety-three chessmen, with their elaborately carved expressions and decorations. The *Proceedings* record that "the natural result of this would have been the acquisition of the entire hoard by the Society," but for some unspecified reason—mostly probably lack of funds—the society missed out.[61]

The chessmen toured the country several times before being split up and distributed among several collectors and institutions in the United Kingdom. Charles Kirkpatrick Sharpe selected ten pieces, and the rest of the collection was offered to the British Museum. Kirkpatrick Sharpe was a noted Scottish antiquary and artist, and he later managed to acquire a lone chessman from the Isle of Lewis. Not much is recorded about this, but after he died in 1851 his collections were sold in Edinburgh. The eleven chessmen were purchased by Alfred Denison, First Baron Londesborough. Lord Londesborough was an avid collector in the 1850s, especially focusing on classical, medieval, and Renaissance decorative pieces. Other objects from his collection are currently in the British Museum.[62]

The *Proceedings of the Society of Antiquaries of Scotland* reported in its 1888 and 1889 volume that the collections of Lord

Londesborough were "recently exposed to sale in London," and that the eleven chessmen were purchased by the Society of Antiquaries for the national museum.[63] They were immediately displayed and have been popular ever since. They currently reside in the *Kingdom of the Scots* section of the museum, in the side meant to show Scottish links with the Norse and Viking cultures. They are also held to say something about the role of sophistication and fun in medieval Scotland, counteracting commonly held assumptions about the backwardness and warlike character of Scottish society at this time.[64] Visitors constantly seek out and are drawn to these pieces.[65] They have been chosen to represent the collections on publications created in the NMS, from maps of exhibits to postcards and replicas in the gift shop. They are the faces of the Museum of Scotland, and as such of Scottish history as a whole.

However, there has been controversy around them as well. How Scottish is something found in the Hebrides, probably made in Scandinavia, and exhibited across the United Kingdom? Communities on the Isles of Lewis and Uig have agitated for the chessmen's return to the Hebrides. Curators at the NMS reject that call, instead saying that if they were to be returned to a "homeland," they should most likely be given to museums in Norway or Iceland. The British Museum has laid claim to its group of the chessmen as symbols of their collection as well. In London, just as in Scotland, you can go home with your very own chessman or a poster proclaiming that you have stood in their presence. Many visitors to the British Museum do not even realize that a smaller number of the figures reside in Scotland. However, at the end of 2007 Alex Salmond, the newly elected Scottish first minister and head of the SNP, promised publicly to bring the British Museum chessmen back to Scotland, a call that was equally celebrated and mocked and that reinflamed older arguments about the ownership of Celtic cultural patrimony in the United Kingdom.[66] These issues are still ongoing, with a compromise brokered in late 2009 that saw twenty-four of the British Museum's chess pieces joining six from the collections in Edinburgh to embark on a traveling exhibition of their own to

Edinburgh, Aberdeen, Shetland, and Stornoway.[67] The chessmen were included in a list of what an independent Scottish government would be able to negotiate for if the 2014 independence referendum succeeded (key items touted before the vote included cultural property such as the chessmen and 8.4% of everything else in British institutions, the rights to North Sea oil, and an open immigration policy).[68]

Given all this controversy and contested identity, it is both easy to see why they would be included in a Highland culture exhibition and also why they might be confusing to the messages of the exhibition. In the exhibition catalogue, the chessmen are the figureheads of the last section, titled "Có leis am Fearann? Who Owns This Land?" A king from the set of chessmen sits impassively looking at the reader, as the page goes on to ask, "Can any single group or person lay absolute claim to this landscape? People past and present have shaped the land. They laid down successive cultural layers that have enriched the landscape, the language, and the traditions of the region. This is the legacy of the Highlands, enhanced by the new Highlanders.... We believe there is a sense in which the land belongs to everyone."[69] By placing the chessmen at this closing point in the narrative, a case is being made for the universality of the Highland experience and culture. In some ways the chessmen are the most "Highland" of the objects in the *Fonn 's Duthchas* exhibition. They meet both of the criteria that the NMS used to designate objects as Highland — they were found in the Highlands and demonstrate the design patterns that have come to be associated with Celtic or Highland goods.[70] There is also no ambiguity about if they are geographically Highland, because if they are accepted as Scottish rather than Norse, the Isle of Lewis is definitively covered under the "Highlands and Islands" designator. However, they are speaking for more than the Highlands exactly because of their aforementioned iconic value. Even if the Isle of Lewis wants them for the Museum Nan Eilean, they are seen to be more powerful than any other type of local archaeological artifacts. They have acquired iconic resonance because of their unique form, imbued as many of them are with a rare and wry humor, and because of their presence in the collections of major institutions. Whether the Museum Nan Eilean would be so keen to have them if they had not already become immersed in this web of iconic meaning in London and Edinburgh is questionable.

So, the Lewis Chessmen were one of the exhibits in *Fonn 's Duthchas*. They were included because of their Highland-specific story and their wider iconic recognition. They also managed to embody part of the story that Highland 2007 wanted to tell—one of a region with a long and glorious history of innovation that led to influences which spread beyond the area to gain worldwide acclaim. The chessmen are considered to be Highland because of their narrative of discovery and material form, even if they are sometimes used by the museum to enhance other sorts of stories as well. Not all the objects in the exhibition met these criteria, however, and thus some had to be framed as Highland in a different manner.

The Union Brooch

The narrative arc in the catalogue for *Fonn 's Duthchas* is very much about the "placeness" of the Highlands—the land, and the people who belong to the land and who have been shaped inextricably by the land. One of the large sections of the exhibition brings this to the forefront by exploring the space the Scottish Highlands landscape has occupied over time:

> The Highlands and Islands are one of the most beautiful regions in the world, but prior to the nineteenth century they were generally seen as cold, sinister places. A different view of the Highlands grew as steamships and railway networks made them more accessible to the new breed of tourist who delighted in this scenery of vast rugged mountains. Although mapped on the very edge of Europe, the Highlands and Islands are at the forefront of global environmental and political issues. The subjects of ownership, land-use and conservation generate huge debate.[71]

This introductory paragraph to the "Mapping the Landscape" section of the exhibition gives way to subsections about maps, geologists, and Highland wildlife. The last subsection is titled "Industry and Infrastructure," and the largest caption is given to object number H.1991.54.1 from the collections of the NMS.

This object is a gold brooch set with "Scotch pebbles," made in Edinburgh in 1893 by Peter MacGregor Westren. It is in the form of "a garter set with two shields surmounted by a crown" and was made to commemorate the Act of Union of 1707 and the marriage of the Duchess of York on July 6, 1893.[72] In its everyday home in what was the Museum of Scotland, this object is displayed in the *Victorians and Edwardians* section, next to other similar brooches. It is neither the most ostentatious nor biggest of the brooches on display, and were it not for the advertising card displayed with it, this particular object would be hard to differentiate from those around it. The advertising card identifies the stones used and labels the object as an "authentic" souvenir of the events mentioned above.

The "Scotch pebble" form of jewelry, though first crafted in the 1820s, developed as a fashion in the 1860s, initially mostly among the English landed classes.[73] This was when Queen Victoria began summering at Balmoral in Scotland, setting off a rage for all things distinctively Scottish. Scotch pebbling was so named because it called for the substitution of polished stones from the beaches and Highlands of Scotland for the more normally used precious and semiprecious stones in ladies jewelry. Most commonly these pebbles were types of agates, but malachites and jaspers were also used, especially those found around the Cairngorm Mountains. Beyond the "what" of the brooch's manufacture, however, it is worth considering the "why" of its story.

This particular object is known as the Union Brooch and was made to commemorate two distinctive historical events—the political Union of the Parliaments, which took place in 1707, and the political marriage-union of Prince George, Duke of York, to Mary of Teck in 1893. The future duchess of York, Princess Victoria Mary Augusta Louise Olga Pauline Claudine Agnes, commonly called May, was a distant relation to the Habsburg court as well as a cousin to Queen Victoria's children. She was first engaged in 1891 to Prince Albert Victor, the heir to the throne, but he tragically died of influenza six weeks after the engagement was announced. Queen Victoria was very fond of May, though, and encouraged the new heir, George, to propose to her in his brother's stead.[74] The couple married in a lavish ceremony in the Chapel Royal of Saint James's Palace on July 6, 1893.

Even with this background and its overtones of Unionism and Victoria, the dual commemorative mission of this gem still comes across as contrived. The royal marriage is an obvious choice for the making of celebratory objects at the time. Including the Union of 1707 seems like more of a handy political statement than an actual clear link. This confusion might be why displays of the object have not put much weight on its stated commemorative value. In the Museum of Scotland, the story the brooch tells is one about the style and craftsmanship of Victorian and Edwardian accessory-makers. In the *Fonn 's Duthchas* exhibition, the emphasis is directed to the land and placeness of the object.

The advertising card that accompanies the brooch devotes some space to telling the buyer about the two events the brooch commemorates. It also notes that the brooch is an entirely authentic souvenir of these events. However, most space on the card is taken up with explaining which stones are used in the decoration. It tells the reader what types of stones they are, their precise origins in Scotland, and a (usually aristocratic) name for each stone. These names probably reflect the people who owned the land from which each pebble was taken. Even the gold of the brooch has a Scottish connection, as it was found, we are told on the card, in the Kildonan gold rush of 1869 and 1870.[75] Finally, there is an outline map of Scotland, which is marked with each location from which pebbles now in the brooch were harvested. It is clear that the placeness of the selected pebbles was as important as the events that the brooch was made to celebrate. It emphasized a Scottish connection to the piece of jewelry by making evident the places that contributed to the making of it. This is why the object finds itself in the "Landscape" section of *Fonn 's Duthchas*, under a level of scrutiny not normally awarded to it. In its form, the Scotch pebble brooch embodies a connection between land and Victorian sentimentality for Scotland, and the presence of an advertising card attesting to this gives the object more aura, more iconic value, than it would have otherwise.

The brooch is "Highland" then not because it was made there or because it says anything about Highland history or culture. It is Highland because it literally encompasses stony fragments of the Highlands. It is made up of bits of the land, each personally labeled and located on the map, and given further weight by the acquiescence of the landlords mentioned on the card. In medieval Scotland, reliquaries, such as the Monymusk Reliquary, were used to carry the body of the saint to far-flung parishioners so that they might stand in the presence of glory. In the nineteenth century new, modern types of reliquaries were created. Some of those were the small "celebrity wood" souvenirs, like Mauchlinware, which gave the buyer a bit of the aura of a famous personage when they purchased an item made of wood from that person's home.[76] This was not a purely Scottish phenomenon, as popular American authors such as Louisa May Alcott wrote of being hounded by celebrity-seekers stripping branches from her garden.[77]

I would argue that items such as this brooch did the same thing—except in this case it was the aura of a place, and all its associated ideas of romanticism and wildness, that you were getting, rather than that of a famous person. This sort of iconic connection to the lands of the Highlands made the Union Brooch an important object in the context of *Fonn 's Duthchas*, where it is not so important in the context of the Edinburgh-situated NMS narrative.

The Cadboll Cup

The process of framing an object for presentation in a new exhibition context also works the other way around. An artifact that is important in Edinburgh can be reframed to be relevant to the Highlands in order to conform to expectations. In creating the Highland 2007 exhibition, the institutions involved were given two mandates from the Scottish Executive. One was to show the best of their collections of Highland objects, and the other was to show as many of them as possible. The point of the exhibition from this political point of view was to expose as many people as possible to the "treasures" of the Highlands held in the collections of the national institutions.[78] Given those imperatives, the focus had to be on powerful objects that were visually arresting and did not require much explanatory context. The Lewis Chessmen, though small in stature, were the sort of visually impressive objects organizers thought audiences would want to see. The National Galleries of Scotland had the large and impressive paintings with iconic Highland scenes. In order to provide a material counterweight to this, the NMS staff was under some pressure to provide "treasures," and this led to Highland connections being overstated or created where academically they might be in doubt.

The Cadboll Cup is a silver mazer from the mid-sixteenth century and was acquired for the museum in 1970 at a cost of £33,000 with help from the National Art-Collections Fund and a special Treasury Grant.[79] It was sold by the Macleod family, in whose care it had been for centuries.[80] The cup had been on long-term loan to the Victoria and Albert Museum and displayed "in facsimile" in the National Museum of Antiquities of Scotland.[81] The issues of authenticity that this brings up are intriguing. The museum already had a version of the object that the casual observer would not have noticed was anything other than authentic—the act of placing an object on display in a museum space to some degree makes it authentic. However, this was not enough for curators when the Museum of Scotland opened. They thus retrieved the cup from the Victoria and Albert in 1997.

The Cadboll Cup is highly decorated with a combination of Renaissance and Celtic iconography chased over both the cup and standing base in a "West Highland character."[82] Little appears to be known about the cup's actual provenance, except that it belonged to the Macleods of Lewis and was rescued from the fire of Invergordon Castle in 1801.[83] There has been argument about whether some of the intricate Celtic decoration was more modern than the object itself, suggesting the piece was originally plainer and decorated later, when fashions (or economics)

The Cadboll Cup, a ceremonial cup or mazer, is an heirloom of the Macleods of Cadboll in Easter Ross, in the Highlands of Scotland. It is highly decorated with twelve panels of knots and flowers outside and a shield flanked with an M and an N inside, dating from the mid-sixteenth century. © National Museums Scotland.

changed. The catalogue for the most recent temporary exhibition in which the Cadboll Cup was featured says that it is "one of the most important cups [though] . . . nevertheless an enigmatic piece."[84] It is missing maker's marks but has stylistic similarities to communion cups and another famous brooch.[85]

The decorative scheme and unfamiliar shapes used in the cup's construction led to thoughts that it might have been assembled from a variety of different parts, including a French wine goblet stem. Sheriff Norman Macpherson, who first presented information about the Cadboll Cup to the Society of Antiquaries of Scotland in 1888, discounted this. He commented, "No doubt any time since the commencement of the Celtic furor, half a century ago, one familiar with Celtic ornament in its various stages prior to the Reformation might have devised similar patterns, but as far as we have been able to judge, no one has."[86] Although he did not expand greatly on why he believed the decoration to be contemporary with the rest of the cup, Macpherson's assertions were later found to be at least somewhat true when a chemical analysis performed on the cup in 1970 found all the silver to be the same composition and age.[87] More recent analysis also found that all the silver in all parts of the cup "had a consistently high silver composition," which seemed to the analysts to suggest that the cup was made by both French and Scottish craftspeople, working together in either country.[88] Much of the decoration on the cup is similar to that on other objects from the West Highlands, though it combines these ribbon and interlace designs with the common Renaissance motifs of foliage and "strapwork with arabesque of leaves." Robert B. K. Stevenson, director of the National Museum of Antiquities of Scotland from 1946 to 1978, was in no doubt that these decorations denoted a "Scottish and probably West Highland origin" for the cup.[89] Modern curators as well see it as Highland, albeit an object that also embodies the "auld alliance" between Scotland and France.[90]

Under this criteria, the Cadboll Cup is a Highland object and worthy of being included in the caravan of treasures making its way through the country as the Highland 2007 traveling exhibition. Nonetheless, curator Hugh Cheape, who was responsible for creating and curating the medieval galleries at the Museum of Scotland, and so under whose domain the cup fell, believed that it is disingenuous to speak of there being any particularly Highland objects at the time that the cup was made.[91] The land now designated and recognized as the Scottish Highlands were not considered separate from the rest of Scotland until much later. In the Museum of Scotland the Cadboll cup is displayed in the Renaissance section, and it is, like many of the objects in that area, meant to demonstrate the links that existed at the time between Scotland and the rest of Europe. It is a central icon of the narrative constructed by curators to highlight the "Scotland as European" element of the pre-Union Scottish kingdom. Nothing is said about its Highland connections, and its French decorative styles are highlighted and used in relation to the other objects displayed in that area to create a cohesive idea of Scotland as part of an European network of trade and culture. The Cadboll Cup, when seen there, stood as a symbol of national connections that, as seen in the earlier discussion of the debate around the provenance of the Prince Charlie canteen set, were not recognized even twenty-five years ago. However, no matter how strong this version of the cup's story is in the permanent galleries, when it was displayed in the context of Highland 2007, it almost entirely lost the European Renaissance narrative. Instead, another version of its story—one that is not necessarily any less correct—was highlighted in order to fit the desired theme.

This Highland-focused narrative is especially important given Highland 2007's sister-event, Homecoming Scotland 2009.[92] For 2009, the Scottish diaspora was "called home" to Scotland through an international marketing blitz. Much of this campaign was illustrated with images of Scottish history, artifacts, and art. It demonstrated how museum artifacts can be used to fulfill certain noncuratorial—business, political, or economic, for example—mandates. The age of modernity or postmodernity has also brought with it a compulsion to market the museum experience in the same ways as any other consumer good. These marketing mandates can do just as much, if not more, to alter existing curatorial and museological narratives than political ones. This need to market the museum and the nation through the museum in Scotland became more and more clear as the Museum of Scotland became more established in the years after its opening.

6
Changing Nation, Changing Museum

2008–2011

The doors to the Museum of Scotland opened on Saint Andrew's Day 1998 to mostly universal acclaim. Before opening a stone had been embedded at the threshold between the Royal Scottish Museum (RSM) and the Museum of Scotland, which was meant to show the two missions. If read from the Museum of Scotland side, the museum's job was to "Show Scotland to the World," whereas from the RSM side, it was "Show the World to Scotland"—a neat division of labor.

A few years on, however, the corporate team of the National Museums of Scotland (NMS) was becoming increasingly dissatisfied with the elision and confusion between missions and institutions. In 2005 they embarked on a study of social attitudes, discovering that to many people, "it was a little bit confusing which museums in Scotland were in our group and which weren't and how they all relate to each other and how they communicated to the outside world. . . . [These things were] perhaps not very clear and very emotionally engaging with the types of audiences we want to attract and feature."[1] The corporate organization had been steadily putting institutions across central Scotland under its wing, including the Museum of Flight, the Museum of Scottish Country Life, Shambellie House Museum of Costume, and the Scottish United Services Museum. Although these were under the control of National Museums Scotland, it was unclear that they were considered part of the national collections and thus part of a Scottish national story. This echoed the results from RSM and Museum of Scotland visitor studies from 1999 to 2003. At first the firm administering the annual studies had applied a quota to make sure that they caught enough respondents who had visited both museums. However, by the end of 2003, they were finding from surveys and anecdotally that people were viewing the site as one museum, not restricting their visit to one museum or the other—and in fact were not really aware when they were in one space or the other.[2]

Given the differences in public perception as well as the changing heritage context of Scotland, the corporate team and trustees decided that it was time to rebrand and reenvision the role of the umbrella organization and of each museum within it. Over the course of a year they "did some consultation with stakeholders internally and with people externally—either who visit regularly, occasionally visit, or never visit, and just kind of explored what they understood about us and what we stood for and so on."[3] The brand is a series of ideas about the institution, organization, or product it represents, but it also has a tangible presence in signs, promotional literature, and other advertising media. Brand identity lets the public know what a cultural product stands for, even if it is something intangible like "Scottish national identity."[4]

Although the NMS as a larger concept and each of its subsidiary museums had been a brand before 2005, it was due for a change as its existing identification no longer seemed to accurately convey the ideas behind the institutions and thus was not functioning effectively. Part of this failure was in not conforming to public perception. There is only so much that a brand can do to alter mass consciousness. Sometimes, if a brand is not managed from the inside, the outside world will do the branding itself.[5] Market research and anecdotal evidence had shown that despite efforts to the contrary, people saw the two connected museums as one entity. Therefore, it was easier to change the brand to reflect the outside hegemony than to continue with a gulf between the corporate identity and the public one. As one museum employee noted, "We found here that everyone is very confused about what the museum is called. The public call it Chamber's Street Museum or the Royal Scottish Museum, or whatever. A whole variation of names, and a lot of people already called it the National Museum of Scotland."[6] With the launch of the new brand for the overall organization of the National Museums of Scotland on October 30, 2006, many names were changed, including that of the complex on Chambers Street. Several things the Heritage Committee members had feared in 1981 had come to pass—the collections of Scotland's past were swallowed up and amalgamated with those of the Royal Scottish Museum, and the "national" word that they had disdained was inserted.[7]

Naming the National

The 2006 rebranding did more than just change the names of the museums, though that was the most obvious effect for the public. The corporate organization became National Museums Scotland, dropping the "of," which was deemed unnecessary. The two institutions on Chambers Street were unified under the new name National Museum of Scotland, and all other museums in the group became unified name-wise by having their purpose bracketed by new bookends of "national" and "Scotland." Thus the former Museum of Flight became the National Museum of Flight Scotland, Shambellie House Museum of Costume became the National Museum of Costume Scotland, and so on. Interestingly, the word "Scotland," though officially in the new names, was deemed to be necessary only in certain contexts where the location might be unclear. The National Museum of Scotland would always be called such, but within Scottish contexts it would just be the National Museum of Flight, the National War Museum, and such. A knowledgeable audience could imply the location, the thinking went, and thus it would not need to be obviously signposted.[8]

These changes in name could be seen as merely a way to integrate a corporate identity and bring a group of museums closer together under the aegis of the larger National Museums Scotland identity. However, the way in which the new names were selected and imposed also tells us something about how the nation of Scotland was perceived and what role these museums—and particularly the newly dubbed National Museum of Scotland—was to have within it. The Williams Committee had argued in 1981 that there was no need for the adjective "national." What had changed between 1981 and 2006?

The most obvious answer is that the nation of Scotland had changed. Although there had been several near misses for political devolution in the 1970s and 1980s, nothing changed in the political arena until the successful devolution referendum of 1997. This change brought the Scottish nation closer than they had been for centuries to having a Scottish state. Movements for devolution, if not outright independence, had long used the idea that the Scottish nation deserved a Scottish state as a rallying call; in 1997 this cry was somewhat met. The political state and the cultural nation of Scotland were the closest to congruent as they had been since the Union of 1707. This was a major shift for the nation, and for its identity, but also a leap into the unknown.

When the Museum of Scotland opened in 1998 the Scottish state was just finding its feet. By 2006, it was well-established as a political entity. It was led by a nationalist party, had continually strengthened its use of devolved powers, and advocated for a move to independence. While a devolved Scotland might not meet all the requirements for a political state—it did not yet have Max Weber's classic formulation of an "agency within society which possesses a monopoly over the legitimate use of violence"—it was tantalizingly close.[9]

Having a state changes the idea of a nation. If a nation is the cultural grouping of people that feel or imagine themselves to be linked, it reacts differently when it is under the rule of a state that it feels comes from outside that imagined community than it does when it is under the control of something from within. The reframing of the names of these national institutions may reflect a larger reframing of the nation that can take place once devolution is established. Culture is one of the aspects over which the

Scottish government has full control. The National Archives of Scotland, the National Library of Scotland, and the National Galleries of Scotland all join National Museums Scotland as the so-called National Institutions under the oversight of the Arts and Culture Department of the Scottish government. Changing the name of the museums integrated them not only into the National Museums group but also into a nation that was increasing asserting its control over aspects of state policy. The "National" tag could be seen as a badge of honor in the newly confident Scottish national state.

Identity and belonging is not just asserted at the highest levels of government, however. It is also signaled in smaller, daily ways among all the members of the nation. Theorist Michael Billig discusses the importance of these "banal" signals of nationalism and identity, concentrating on the implicit identifying that goes on with "deixis," or a "continual pointing to the national homeland."[10] The Museum of Scotland may have implied that national connection, but it did not draw the audience into the nation explicitly. This fact becomes even more important if we return to the original, pithy message of the Museum of Scotland. It was to show Scotland to the world. "The world" is necessarily outside the nation of Scotland. Thus, while members of the Scottish nation may implicitly know that a Museum of Scotland is a museum of the nation, outsiders may not. The change in name flags the museum's mission more clearly as somewhere that the outsider or tourist may go to explore things that are not of their national experience. By reiterating the "national" label over and over, it asserts continually to both outsiders and insiders that here is a nation that can be made explicit, rather than continuing to be tacit and under the control of others.

There is also a strong value connotation to the word "national." It has the weight of authority and truth behind it, as only "official" things are given the honor of being deemed "of the nation." Adding "national" to the name of the Museum of Scotland served several purposes. Museum marketing director Catherine Holden said that "it's clarifying that these [museums] are the ones that have national status, and I think it is also an important quality stamp, so they are of national status and we want to recognize that in their naming, and also for people who are perhaps not frequent visitors, it says to them this is something worth seeing. It has a validity and encourages people to visit."[11] Because of the weight that we give to nations in modern society, people recognize something national as something inherently more important, and more worth their time, than something not officially national. They also see it as something they should have seen or with which they should have been involved. As a member of the nation, you are expected to engage with the daily activities and identities of the nation, and as a visitor to another nation, you are meant to gaze on them from afar. Both these things would now be available at national institutions. A simple change of name can remind people of their obligation to the nation. This was easily identified right after the change in names at National Museums Scotland. Holden continues, "And in fact we've just done some research looking at awareness of the museums. And we asked people whether they've heard of the old names of those museums, and then we asked if they'd heard of the museums with their new names and awareness went up, even though it's exactly the same thing. But suddenly because it's the *National* Museum of Costume people think, yeah, I should have heard of that, I should have been there."[12] In the past national identity, with its value and weight, could be taken for granted. This allowed the committee members of 1981 to say that many great national institutions omit "national" from their name.[13] But the situation in Scotland and the world had changed to an extent where the explicit flagging for the nation at every turn became helpful in attracting visitors, funding, and quality assessments— the essential nutrients of a modern museum.

The name change, in addition to increasing the positive attributes given to the museum, also eliminated some negative ones. While getting permission to remove the "Royal" sobriquet from the Royal Scottish Museum was time-consuming and somewhat controversial, it also removed the negative connotations that the old name might have had in devolved Scotland.[14] The change emphasized that Scotland as a nation, rather than the monarchy, was in charge of official history, and also brought the contents of the institution in line with what was promised on marketing material. It eliminated the possibly apocryphal worry that tourists encountering a "Royal Museum" would expect a museum of the monarchy, rather than one of the nation.[15]

The Image of the Nation

The name was not the only change to occur during the rebranding. These name changes were distilled down into a visual form—a new logo. Previously each of the museums had had its own logo, a visual symbol of its contents or purpose. The Museum of Scotland used a thistle, usually acknowledged as a symbol of Scottishness, and the RSM had a lion rampant, the symbol of the royal family in Scotland. The other museums in the group had other visual incarnations of purpose. All of these were consigned to the dustbin, however, when the rebrand occurred. In the newly integrated and newly national National Museums Scotland, all subsidiary museums shared the same logo, called the museum mark. The official brand guidelines say that "the mark represents the experience of enquiry and exploration, discovery and enjoyment. Graphically this is represented as questions and exclamation marks and suggests a cyclical process—visitors ask us for information, and we seek their views and challenge them to think in new ways as part of an ongoing dialogue."[16] The mark, made up of two question marks and two exclamation marks meeting in the middle to form a saltire cross, also mirrors the shape of the Saint Andrew's Cross flag of Scotland. This logo is on everything from the signs at the entries of the buildings to official maps, from bags at the museums shops to staff nametags. The idea is that every time the mark is seen it conjures up a set of very specific ideas having to do with the whole spread of national museums in Scotland.

In that way a logo functions in much the same way as any other museum icon. It is one small form standing in for and representing many larger ideas. The Museum of Scotland was from the beginning, as we have seen in earlier sections of this work, intended to be heavily based on iconic objects. This approach, with the rebranding, was only intensified as the museum itself was iconized. The logo was meant to bring forward ideas of a newly strong and political Scottish nation, to encourage thinking about exploration and discovery, and to do all that from just one small visual source.

The brand guidelines established by National Museums Scotland are full of small details about the new corporate typeface and how exactly the logo should be used, but they also positioned all of these supposedly trivial details in context. "What is a brand?" the guidelines ask. The answer: "A brand is much more than a logo. It is an intellectually and emotionally engaging idea that helps organizations make decisions about the future. A unique brand idea provides internal focus and helps organizations stand out. When the idea is expressed properly, it creates stronger bonds with the audience."[17] This is, in essence, the idea behind any brand or corporate identity. The unified design that underlies each brand can be used to convey a larger idea that might not be clear from outside.[18] The brand in this way is as much an icon as the objects profiled. Brands are created to be iconic in that everyone who looks at them immediately connects them to a series of larger ideas. In the case of corporate brands, these might be ideas about the refreshing nature of a fizzy drink. Although museums hold themselves apart from that sort of overtly commercialistic world, the museum experience is increasingly a commodity. Reenvisioning the set of reflections that go along with its iconic value allowed the museum to control what people are consuming as surely as if they shifted the stock in the museum shop.

Icons Inside

Sometimes rebrandings are purely cosmetic and that regardless of new name or new logos, little inside is altered. However, things changed on the inside of the NMS—or at least the way the inside was presented—as well. With the integration of the RSM and the Museum of Scotland, the scope of objects on display shifted considerably. The Royal Museum, because of its industrial and scientific background, displayed a wide range of objects, generally arranged into a series of thematic galleries. Thus *Art and Industry since 1850* shared the ground floor with *British Animals* and *World in Our Hands,* about the science of ecological change, while upstairs the East Asian Art Gallery connected to *Modern Jewelry* and then left you in *Ancient Egypt.* With the rebranding, all of this was now part of the National Museum of Scotland. Where before only the objects relevant to the history of Scotland had been labeled as being in any way national, now everything was.

In this way the new NMS mirrors other institutions considered to be national but yet say very little about the history of the nation. The British Museum is intended to be, and widely perceived to be, a national museum. So is the Louvre in France. Nonetheless, these are both closer to what scholars Carol Duncan and Alan Wallach term a "universal survey museum," where the wealth and strength of the nation is shown not by its own objects but by how much of a complete set of things the nation has from other places.[19] While Duncan and Wallach focused primarily on art museums and their aims to collect all the right, internationally important artists, the same argument can be held for internationally important national museums of objects. The British Museum and others like it say little or nothing about the nation in which it is situated, other than drawing a picture of past empire and glory through the sheer value and breadth of its collections. With the addition of the RSM collections, the NMS became an intriguing hybrid of a small-scale universal survey museum and a self-consciously national history museum.

The corporate leaders of the museum realized that something more had to be done to unify the collections than merely gluing a new logo on things, and so they envisioned a completely new and all-encompassing role for objects within the renamed space. When doing the research leading to the rebranding, the marketers noticed that the museum had "really diverse audiences, really diverse objects, so we said 'What unites everything that we do?' And we really came to the idea that it is the things, that we have the real things, and particularly in a virtual world that is increasingly a valuable commodity. We have the real things and the revealing stories behind them."[20]

While this is the main idea of any museum, this idea of "real things . . . revealing stories" became the major theme of the rebrand—as well as the tagline on new banners and advertising—and it served to further highlight how iconic objects are created and manipulated to serve the museum. Unlike with the initial development of the Museum of Scotland, where the objects were meant to tell the story on their own, during the rebrand much more emphasis was put on drawing the story out of the object and making it explicit. According to Catherine Holden, "For some people who are perhaps not regular visitors the objects might be interesting, but it is the stories behind them that were even more interesting . . . which meant that in our literature and other things we started to focus on the objects and the stories behind them." Here again the ideas of enquiry and exploration first hinted at in the new logo returns. The corporate marketers wanted to make people aware of the stories behind the objects, but given the recent trend for increasing interactivity in museums, the other buzzword was audience engagement. So, Holden continued, "as well as objects we usually try and put a question, you know, something that catches attention and tries to involve someone in the objects."[21] The objects were still there as icons—meant to represent ideas larger than themselves—but they were also being used as hooks to engage an audience in their story, or whatever version of their story the museum wanted to tell.

New Museum, New Icons?

One of the main public complaints when the Museum of Scotland first opened was that the space was confusing and that there were not enough signs telling visitors where they were or how to move around. This was an aesthetic and architectural decision and had been modified only slightly since opening. The rebranding addressed these issues and made some major changes. Large, freestanding signs appeared in all the galleries of what used to be the Museum of Scotland overnight. These signs laid out the themes that would be encountered in the gallery to follow, and they each focused on one particular object that was located within it. These objects were a mix of recognized icons, such as the Lewis Chessmen, and new objects elevated to icon status. Holden explained this combination:

> There are some things that we think are iconic, and particularly people that don't visit that much, they can be more motivated by a sort of celebrity object, something that is immediately recognizable, like Jackie Stewart's Formula One helmet or the Lewis chessmen. . . . So we wanted to really capitalize on those things, which are really strong assets of ours, but also for the people who perhaps feel they've been there, and done that, seen the Lewis Chessmen, we needed to intrigue them a little bit, in some of the more unexpected objects in the museum.

The objects were acting as guides in the narrative of the galleries, and also as literal signposts along the journey. She continued, "Our research has shown in the Royal Museum part of the building that they tend to stay on the ground floor, in the main hall and the immediate galleries. Very few people, like 10 percent of people, actually go upstairs, so to some extent we picked things that try to encourage people to go and explore, find other things that they perhaps weren't expecting."[22] The objects, newly given icon status, were engaging people and luring them deeper into both the story and the space of the rebranded nation.

It is clear from the blockbuster exhibition phenomenon that certain categories of objects naturally attract the most attention from audiences. Among those, themes of opulence or tragedy are foremost. These blockbuster-marketing techniques were also applied to the selection of icons for the new signs and narratives that went along with the rebranding. Previously overlooked objects that fit those storylines were given prominence. Tracing what these objects were made to say can tell us a lot about how curators constructed new narratives to make sense out of a suddenly expanded collection and remit. Objects to highlight were selected on the basis of four criteria. Each object had to be visually striking, have an interesting story, represent the collections, and speak to different audiences.[23] The final choices were made by the marketing team, in consultation with the curatorial, education, and design departments. Once objects were selected they were used by the rebranding effort in a variety of ways. Perhaps most obviously a series of large banners outside the building advertised the museum. Each one featured a different object and question relating to the object along with an exhortation to "come inside to find out" the answer. The same group of objects and questions also appeared throughout new museum publications, such as maps and calendars of events. This meant that the objects were being rebranded alongside the museum.

Mary's Jewels

In the Museum of Scotland half of the museum, one of the most obviously rebranded objects was a set of jewelry associated with Mary, Queen of Scots. It was featured on one of the aforementioned new signs, which was placed right at the entry to the *Kingdom of the Scots* gallery. This space had been home to only two objects, one of which was the Monymusk Reliquary. The reliquary had been placed there at the entry to the gallery, all alone in a white space, to highlight its role as an icon of the narrative to come, leaving the space around it unadorned except for a small Pictish cross and a quote from the Declaration of Arbroath, a letter to the pope written in 1320 that is considered a declaration of Scottish independence. This design decision enhanced the reliquary's aura and strengthened its iconic value. However, now that the same space was dominated by a freestanding sign touting the narrative explicitly, rather than letting the object draw people in quietly.

The main image on this sign is that of a heart-shaped gold and enamel pendant set with rubies, diamonds, and a cameo of Mary, Queen of Scots. The same picture of the pendant was used on an exterior banner, where it is found with the words, "Who treasured me? Come inside to find out."[24] With the visitor's interest piqued by this repetition, the sign has the effect of speeding people past the actual objects in the room in favor of finding this new, rebranded icon. It can be found in a case of jewelry next to the "authentic replica" of Mary, Queen of Scots' coffin.[25] In the case is the pendant and several other pieces of jewelry—a necklace of gold filigree beads, some painted miniatures, and a gold enameled locket. The whole case is labeled as containing the "Penicuik Jewels," which refers to a suburb of Edinburgh where Mary lived and a family, the Clerks, who were her supporters.

While the Penicuik Jewels are important and interesting, the cameo in question does not belong with them. Indeed, the Penicuik Jewels perhaps have more authenticity as relics of Mary but are not chosen as icons of her. The jewels were long in the possession of the Clerk family of Penicuik, who had acquired them by a member of the family marrying the great-granddaughter of Giles Mowbray, who was one of Mary's servants while she was imprisoned in England. Just before her death, Mary gave bits of jewelry to each of her servants.[26] The gold filigree necklace was probably made from beads of several bracelets given to Mowbray by Mary. The miniatures were likely not from Mary herself but rather made to commemorate her and her son.[27] However, the necklace is the closest to an actual piece of jewelry worn by Mary that the museum has. This relic of the queen was donated to the museum after the efforts of two dedicated gentlemen (one of whom later wrote the book about them) raised enough money in public donations to buy the objects at a sale in London in 1923.[28] The lot that contained the Penicuik Jewels also contained a fan of yellow silk and silver tissue with an ivory knob, "a Ryal of Mary and Henry, 1565, one or two threads of Prince Charles' hair, a leather-covered casket, a small pair of scissors in silver filigree case; and a reticule and handkerchief."[29]

The Penicuik Jewels have been exhibited just as many times as the cameo and have a close personal relationship to Mary in their provenance. The cameo, on the other hand, was very likely not Mary's at all but rather commissioned by her for distribution to her friends and supporters. It was bought by the museum in 1959, after it came up for sale in London. A special grant from the Treasury Department was needed, as well as money from the

National Art Collections Fund and the museum itself. The identification of the cameo as Mary was "confirmed by the Scottish National Portrait Gallery and by their colleagues in London"; thus it was authenticated as of Mary in form, if not exactly in provenance.[30] That remained a bit fuzzier, and like we have seen in the case of the Monymusk Reliquary, what was first unknown has seemed to become slightly more solid, just due to the passing of time.

The first reports about the cameo noted, "The history of the jewel is unknown. There is evidence, however, that mid-sixteenth-century monarchs were in the habit of giving mounted cameos of themselves as marks of favor; it is suggested that this elaborate jewel was probably given in return for a service of considerable importance."[31] In 1986 the cameo was featured in a book on Mary, Queen of Scots, where its caption read, "Sixteenth century Scottish jewel made with a French cameo of Mary; probably a gift by her to one of her supporters."[32] By 1990, when the cameo was in an exhibition about the Stewart family, the caption read, "The cameo illustrated is one of several of the Queen to have survived, and could have been commissioned by Mary from France or Italy for distribution to friends and supporters."[33] So over the course of about fifty years, nothing new has actually been learned about the cameo, but it is presented in a variety of different ways, each of which removes the object a little bit from Mary herself. First she gave it away in return for a great service, then she gave it to one of her supporters, and in the end it is just one of many objects commissioned by her to be distributed on her behalf.

These subtleties are not elucidated in the rebranding of the object, however. The correct answer to the question, "Who treasured me?" is evidently meant to be Mary, Queen of Scots. She is the icon, and an association with her is created in this object—which was probably selected over the more historically accurate relics of the Penicuik Jewels because it is more instantly recognizable. In the context of the rebranding, iconicity of form is just as important, if not more so, than iconicity of narrative. Thus, one object that is only tangentially related to a popular and tragic icon of history is made to stand in for her and her much more complicated story, just because it happens to be recognizable and saleable.

Egypt in Scotland

Sometimes, however, it is not just one object that gets attention. Rather it is the sheer weight of a mass of artifacts, with one delegated to serve for the whole. In this case the one is a representative not only of a larger idea but also a larger collection. The majority of the Egyptology collection in the NMS was collected in the early twentieth century by the notable archaeologist William Flinders Petrie. One of the most important archaeologists and contributors to development of thought about ancient Egyptian society and material culture, he developed scientific methods for archaeology and believed that knowledge could only be gained by attention to the smallest details.[34] He was a member of the British School of Archaeology, and his work was partially funded by the public and the Royal Society of Edinburgh so that it could acquire Egyptian artifacts for its museum. These objects had weight even at the beginning of their museum life. Just as Petrie was to start a new excavation, James J. Dobbie, then director of the RSM, put out a heartfelt plea. He argued it "would be a reflection upon our national spirit as well as an irreparable loss to our museums" if foreign governments had to fund the excavations. He went on to say,

> Hitherto we in Scotland have given but meager support to the work of exploration in Egypt, and the museum's claims upon the results has been a proportionally restricted one. In England, on the other hand, the contributions are on a much more liberal scale and bear fruit each year in the addition of many valuable objects to the English collections. I would ask that a similar public-spirited liberality should secure for us such a share of the results of Professor Petrie's labors as would help to place our collections on a level with those of England. I am not here referring to the great collections of the British Museum, which are on a level by themselves. But it is surely neither idle nor presumptuous to attempt to place

our Egyptian collections at least on an equal footing with those of Manchester, Liverpool, Oxford, or Cambridge, to which at present they are inferior both in extent and in the variety and beauty of the objects which they contain.[35]

Being able to claim some of the many objects at that time flowing out of Egypt into the coffers of museums worldwide was seen as a necessary thing to retain the prestige of the collection as a whole. If Scotland missed out on these objects, the tacit understanding was, its museum would be seen as inferior. Egyptian artifacts fell into the universal survey idea of "things you must have" in order to be a complete collection.

Of course, they were then and have always been a big crowd-pleaser. The first modern "blockbuster" exhibition was of objects from the tomb of King Tutankhamen, and they remain a go-to subject when visitor numbers need to be increased.[36] Even in the early twentieth century, the public responded. Dobbie wrote that "it is unnecessary to enlarge upon the great and growing interest which the general public exhibit in the history and antiquities of Egypt, and the importance, from this point of view, of augmenting and improving our collections."[37] His plea for public donations for Petrie in order to stake a claim for Scotland to the treasures uncovered succeeded. Within three years the Egyptian collection in Edinburgh was so large that the RSM presented it evidence of the need to expand. In 1909 the Egyptian collection was redisplayed and recased, creating an "open and clear" display that attracted new visitors and made the objects seem new and exciting. The annual report for that year reported, "The effect referred to is really dependent on the provision of suitable space for the proper exhibition of the collection, and establishes a visible proof that the need for greater accommodation for the other sections of the museum is actual and urgent."[38]

The impetus for the recasing, other than to show need for new space, was the procurement of another group of new objects from Petrie, whose connection with the RSM had flourished. He routinely traveled to give lectures in Scotland about his most recent finds.[39] This new collection was "a group of objects, one of the most important ever brought to this country from Egypt."

A burial, it included the mummy of a woman and all the objects found in the tomb with her: "Professor Petrie states confidently that no complete burial group containing such unique objects is to be found in any museum out of Cairo. The whole contents of the tomb are shown in a large case in which the objects are placed as nearly as possible in the relative positions in which they were discovered."[40]

Again we see that it is not the one glorious object that is important, but the mass of them, and the having of something that no one else displays. This attitude was not uncommon in the early twentieth century. Museums tended to focus more on the treasure or exotic value of their objects, and display rhetorics preferenced the mass over the singular in designing exhibits.[41] Nonetheless, while the majority of other objects in the RSM or the NMS are displayed very differently now than in the past, the Egyptian displays have remained relatively static. They experienced some changes—most notably in the 1970s, when they were joined by four huge murals representing aspects of life in Egypt, which remained there for more than thirty years—but then reverted to something very similar to their first displays in the National Museum of Antiquities.[42] Unlike in other parts of the museum, the trend for the singular and iconic has not triumphed among the Egyptian artifacts. They remain displayed together, with the burial group still exhibited in a similar fashion to how it was discovered in 1909.[43]

In the course of the rebranding, certain objects from the collections were chosen to be icons of the new museum and to serve as signposts through the journey. One of the Egyptian artifacts served in this capacity, placed on an outside advertising banner with the question, "Where did I rule?"[44] However, unlike the Mary, Queen of Scots, jewelry and other objects raised to the position of icon, it is not immediately evident which of the many sarcophagi or burial figurines appears on this banner. The object is not presented in enough detail for the small differences that identify each sarcophagus to be visible, and since there is no sense of scale given, it could well be one of the many miniature figures of sarcophagi, called shabtis and meant to represent servants for the afterlife, that exist in the collection. A visitor looking at that marketing material would not necessarily know which object it is. Thus, even now it is the mass of the collection that is being highlighted, rather than the more common, rare, and solitary object that stands alone. The collection and the multitude become the object. The story of the real, individual object has been swallowed by the need to emphasize the scope of the collection as a whole.

The two rebranded objects—the Mary, Queen of Scots, jewelry, and the Egypt collection—both highlight different parts of the collections of the NMS and appeal to different audiences. By presenting them in the same way through the newly rebranded marketing campaign, the corporate heads of the museum were attempting to infuse continuity into what had been two very different institutions. To some extent they have succeeded. However, each of the two objects profiled here remains rooted in the separate narratives and display styles of its "home" institution. A museum built on icons stays that way, as does a museum built on a mass of global collecting. Still, that gap may be about to narrow.

Moving the Past Forward

Another major issue for the NMS, other than the rebranding, was the Royal Museum Project. From April 2008 until the summer of 2011 the RSM was closed to visitors while undergoing a major overhaul of both building and the artifactual narratives contained within the space. This was another reenvisioning of the Scottish past as seen in an ever-changing Scottish present. The Royal Museum Project was about reinvigorating the Victorian building that had been so iconic to the Edinburgh landscape but now no longer worked in a world of step-free access and interactive exhibitions. It was also about yet another—the last?—name change for a space that has had a lot of them. And again, it was the continuation of a conversation from 1780 onward in Scotland: nations and their need for a national museum. As the Royal Museum Project came to a close, all trustees were issued a gold brochure. In this, Professor Tom Devine, Sir William Fraser Chair of Scottish History and Palaeography, director of the Scottish Centre for Diaspora Studies at the University of Edinburgh, and frequent consultant at the Museum, wrote, "No nation should be without a national museum. It is through its physical artefacts from the past that the people of a nation can truly understand how they came to be."[45]

The NMS organization was awarded £34 million of funding by a combination of the Heritage Lottery Fund and the Scottish government in 2008, and they added to that with donations from charitable trusts, corporate sponsors, and individual donations. In total, the Royal Museum Project cost about £46.4 million. It was meant to "create a world-class, 21st century visitor experience for Scotland, and a showcase for international visitors."[46] The renovation created a new ground level entrance to the RSM building and sixteen new galleries, and doubled the amount of objects on display. A major part of the campaign for the Royal Museum Project (subtitled "Making a world of difference") was that they were creating a national museum fit for the twenty-first century. Another line used in the same campaign was celebrating Scotland's contribution to the world.[47]

The RSM half remained, however, a basically thematic and noniconic museum. The major sections of the museum after renovation focus on the natural world and world cultures—both areas that were covered in the museum already. The difference, other than an obvious update to display style, can be found as a result of the museum's new identity as one half of the NMS. The RSM had always been more a museum *in* Scotland than a museum *of* Scotland. Now that changed. In the planning process Catherine Holden explained it: "What we want to do is make sure that threaded throughout the Royal Museum's exhibitions are stories about . . . why they're here in Scotland, what have they got to do with Scotland, and often about the people who went out and collected and found the objects or invented the objects who were Scots or traded with people internationally and so on."[48]

This was made clear by the chairman of the Board of Trustees, Angus Grossman, who said in a brochure made for the opening,

"We can tell great stories about the world, but also about how the Scots saw that world and how they had such a disproportionate impact on it."[49] In selecting the key objects for the first spaces of the new museum, David Forsyth, senior curator of Scottish social history and diaspora, said that he believed they are "representatives of collections that belong to Scotland but speak of the world around us. In particular they show how Scots have made connections and exerted influence across the globe and tell a broader story."[50] To do that, each new highlighted object brought out for the bigger space created in the renovated Royal Museum had an unexpected Scottish story. As museum director Gordon Rintoul said in a preview of the museum in the *Scotsman* magazine on the opening weekend, "Every object in the museum is either Scottish or it was a Scot who brought it back or discovered it. Every item has a story and we want to tell it."[51] They did tell these stories in media accounts at the opening, making clear that the point was to "unite the collection with a Scottish narrative."[52] Sometimes the theme was taken further, as in one article that proclaimed, "Revamped Museum Is Hailed as New Symbol of a Nation."[53]

One object mentioned in media reports many times was the large *umete*, or wooden feast bowl, from Atiu, one of the Cook Islands in the South Pacific. The bowl, 144 inches long, 38 inches wide, and nearly 36 inches tall, was carved from a single piece of tamanu wood. It makes an impressive statement sitting on a plinth in the Victorian entrance hall of the museum. Its Scottish story comes via a Tahitian princess who married not one but two Scottish businessmen—one at a time, of course. Princess Titaua inherited the feast bowl from the women in her family and then brought it into her new family. Her first husband was John Brander, a Scot-Polynesian trader. When he died and left her a young widow, she married George Darsie, another Scot in the area. She and her second husband managed a plantation together and then retired to his hometown of Anstruther in Fife. They brought the bowl and other South Seas collectables with them. In 1895 George Darsie sold them to the RSM.[54] Gordon Rintoul specifically mentioned this as his favorite object and the one he felt "encapsulate[d] this whole wider Scottish story."[55]

After the rebrand and the reopening, the displays of the former Museum of Scotland half of the building remained as they were, with a very few exceptions. They persisted in telling a basically chronological story of Scottish history through material culture. On the other side of a wall, the former RSM displays are, in their own way, now doing the same thing. Scottish identity was threaded throughout each new narrative, whether about the stars, the animals, or the culture of the South Sea islands.

Scotland and the World

The displays of the two formerly separate museums are meant to be complementary, but the public may continue to regard them as separate. Alternately, the two museums may appear too repetitive, and visitors consider it necessary to view only part of the museum. The 2012 survey found that the physical link between the two remained unclear, although Scottish history content was an acknowledged interest with many visitors.[56] They simply were not sure how to get there.

Visitors have a way of creating their own narratives, which sometimes correspond with what is expected and sometimes go off in other directions altogether. This is a common issue when museums try to rebrand or renovate. Curatorial and public viewpoints may be opposed, fashions may change faster than museums can adapt, and different audiences can be brought in at a cost of alienating established ones. Thus, the decision about how to "brand" a new or renovated museum is a critical one. The brand has to encompass what the institution stands for and speak to its audiences, collections, and missions.

The new NMS brand is one about stories, Scottishness, and diversity. Of course, it is hard to tell now exactly how the messages in the new galleries of the NMS are read by visitors. The idea is to have narratives of identity threaded through every exhibit, but it is not clear yet if audiences are actually perceiving them. Nothing came up about it in the evaluation of the galleries completed in 2012. In fact the most overtly Scottish part of the new space—the *Discoveries* gallery—was noted as a "hidden gem" that visitors did not realize had Scottish content until they had read three or more object labels. However, this survey only spoke to 168 visitors from September 2011 to September 2012, so the results are interesting but fairly insignificant.[57] However, it seems that the links between the two buildings remain unclear. The weight of the complicated institutional and architectural history is still evident, despite official publications increasingly moving to call the former Museum of Scotland space a "1998 extension that introduced the Scottish galleries."[58]

This gentle rewrite of history is just the next step in a process that is looking to embed the Scottish museum narrative wholly into the universal one. Visitors may not be noticing it, or at least they may not be noticing it enough to mention it to consultants administering response surveys, but I believe it is still critically important to examine. Just the curatorial act of putting those narratives together, and of reenvisioning the collections to center Scottishness, is an undertaking worthy of consideration—regardless of whether visitors ever read it that way.

When the NMS was first born as one cohesive whole on paper in 2006, it held side-by-side narratives of national history through objects. Both halves presented a different version of the nation, reflecting different times in society and different potential audiences. The older version, that of the Museum of Scotland, was the material manifestation of a nation unsure of itself. The weaker or less recognized a nation is, the more it must use obvious tools of nation creation. When the Museum of Scotland was planned and first opened, its audience could not be expected to know or assume the history of the nation. The Museum of Scotland thus had to act in almost the same way as the first postcolonial museums—using the space for a constant reiteration of national history, complete with an implied oppressor and a narrative of struggle.[59] To fund the new museum, the planners had to rely heavily on expatriate donors, a group whose national identity is strengthened by being physically removed from it. The projected audience for this museum was tourists who needed to be told a history of Scotland that was more than tartan and bagpipes, and a national populace who had, by dint of British standardized curricula, been taught very little about how Scottish history differed from British history. Because the apparatus of a state to enforce national identity through banal, everyday means was lacking, the museum had to do it much more overtly.

Meanwhile, before 2006 the RSM was seen as a place for local, repeat visitors and for children to wander.[60] When thinking of the space, people said things like "unchanging" and "nostalgic" as well as "breadth of appeal." These research consultants noted the same problems with the name, saying, "Users do not refer to the museum in a consistent manner, and that the name *Royal Museum* is rarely used. The museum is described variously as *The Museum*, the Scottish Museum, the Chambers Street Museum, and the National Museum." In 2003, the particular solution given to this problem was to strengthen the brand of the RSM and to further increase differentiation between the Royal Scottish Museum and the Museum of Scotland, as people were confused about having two museums on one site.[61] However, as we have seen, before long, this was given up as fruitless. There was no sense fighting against public opinion that was telling you, in a way, what it needed—a larger, more universal NMS that took in everything on Chambers Street.

This is why I do not think it is that important if visitors actively notice what the curatorial team have done to thread Scotland throughout the narratives in the new space. Whether or not visitors recognize it, the narrative is there, and it was a decision that could not have been made in an earlier time of the museum's, or the nation's, life. This particular space had to go through a lot of changes to get to this point: in name, mission, collections, and institutional structure. In that, it mirrors its older (1780) yet newer (1998) half, the former Museum of Scotland.

In the meantime change has been happening outside the museum walls as well. With devolution established and thriving, nationness in the museum can be more overtly presented.[62] The message in many universal survey-type museums is that the nation is so well recognized no direct statements need to be made about it.[63] The post-2011 NMS is a bit of a hybrid—more national than that, less national than before. The museum parallels the nation—as the nation gets stronger in itself, so does the national identity in the museum.

Visitors entering the NMS know that they are stepping into national space by stepping through the door with that label, clutching the map with that insignia, passing greeters with those nametags and signs with those logos. This is the power of a name and the power of branding—as well as the power of a national museum. We have come to think, from the eighteenth century until today, that every nation needs one. And so, since 1998, Scotland has had not one but two incarnations of their museum. The differences are illuminating.

The first objects you would have seen as you entered the Museum of Scotland in 1998 were a carved stone Pictish cross, the Monymusk Reliquary, and the statue of Saint Andrew.[64] These are all very traditional images of Scotland. The Monymusk Reliquary is, as discussed previously, on Scottish banknotes, and the others are likely to feature heavily on tourist postcards. Together they represent an established visual culture version of Scotland, for an audience that wants or needs that, by curators that have not had space to do even the simplest version of their story ever. In contrast, the first objects you see as you enter the new main doors to the renovated NMS are an Assyrian relief, a fossilized tree slice, and a helmet. Again, like everything else in the museum, these have Scottish connections, but the impression they leave is entirely different. They are items that challenge the vision you may have about Scotland as a place of Pictish carved crosses and medieval relics. It expands and globalizes the nation while still leaving what is now called "the Scottish Galleries" there—for those who can find them in what remains a troublesome space.

The rebranding of the Royal Museum and the Museum of Scotland to create the NMS was an exercise in critical analysis, to look at what and who the nation is today and what the role of national history and national institutions within it should be. It called for the creation of new icons to support new narratives and new, larger ideas. It is reflective of the changes that have gone on in Scotland over the last decade and is part of a larger context in

Edinburgh, Scotland, and beyond. In that way it encapsulates all of the issues that we have carried through the various moments in time profiled here. The NMS comes out of all of them, and incorporates some of everything it has seen within its walls, over the span of time. More than just a logo, a musty attic, or a place of entertainment, the new national museum itself is an iconic object for Scotland.

Conclusion

In March 2017 Nicola Sturgeon, the first minister of Scotland, called for a second referendum on Scottish independence in light of the recent vote to pull the United Kingdom out of the European Union.[1] Scotland has long had closer links to Europe than the rest of the United Kingdom, as objects such as the embellished canteen given to Charles Edward Stewart showed.[2] Sixty-two percent of Scots voted to stay in Europe, while overall in the whole of the United Kingdom, the "leave" vote was 53.4 percent. All Scottish counties voted to stay.[3] Given those results, it makes sense that another independence referendum be called, as a major decision is about to be taken against the wishes of a majority of Scots. However, it also makes it difficult to decide when to end a study like this. Scottish identity is changing. It always has been, as Scots continuously negotiate their relationship to the British state, to their own incarnations of statehood, and to how they represent that identity in museum spaces.

Emphasizing Scottishness

Any point at which analysis stops must be arbitrary, as the change that is central to the museum project continues regardless. In the particular case of the National Museum of Scotland (NMS), that is especially true. The museum profiled here is already a historical artifact itself, as the museum continues to integrate itself after the huge rehang and reopening of 2011. That created one complete national museum, from the stunning animal galleries to the *Windows on the World* artifact wall, the largest single museum display in the United Kingdom, to the Scottish artifacts profiled here. The mission of the renovation was to refresh the space and galleries of the Royal Scottish Museum but also to better integrate the history of Scotland into every exhibited narrative.

This was done by reenvisioning the collection, having it speak not just about the wider world but about the Scottish adventurers and diaspora communities that brought objects back to Edinburgh. Nearly every artifact now includes a narrative about its journey into the museum's coffers, opening a discussion about how Scottish travelers spread across the world and contributed to the development of science, government, and other fields of endeavor.

Most clearly this is done in the new *Facing the Sea* gallery space—the only museum space dedicated to the culture of the South Pacific anywhere in the United Kingdom. The narratives presented in *Facing the Sea* tell the average visitor a fair amount about the unique history, culture, and material goods of the islands. Yet they do this while also shining a light on Scottish travelers to the Pacific Islands and on a Tahitian princess who married a visiting Scottish businessman and moved to central Scotland. Each exhibited object is framed by its connection to Scotland, however tenuous that might be.

This approach—of telling the story of the nation through the contributions of particular individuals—began in the museum in July 2008, when a new permanent gallery covering Scottish history from World War I to the present opened in the former Museum of Scotland section. This was the first time in nearly a decade that modern history was a part of the museum. The twentieth-century gallery that was in the museum on opening day in 1998 was always meant as a temporary solution and closed soon afterward. The new permanent displays are in two interconnected galleries. One, the *Scottish Sporting Hall of Fame*, has been open since June 2006 and runs down the center of the gallery space. It is self-contained but also connects to many of the display and content ideas in the larger gallery that surrounds it. The rest, which is called *Scotland—A Changing Nation*, takes five main themes to construct a vision of Scotland in the twentieth and twenty-first centuries: "War," "Industry," "Daily Life," "Leaving Scotland," and "The Voice of the People."

Like the recently completed Royal Museum Project, the modern Scotland gallery stepped away from the white walls and

Conclusion

solitary objects of the lower floors of the museum. Instead, there is a multiplicity of colors, images, sounds, and text in which the objects sit embedded. The entry panel to the gallery lays this out as a display philosophy: "Through personal stories, film, music, poetry, *and objects*, we hope you will discover both well-known and less-expected aspects of Scottish life."[4] The textual placement of objects at the end of this list of encounters mirrors the fact that the object is very much the last part of the gallery that visitors see. It is not that there is a lack of objects but rather that they are so deeply embedded in this framework of visuals, film, and continuous sound that they act as interesting illustrations rather than key parts of the narrative.

This was a way to represent the cultural cacophony of modernity in a completely different way than was possible in the measured and organized exhibitions of things that have been consigned to the past. Film, sound, and photographs are objects in their own right and can be icons of the historical narrative as successfully as traditional objects. However, the inclusion of these new types of artifacts changes the types of stories that can be told in the gallery. This has led to material being displayed largely in grouped exhibition cases that contain thematic displays of artifacts, rather than the solitary objects that are more common throughout the rest of the museum.

The "personal stories" promised at the entry are represented by small cases of objects, each topped by a picture and small biography. The people profiled vary from noted political campaigners to pop stars and organic farmers. The objects displayed are largely forgettable, making the display about the person and the iconic personality presented there. The marketing tagline for the new gallery, repeated in advertisements in many different contexts in the months after it opened, was "Made in Scotland, from Stories," which reflects both the 2006 rebranding phrase of "real things . . . revealing stories" and also the culturally iconic advertising slogan from Irn-Bru, which had celebrated the drink that is more popular in Scotland than Coca-Cola, as being "made in Scotland, from Girders."[5]

Both the 2008 modern gallery and the much larger 2011 project have changed the NMS considerably, both aesthetically and conceptually. Perhaps the focus has shifted from telling the story of the nation through objects to telling the story through people. However, the two are inextricably linked. By more closely entwining the stories of the nation's material culture with the stories of its people, the NMS has acknowledged the power that objects have to tell multiple stories. Very few artifacts were added to the collection. Instead, existing collections were relabeled to fit what museum staff decided needed to be said to a nation that is increasingly confident about its own identity and place in the world. Because they can be fit to many contexts, as well as stand without any, museum artifacts act as a perfect canvas for the performance of whichever identity is to star at any given time. For this reason iconic objects have become the central focus of this book. Tracing them through the various exhibitions, galleries, and narratives where they can be found serves to highlight the ways in which historical truth is manipulated and constructed in the museum. It is not the one singular, authentic truth that is encountered there but rather the latest incarnation of an ongoing process of identity creation and its public production within the space of the museum.

Politics and Nationhood

Outside the walls of the museum, Scottish identity has also continued to change and evolve. When the Scottish National Party (SNP) first gained power in Scotland in May 2007, it proposed a national referendum on Scottish independence to be held in 2010. However, it soon became clear that public opinion was not strongly behind moving that quickly. A previous independence campaign had failed in 1979, so of course appetites were not high for risking another loss. In the meantime, though, the devolved government, under the leadership of the SNP, continued to gain more powers and used them in ways that differentiated Scotland from England and Wales—such as eliminating charges for prescription drugs and not charging tuition fees to university students. These were all signs of a more confident government, and a more confident nation.

When the next Scottish election arrived in May 2011, the public perception and culture had shifted enough that an independence referendum could be put on the table again. The SNP won an even larger majority and promised a vote in the second half of the term. On July 29, 2011, the refurbished NMS opened, with its newly persistent narratives of Scottishness around the world. Then in October 2012 the then-Scottish government and the government of the United Kingdom reached the Edinburgh Agreement, allowing for a simple yes-or-no vote on Scottish independence to be held on September 18, 2014.[6]

The agreement for a referendum was the culmination of the centuries-long fight for acknowledgment of Scottish distinctiveness. After the trauma of the Jacobite wars, proponents of Scottish nationhood had moved slowly and carefully in order to establish their claims of Scottish national character without too overtly challenging British power structures. They first worked through culture and history. This dates back to the establishment of the Society of Antiquaries of Scotland in 1780 and their Scottish antiquarian collection. Once that was done, proponents of Scottish nationalism could push for governmental recognition of Scottish culture as the next step in demonstrating that Scotland was a separate space. The collection and its public display allowed Scotland to network with other international museums and collections, and thus see its history and material culture in new ways and new contexts. Meanwhile, the push continued for true recognition of Scotland as a nation, and thus for there to be a *national* museum.

Once the national museum was granted funding, planned, and opened, there was a fifteen-year process of gradual change in how identity and history was presented there. This moved in tandem with the gradual change of Scottish devolution and politics, as well as the larger cultural and social milieu in which it was embedded. Over the period from 1998 to 2014, the sense of Scottish distinctiveness from England and Wales grew stronger, Scottish parliamentary powers increased, the national museum presented Scottish history more forthrightly, and the Scottish nationalist movement came into the center of politics. These issues are all intertwined.

The September 2014 Scottish independence referendum failed, despite what was looking like a very tight race up until the last minute. Within two weeks, there was a display on the event in the twentieth-century gallery at the NMS, showing banners and signs from both sides of the fight—the "Yes" and "Better Together" campaigns, and a short explanatory label. This quick response time shows that the NMS is now attempting to do more of what the Smithsonian National Museum of American History does, which is collect things of national importance as and when they are happening. No longer are museums silent repositories of the ancient. Instead, they actively respond to current events, to history in the making. This will continue to be an important role for the NMS in the years to come. Scotland's identity and position within Britain and the world remain in flux. The ongoing debate about how to navigate Brexit may test those further.

What Does This Mean for the Museum?

There are always three intertwining layers of museological narrative. First is the museum, a space and institution that, though it has been examined before, has never been looked at in all of its historical and social context, and in concert with its contents. The museum in previous work has either been seen as a universal and new type of institution, without many nationally contingent specifics, or as a new type of event tied strongly to the eighteenth and nineteenth centuries. Understanding both these kinds of museum narrative is critical, but it is not enough. Particular nations and contexts lead to the creation of particular museums. The resulting institution cannot be fully understood without looking at where it came from and the dilemmas and controversies it had to address in the process of formation. Also crucial, and often missing, is the concept of continuous change. This book has not only looked at how the NMS was created but also how it has continued to change in order to better reflect the nation that it represents. Creating this long history of the museum allows for the development of a more nuanced idea about the relationship between history and modernity, between a museum and its public, and between culture and politics.

The second level of narrative, that of the exhibition, is where the ongoing life of the museum really begins to emerge. Too often temporary exhibitions have been considered in isolation, rather than as part of a larger narrative. Each exhibition is influenced not only by its time and context but by the shows that have gone before and what is planned for the future. These exhibitions, their storylines, and the important objects they both use and produce are windows into the soul of the museum project. These exhibitions' main product, exhibition catalogues, are artifacts themselves, produced to reflect certain goals and aspirations of the exhibition and its creators. While generally considered a popular commodity rather than a historical source, catalogues provide an important insight into the exhibition world. They can be a significant primary source for scholars of the museum world, containing as they do the permanent textual form of something originally meant to be both temporary and artifact-based. The relationships between the museum and the exhibitions it has hosted, between past and present exhibitions, and between the museum show and its catalogue form are all critical to a deeper understanding of the public role played by history.

The most detailed level of narrative is that of the artifact. This too is an aspect of historical and sociological study of the museum that scholars have missed. Objects are the heart of the museum enterprise. They and their extraordinary capacity for multivocality are what make the constantly shifting narratives of the museum possible. From the great bulk of the Newcomen engine to the tiniest of the Lewis Chessmen, each artifact in any museum is responsible for supporting a great weight of history and for conveying that historical story to the visitors who pass by it each day.

Recently, museum studies has emphasized how visitors receive and understand the narratives of a museum, and how their personal experiences alter the curatorially created narratival hegemony. This is undoubtedly important. However, it is also important that the objects and their stories do not become entirely reliant on the impressions of the individual visitor. Each object has been selected to play a particular part in whatever narrative is momentarily given precedence. Regardless of whether this narrative is being read "correctly" by visitors, it was created to fulfill specific goals within its museum, gallery, or exhibitionary context. Just as each exhibition is connected to the ones before and after, in a larger historical and museological story, so too is each object. They create and recreate the artifactual narratives that underlie the larger ones of exhibition and museum. Tracing a series of objects through a portion of their lives allows for the examination of the changing ways objects are read in different times and spaces, as well as identifying the ways in which they can be made to tell a wide variety of stories suiting a variety of needs.

Scotland's museum history is unique in its particular twists and turns. However, it also follows certain universal patterns. National museums are not merely the holders of national history and material culture. Instead, they, through their temporary exhibitions, constant institutional changes, and ever-shifting artifactual narratives, create and reflect contemporary visions of the nation and aspirations for its future development. This new viewpoint places the museum at the center of the modern national project, creating and upholding the public view of history.

Whatever the next incarnation of Scottish cultural and political identity, the museum and its artifacts will be there to tell its stories. It has been doing that since 1780, through thick and thin, through ups and downs, and it will continue to do so. And that is the beauty of artifactual narratives—they are endlessly flexible. They adjust to the circumstances at hand, can be read by whichever visitor is there, and manipulated by whichever curator is in charge. Whether or not Scotland ever again becomes an independent state, it is a unique nation, with unique objects, and it shows these in its unique national museum space.

Notes

Beginnings

1. Scotinform, "Royal Museum Project Evaluation of Galleries Executive Summary," November 2012, 1, 069(411) NMS 2012, National Museum of Scotland Archives, Edinburgh (hereafter NMS Archives); Draft Report, September 2012, 2, NMS Archives.
2. Mike Wade with Sue Mitchell, *On the Trail of Scotland's Past* (Edinburgh: NMS Publishing, 1998).
3. See, for example, Nina Simon, *The Participatory Museum* (Santa Cruz, CA: Museum 2.0, 2010); John H. Falk and Lynn D. Dierking, *The Museum Experience Revisited* (Walnut Creek, CA: Left Coast Press, 2012); Elizabeth Wood and Keirsten F. Latham, *The Objects of Experience: Transforming Visitor-Object Encounters in Museums* (New York: Routledge, 2013); and Peter Samis and Mimi Michaelson, *Creating the Visitor-Centered Museum* (New York: Routledge, 2017).
4. See, for instance, Suzanne Macleod, Laura Hourston Hanks, and Jonathan Hale, eds., *Museum Making: Narratives, Architectures, Exhibitions* (New York: Routledge, 2012); Suzanne Macleod, *Museum Architecture: A New Biography* (New York: Routledge, 2013); and Gail Dexter Lord and Ngaire Blankenberg, *Cities, Museums, and Soft Power* (Washington, DC: American Association of Museums Press, 2015).
5. See Neil Larson, *Determinations: Essays on Theory, Narrative, and Nation in the Americas* (London: Verso, 2001); Tatjana Aleksic, ed., *Mythistory and Narratives of the Nation in the Balkans* (Cambridge: Cambridge Scholars, 2007); and Sheila Miyoshi Jager, *Narratives of Nation-Building in Korea: A Genealogy of Patriotism* (New York: Routledge, 2016).
6. Ernest Gellner, *Nations and Nationalism* (Oxford: Blackwell, 1983); Benedict Anderson, *Imagined Communities: Reflections on the Origin and Spread of Nationalism*, 2nd ed. (London: Verso, 1991); E. J. Hobsbawm, *Nations and Nationalism since 1870*, 2nd ed. (Cambridge: Cambridge University Press, 1992); M. Hechter, *Containing Nationalism* (Oxford: Oxford University Press, 2000); L. Greenfeld, "Modernity and Nationalism," in *The Sage Handbook of Nations and Nationalism*, ed. G. Delanty and K. Kumar (London: Sage, 2006), 157–68; Daniele Conversi, "Nationalism and Modernity," *Journal of Political Ideologies* 17, no. 7 (2012): 13–34.
7. Fiona McLean, "Museums and the Construction of National Identity: A Review," *International Journal of Heritage Studies* 3, no. 4 (1998): 244–52; Peter Aronsson, "Explaining National Museums: Exploring Comparative Approaches to the Study of National Museums," in *National Museums: New Studies from around the World*, ed. Simon Knell, Peter Aronsson, and Arne Bugge Amundson

(London: Routledge, 2011), 29–54; Sharon J. MacDonald, "Museums, National, Postnational, and Transcultural Identities," in *Museum Studies: An Anthology of Contexts,* ed. Bettina Messias Carbonell (London: Blackwell, 2012), 273–86.

8. For more on the history and naming of the Industrial Museum, see Geoff Swinney, "Towards an Historical Geography of a 'National' Museum: The Industrial Museum of Scotland, the Edinburgh Museum of Science and Art and the Royal Scottish Museum, 1854–1939" (Ph.D. thesis, University of Edinburgh, 2013), https://www.era.lib.ed.ac.uk, and C. D. Waterston, *Collections in Context: The Museum of the Royal Society of Edinburgh and the Inception of a National Museum for Scotland* (Edinburgh: National Museums of Scotland, 1997), 87.

9. Waterston, *Collections in Context,* 102, 124.

10. This sentiment came from George Wilson, the first curator of the Industrial Museum, in a lecture in 1854.

11. *Making a World of Difference,* campaign manual, RMP.2012.0020, 5, NMS Archives.

12. "New Art and Science Galleries Now Open: Ancient Egypt and East Asia," National Museum of Scotland, http://www.nms.ac.uk.

13. Colin Kidd, *Union and Unionism: Political Thought in Scotland, 1500–1800* (New York: Cambridge University Press, 2008); J. Wormald, "The Happier Marriage Partner: The Impact of the Union of the Crowns on Scotland," in *The Accession of James I,* ed. G. Burgess, R. Wymer, and J. Lawrence (London: Palgrave Macmillan, 2006), 69–87.

14. Murray Pittock, "Scottish Sovereignty and the Union of 1707, Then and Now," *National Identities* 14, no. 1 (2012): 11–12.

15. Murray Pittock, *The Myth of the Jacobite Clans: The Jacobite Army in 1745,* 2nd ed. (Edinburgh: Edinburgh University Press, 2009).

16. Matthew P. Dziennik, "Liberty, Property and the Post-Culloden Acts of Parliament in the Gàidhealtachd," in *Liberty, Property and Popular Politics: England and Scotland, 1688–1815: Essays in Honour of H. T. Dickinson,* ed. Gordon Pentland and Michael T. Davis (Edinburgh: Edinburgh University Press, 2016), 58–72.

17. Dauvit Broun, Richard Finlay, and Michael Lynch, eds., *Image and Identity: The Making and Re-making of Scotland through the Ages* (Edinburgh: John Donald, 1998); Hew Strachan, "Scotland's Military Identity," *Scottish Historical Review* 85, no. 2 (1998): 315–32; Juliet Shields, "From Family Roots to the Routes of Empire: National Tales and the Domestication of the Scottish Highlands," *ELH* 72, no. 4 (2005): 919–40.

18. Steve Murdoch and A. Mackillop, eds., *Fighting for Identity: Scottish Military Identity, c. 1500–1900* (Boston: Brill, 2002); A. Mackillop, *"More Fruitful than the Soil": Army, Empire, and the Scottish Highlands* (Edinburgh: Tuckwell Press, 2001).

19. Graeme Morton, *Unionist Nationalism: Governing Urban Scotland, 1830–1860* (Edinburgh: Tuckwell Press, 1999).

20. The earl was very interested in antiquarianism and Scottish politics for much of his life even before founding the Society of Antiquaries of Scotland. He had been a member of the Society of Antiquaries and the Royal Society in London since 1764. See Emma Vincent Macleod, "Erskine, David Steuart, Eleventh Earl of Buchan (1742–1829)," in *Oxford Dictionary of National Biography,* ed. H. C. G. Matthew and Brian Harrison (Oxford: Oxford University Press, 2004), 18:524–27.

21. David Stewart Erskine, Eleventh Earl of Buchan, *Discourse Delivered at a Meeting for the Purpose of Promoting the Institution of a Society for the Investigation of the History of Scotland and Its Antiquities* (Edinburgh, 1780), 4.
22. The Society of Antiquaries (England) was started on December 5, 1707, though was only in operation continuously from 1717; it received its royal charter in 1751.
23. Buchan, *Discourse*, 13.
24. R. B. K. Stevenson, "The Museum, Its Beginnings and Its Development, Part I, to 1858: The Society's Own Museum," in Bell, ed., *The Scottish Antiquarian Tradition*, 33.
25. William Smellie, *Account of the Institution and Progress of the Society of Antiquaries of Scotland* (Edinburgh, 1782), 1–2.
26. Ibid. 25.
27. Society of Antiquaries of Scotland, https://www.socantscot.org.
28. David Stewart Erskine, Eleventh Earl of Buchan, quoted in Smellie, *Account of the Institution*, 16.
29. Marinell Ash, "David Laing, Daniel Wilson, and Scottish Archaeology," in Bell, ed., *The Scottish Antiquarian Tradition*, 96.
30. Ibid., 102.
31. "Old and New Towns of Edinburgh," UNESCO World Heritage Centre, http://whc.unesco.org; E. Patricia Dennison and Michael Lynch, "Crown, Capital, and Metropolis: Edinburgh and Canongate, the Rise of a Capital and an Urban Court," *Journal of Urban History* 32, no. 1 (2005): 22–43; Volker M. Welter, "History, Biology, and City Design: Patrick Geddes in Edinburgh," *Architectural Heritage* 6, no. 1 (1995): 60–82.
32. Society of Antiquaries of Scotland, minute book, 1844. 069(411) Edi 1844, NMS Archives.
33. Walter Scott and George, King of Great Britain, *Hints Addressed to the Inhabitants of Edinburgh, and Others, in Prospect of His Majesty's Visit* (Edinburgh: Bell and Bradfute et al., 1822).
34. Richard W. Butler, "The History and Development of Royal Tourism in Scotland: Balmoral, the Ultimate Holiday Home?" in *Royal Tourism: Excursions around the Monarchy*, ed. Phillip Long and Nicola J. Palmer (Buffalo, NY: Channel View, 2008), 51–61.
35. Hugh Cheape, "The Society of Antiquaries of Scotland and Their Museum: Scotland's National Collection and a National Discourse," *International Journal of Historical Archaeology* 14, no. 3 (September 2010): 357–73.
36. Bruce G. Trigger, "Daniel Wilson and the Scottish Enlightenment," *Proceedings of the Society of Antiquaries of Scotland* 122 (1992): 61.
37. Hugh Cheape, curator of Scottish history, interview by author, May 23, 2005, February 9, 2007.
38. Stevenson, "The Museum, Part I," 80.
39. *Proceedings of the Society of Antiquaries of Scotland* 1 (1852).
40. R. B. K. Stevenson, "The Museum, Its Beginnings and Its Development, Part II: The National Museum to 1954," in Bell, ed., *The Scottish Antiquarian Tradition*, 143.
41. See Nick Prior, *Museums and Modernity: Art Galleries and the Making of Modern Culture* (Oxford: Berg, 2002), chap. 2.

42. Anderson, *Imagined Communities*, 183.
43. Michael Billig also discusses the ways in which national identity is reinforced by small acts like this. See Billig, *Banal Nationalism* (London: Sage, 1995).
44. George Dalgleish, curator of Scottish decorative arts, interview by author, June 10, 2005.
45. For more on this, see Anthony Smith, "Nations and History," in *Understanding Nationalism*, ed. Monserrat Guibernau and John Hutchinson (Cambridge: Polity, 2001), 8.
46. The National Museum of Ireland opened in 1890. The National Museum of Wales opened in 1902.

Chapter 1: The Smithsonian Inspires

1. Edwards Park, *Treasures of the Smithsonian at the Royal Scottish Museum* (Washington, DC: Smithsonian Books, 1983).
2. "About the Smithsonian," Smithsonian Institution, http://www.si.edu.
3. As seen in a series of banners throughout the Smithsonian Castle building in Spring 2008. The slogans were also used in media reports from 1981, 1996, and 2012. See Jonathan Yardley, "America's Attic: What We Make Is What We Are," *Washington Post*, December 6, 1981, https://www.washingtonpost.com; Nona Yates, "'America's Attic': LA Is First Stop for a Traveling Exhibit Marking the Smithsonian's 150th Anniversary," *Los Angeles Times*, February 1, 1996, http://articles.latimes.com; and Liz Halloran, "'America's Attic' Team Dredges Convention for Historical Riches," NPR, September 6, 2012, http://www.npr.org.
4. Sheila Brock and Alison Harvey, eds., *Royal Scottish Museum Final Report, 1983–84–85* (Edinburgh: National Museums Scotland, 1986), 64. The report says 98,000 visitors, though press releases at closing reported 100,000.
5. I am indebted here to conversations with the librarians of the National Museum of Scotland in April 2017, as well as to Jenni Calder, "The Royal Scottish Museum in Retrospect, 1854–1985," in Brock and Harvey, eds., *Royal Scottish Museum Final Report*, 13–16.
6. Catherine Holden, director of marketing, National Museums Scotland, interview by author, March 13, 2007.
7. See Isabelle Vautravers-Busenhart, "Special Exhibitions and Festivals: Culture's Booming Path to Glory," in *Arts and Economics*, ed. Bruno S. Frey (Berlin: Springer, 2000), 67–93. See also Smithsonian Office of Policy and Analysis, "Exhibitions and Their Audiences: Actual and Potential," September 2002, https://www.si.edu.
8. Vautravers-Busenhart, "Special Exhibitions and Festivals."
9. Frank Dunlop, quoted in R. W. Apple, "Major US Role Set for Edinburgh," *New York Times*, June 19, 1984.
10. "Hosting Museum Facilities Report for the Royal Scottish Museum," box 25/28, Smithsonian Institution Traveling Exhibition Service, Exhibition Records, ca. 1977–99, 00–069, Smithsonian Institution, Washington, DC (hereafter SI Archives).

11. Summary results of elections of 1979, 1983, and 1987 can be found on David Boothroyd's website, "United Kingdom Election Results," http://www.election.demon.co.uk.
12. For much more on this, see Jonathan Hearn, *Claiming Scotland: National Identity and Liberal Culture* (Edinburgh: Edinburgh University Press, 2000); David McCrone, *Understanding Scotland: The Sociology of a Nation*, 2nd ed. (London: Routledge, 2001); Murray Stewart Leith and Daniel P. J. Soule, *Political Discourse and National Identity in Scotland* (Edinburgh: Edinburgh University Press, 2011); and Susan Condor and Jackie Abell, "Vernacular Constructions of 'National Identity' in Post-Devolution Scotland and England," in *Devolution and Identity*, ed. John Wilson and Kathryn Stapleton (London: Routledge, 2016), 51–76.
13. Mary Bryden, "Shaping and Selling the Idea: How the Product Was Presented," in *Heritage and Museums: Shaping National Identity*, ed. J. M. Fladmark (London: Routledge, 1999), 30.
14. Sheila Brock, "*Treasures from the Smithsonian* Review," in Brock and Harley, eds., *Royal Scottish Museum Final Report*, 63.
15. John E. Reinhart and Ralph C. Rinzler, foreword to Park, *Treasures of the Smithsonian*, 5.
16. Brock, "*Treasures from the Smithsonian* Review," 64; emphasis added.
17. "Memorable Outing," *Sunday Express Magazine*, August 12, 1984.
18. Eight of nineteen articles have a variation of the Smithson-to-Scotland story.
19. "Visual Wonders Proudly Unveiled," (London) *Times*, August 14, 1984.
20. Abby Wasserman, "Smithsonian Featured at Edinburgh Festival," *Torch: A Monthly Magazine for the Smithsonian Institution*, August 1984.
21. S. Dillon Ripley, quoted in "*Treasures from the Smithsonian Institution* Travels to Scotland's 1984 Edinburgh Festival," Smithsonian Institution, press release, March 30, 1984, box 25/28, 00–069, SI Archives.
22. S. Dillon Ripley to Queen Elizabeth II, October 28, 1983, box 25/28, 00–069, SI Archives.
23. Royal Scottish Museum, press release, March 12, 1984, box 25/28, 00–069, SI Archives.
24. See S. M. Davies, "The Co-Production of Temporary Museum Exhibitions," *Museum Management and Curatorship* 25, no. 3 (August 2010): 305–21.
25. For more on the International Festival and its history, see George Bruce, *Festival in the North: The Story of the Edinburgh Festival* (London: Hale, 1975); Eileen Miller, *The Edinburgh International Festival, 1947–1996* (Aldershot, England: Scolar Press, 1996); and Jen Harvie, "Cultural Effects of the Edinburgh International Festival: Elitism, Identities, Industries," *Contemporary Theatre Review* 13, no. 4 (2003): 12–26.
26. Frank Dunlop to S. Dillon Ripley, August 17, 1983, box 42/48, Smithsonian Institution Assistant Secretary for Public Service Subject Files, ca. 1968–88, 00–0367, SI Archives.
27. "One Man's Plan for the Athens of the North," (London) *Sunday Times*, August 19, 1984.
28. The contributions of the Sackler collection collectively are mentioned twelve times in the nineteen U.K. newspaper articles that reviewed the exhibition. The only object mentioned more frequently was the lunar rover or "moon buggy."

29. S. Dillon Ripley to Ralph Rinzler, memorandum, "Edinburgh Festival Miscellany," October 20, 1983, box 42/48, 00–0367, SI Archives.
30. "Partial List of Contacts Made by Ralph Rinzler on Behalf of the SI Edinburgh Program during His October Visit," n.d., box 42/48, 00–0367, SI Archives.
31. S. Dillon Ripley to Norman Tebble, December 30, 1983, box 42/48, 00–0367, SI Archives.
32. S. Dillon Ripley to Frank Dunlop, January 24, 1984, box 42/48, 00–0367, SI Archives.
33. Nina Burleigh, *The Stranger and the Statesman: James Smithson, John Quincy Adams, and the Making of America's Greatest Museum, The Smithsonian* (New York: HarperPerennial, 2004).
34. James Smithson, quoted in Charles Minor Blackfield, "The Smithsonian Institution," *North American Review*, January 1909, 94.
35. George Thomas, *The Founders and the Idea of a National University: Constituting the American Mind* (New York: Cambridge University Press, 2015), 81.
36. See Richard Franklin Bensel, *Yankee Leviathan: The Origins of Central State Authority in America, 1859–1857* (New York: Cambridge University Press, 1990), chap. 1.
37. House report, December 21, 1835, in (Washington, DC) *National Intelligencer*, February 17, 1836.
38. Blackfield, "The Smithsonian Institution," 95. This amount, $508,318.46, is also mentioned in every other history of the Smithsonian. Googling this number will bring you to accounts of the Smithsonian's founding.
39. This was led by Representative Joel R. Poinsett of South Carolina. Denise Meringolo, *Museums, Monuments, and National Parks: Towards a New Genealogy of Public History* (Amherst: University of Massachusetts Press, 2012), 15.
40. William Darlington, *A Plea for a National Museum and Botanic Garden to Be Founded on the Smithsonian Institution at the City of Washington* (West-Chester, PA: N.p., 1841).
41. "An Act to Establish the 'Smithsonian Institution' for the Increase and Diffusion of Knowledge among Men," August 10, 1846, Smithsonian Institution Archives, Smithsonian Libraries, http://www.sil.si.edu.
42. For more on the Smithsonian, American national identity, and science, see Meringolo, *Museums, Monuments, and National Parks*.
43. As of October 2017, the Smithsonian claims to have 154 million objects and pieces of art in its collections. "Smithsonian Collections," Smithsonian Institution, https://www.si.edu.
44. S. Dillon Ripley, foreword to Park, *Treasures of the Smithsonian*, ix.
45. Notes from "Edinburgh Festival Catalogue" meeting, January 20, 1984, box 13/18, Smithsonian Institution Traveling Exhibition Service, Exhibition Records, ca. 1963–2005, 06–059, SI Archives.
46. See Robert C. Post, *Who Owns America's Past: The Smithsonian and the Problem of History* (Baltimore: Johns Hopkins University Press, 2013), and William S. Walker, *A Living Exhibition: The Smithsonian and the Transformation of the Universal Museum* (Amherst: University of Massachusetts Press, 2013).
47. Amy Henderson and Adrienne L. Kaeppler, introduction to *Exhibiting Dilemmas: Issues of Representation at the Smithsonian*, ed. Amy Henderson and Adrienne L. Kaeppler (London: Smithsonian Institution Press, 1997), 5.

48. The slippers remain wildly popular. In October 2016, the NMAH used Kickstarter, a crowdfunding platform, to raise $300,000 to conserve the slippers. The campaign was incredibly successful, going over the goal in seven days, starting on October 17, and announcing the goal met just before midnight October 23. https://www.kickstarter.com; Camila Domoske, "Save the Ruby Slippers: Smithsonian Seeks Funds to Preserve Dorothy's Shoes," NPR, October 20, 2016, http://www.npr.org; Peggy McGlone, "Smithsonian Exceeds $300,000 Kickstarter Goal to Preserve Dorothy's Ruby Slippers," *Washington Post*, October 24, 2016.
49. For examples of this attitude, see "Inspired by Judy's Magic Shoes," *Edinburgh Evening News*, August 8, 1984.
50. "Treasures from the SI—August 12–November 4, 1984, Royal Scottish Museum Edinburgh Object List," n.d., box 3/3, Smithsonian Institution Traveling Exhibition Service, Exhibition Records, 1983–89, 01–133, SI Archives.
51. Donald McClelland to Douglas E. Evelyn, deputy head of NMAH, March 6, 1984, box 42/48, Smithsonian Institution Assistant Secretary for Public Service, Subject Files, ca. 1968–88, 00–0367, SI Archives.
52. Royal Scottish Museum, press release, March 12, 1984.
53. "Preliminary Object Selection List," n.d., box 25/28, 00–069, SI Archives.
54. "Debate on Exhibition Title," n.d., box 25/28, 00–069, SI Archives.
55. Other options included *Treasures from the Museums of the Smithsonian, Treasures from the Smithsonian Museums, America's Smithsonian: Treasures from Its Museums,* and *America's Smithsonian: Treasures from Its Collections*. Ibid.
56. Brock, "*Treasures from the Smithsonian* Review," 63–64.
57. S. Dillon Ripley to Laurence J. Korb, May 18, 1984, box 25/28, 00–069, SI Archives.
58. Norman Tebble, introduction to *Royal Scottish Museum News*, Summer 1984.
59. Donald McClelland, quoted in *"Treasures from the Smithsonian Institution* Review," *Royal Scottish Museum News*, Festival 1984.
60. Walker, *A Living Exhibition*.
61. Post, *Who Owns America's Past*.
62. Lois Marie Fink, *A History of the Smithsonian American Art Museum: The Intersection of Art, Science and Bureaucracy* (Amherst: University of Massachusetts Press, 2007); Meringolo, *Museums, Monuments, and National Parks*.
63. See James B. Gardner, "Contested Terrain: History, Museums, and the Public," *Public Historian* 26, no. 4 (Fall 2004): 11–21, for a curatorial perspective on why the Smithsonian is held to such standards of authenticity. For related academic perspective, see Brenda M. Trofanenko, "The Educational Promise of Public History Museum Exhibits," *Theory and Research in Social Education* 38, no. 2 (2010): 270–88.
64. Ripley, foreword.
65. An online version of the exhibit can be seen here: *Julia Child's Kitchen at the Smithsonian*, Smithsonian National Museum of American History, http://americanhistory.si.edu. For more on it, see Sarah Conrad Gothie, "No Food and Drink in the Museum: The Challenges of Edible Artifacts," in *The Food and Folklore Reader*, ed. Lucy M. Long (London: Bloomsbury Academic, 2015), 395–405.
66. This process is meticulously laid out in a press fact sheet in the *Julia Child's Kitchen* exhibit, http://americanhistory.si.edu.

67. Peggy Loar to Ralph Rinzler, "Smithsonian Participation at the Edinburgh Festival," October 4, 1983, box 42/48, 00–0367, SI Archives.
68. James Goode to Ralph Rinzler, "Edinburgh Festival Ideas," November 1, 1983, box 42/48, 00–0367, SI Archives.
69. Mary Dillon, quoted in Wasserman, "Smithsonian Featured at Edinburgh Festival."
70. Many of the exhibitions profiled in books such as Ivan Karp and Steven D. Levine, eds., *Exhibiting Cultures: The Poetics and Politics of Museum Display* (Washington, DC: Smithsonian Institution Press, 1991), and Bruce W. Ferguson, Sandy Nairne, and Reesa Greenberg, eds., *Thinking about Exhibitions* (London: Routledge, 1996), reflect the change in museum display modes.
71. Wasserman, "Smithsonian Featured at Edinburgh Festival."
72. From the will of Benjamin Franklin, codicil, July 17, 1788, Franklin Papers, Yale University, New Haven, CT, 46:u20, http://franklinpapers.org.
73. Steven Lubar and Kathleen M. Kendrick, eds., *Legacies: Collecting America's History at the Smithsonian* (London: Smithsonian Institution Press, 2001), 64.
74. See Joseph Amato, *On Foot: A History of Walking* (New York: New York University Press, 2004), and Thorstein Veblen, *The Theory of the Leisure Class: An Economic Study of Institutions* (New York: Macmillan 1912), 171.
75. For more on the cap of liberty, see Jennifer Harris, "The Red Cap of Liberty: A Study of Dress Worn by French Revolutionary Partisans, 1789–94," *Eighteenth-Century Studies* 14, no. 3 (Spring 1981): 283–312. See also James Epstein, "Understanding the Cap of Liberty: Symbolic Practice and Social Conflict in Early Nineteenth-Century England," *Past and Present* 122, no. 1 (February 1989): 75–118.
76. "The Statue of Freedom," Architect of the Capitol, June 21, 2016, http://www.aoc.gov.
77. Donald McClelland, quoted in Wasserman, "Smithsonian Featured at Edinburgh Festival."
78. Edward Gage, "Smithsonian Gift-Horse a Winner," *Scotsman*, August 13, 1984.
79. "Exhibitions," National Museum of American History, http://americanhistory.si.edu.
80. The walking stick is mentioned by name in only four of the nineteen British newspaper preview or review articles.
81. Karen Fort, quoted in Wasserman, "Smithsonian Featured at Edinburgh Festival."
82. See Michael Billig, *Banal Nationalism* (London: Sage, 1995).
83. "Receipt of Delivery, George Washington's Walking Stick," box 25/28, 00–069, SI Archives.
84. The ongoing icon status of the ruby slippers became clear when they were a starring feature of New York Fashion Week 2008, being reinterpreted by many important designers as part of a major display. See Eric Wilson, "We're Off to See the Ruby Slippers," *New York Times*, July 17, 2008.
85. Ralph Rinzler to Executive Committee Members, "Interim Report on Edinburgh Festival Participation," August 21, 1984, box 25/28, 00–069, SI Archives.
86. See Sheila M. Brock, education officer at RSM, to Donald McClelland, February 13, 1984, box 25/28, 00–069, SI Archives.

87. Locations included the Broward County Fair and the South Florida Fair. See itinerary and memo from "Vera" to "Fred/Janet/Gwen," "Mini-Treasures," May 31, 1985, box 39/105, Smithsonian Institution Traveling Exhibition Service, Public Relations, Records, 1975–89, 487, SI Archives.
88. Rinzler to Executive Committee Members, "Interim Report," August 21, 1984, box 25/28, 00–069, SI Archives.

Chapter 2: Scotland, for Scotland

1. National Heritage (Scotland) Act 1985, passed April 4, 1985, National Archives, http://www.legislation.gov.uk.
2. Data gathered in interviews.
3. National Heritage (Scotland) Act, § 4.
4. Alexander Broadie, *The Scottish Enlightenment: The Historical Age of the Historical Nation* (Edinburgh: Birlinn, 2002).
5. Magnus Magnusson, foreword to *The Wealth of a Nation in the National Museums of Scotland*, ed. Jenni Calder (Glasgow: Richard Drew, 1989), viii–ix.
6. Allen Wright, "Making a Point about Penury," *Scotsman*, June 5, 1989.
7. Walter Benjamin, "The Work of Art in an Age of Mechanical Reproduction," in *Illuminations*, ed. Hannah Arendt (New York, Schocken Books, 1968), 217–51; Ruth Rentschler, Kerrie Bridson, and Jody Evans, "Exhibitions as Sub-Brands: An Exploratory Study," *Arts Marketing: An International Journal* 4, nos. 1–2 (2014):45–66.
8. I am indebted here to conversations with and comments from Geoff Swinney, curator of fish and mollusks, NMS, who was one of the curators involved in *The Wealth of a Nation*. We spoke on February 7, 2009.
9. Artfund, Art We've Helped Buy, "Monymusk Reliquary, Unknown Artist," National Museum of Scotland, 1933, https://www.artfund.org.
10. Michael Lynch, Sir William Fraser Professor of Scottish History and Palaeography at the University of Edinburgh, trustee of NMS, and historical consultant to Museum of Scotland Project, interview by author, June 9, 2005.
11. "Scotland in History, 1100–1707—Ground Floor Gallery Storyboard," Museum of Scotland Project, October–November 1993, 8, National Museum of Scotland Archives, Edinburgh.
12. Wright, "Making a Point about Penury."
13. Joseph Anderson, "Notice of an Ancient Celtic Reliquary Exhibited to the Society by Sir Archibald Grant, Bart., of Monymusk," *Proceedings of the Society of Antiquaries of Scotland* 14 (1879–80): 435.
14. Francis C. Eeles, "The Monymusk Reliquary or Brecbennoch of St. Columba," *Proceedings of the Society of Antiquaries of Scotland* 68 (1933–34): 436.
15. Anderson, "Notice of an Ancient Celtic Reliquary," 435.
16. Joseph Anderson, "The Architecturally Shaped Shrines and Other Reliquaries of the Early Celtic Church in Scotland and Ireland," *Proceedings of the Society of Antiquaries of Scotland* 44 (1909–10): 264.
17. Ibid.
18. Eeles, "The Monymusk Reliquary," 436.

19. As of spring 2017, the label on the Monymusk Reliquary still says that it is the *brecbennoch*, a relic of Saint Columba, and was with the troops at Bannockburn. The text on the NMS's website says, "Since the 19th century it has been identified by some with the tradition of the Brecbennach of St Columba which was carried before the Scottish army in battle. However, recent research has questioned this tradition and highlighted there is very little evidence to substantiate it." http://www.nms.ac.uk.
20. Robert Anderson, quoted in Catherine Lockerbie, "A Proud Nation Prepares to Show Off Its Treasures," *Scotsman*, January 20, 1989.
21. Carol Duncan, *Civilizing Rituals: Inside Public Art Museums* (New York: Routledge, 1995), 17.
22. *Saint Andrew: Will He Ever See the Light?* (Edinburgh: National Museums of Scotland, 1987).
23. Stephen Greenblatt, "Resonance and Wonder," in *Exhibiting Cultures: The Poetics and Politics of Museum Display*, ed. Ivan Karp and Steven D. Levine (London: Smithsonian Books, 1991), 42.
24. Ibid., 45.
25. Magnusson, foreword, vii.
26. Ibid.
27. Geoff Swinney, interview by author, February 7, 2009.
28. Wright, "Making a Point about Penury."
29. The 1980s was the age of the "white cube" museum design aesthetic, privileging open space and emptiness. See Brian O'Doherty, *Inside the White Cube: The Ideology of the Gallery Space* (Berkeley: University of California Press, 1999).
30. Geoff Swinney, interview by author, February 7, 2009. See also Jenni Calder, ed., *The Wealth of a Nation in the National Museums of Scotland* (Glasgow: Richard Drew, 1989), 128–29.
31. Barbara Buchan, "The Director Has a Dream," *Edinburgh Evening News*, June 2, 1989.
32. Rena Boyd, "Riches of Scotland: Capitol Exhibits Nation's Wealth," *Edinburgh Evening News*, January 20, 1989.
33. Lockerbie, "A Proud Nation."
34. John H. Falk and Lynn D. Dierking, *The Museum Experience Revisited* (New York: Routledge, 2012).
35. See work such as Eileen Hooper-Greenfield, *Museums and the Shaping of Knowledge* (London: Routledge, 1992), and the education section of Sharon MacDonald, ed., *A Companion to Museum Studies* (Oxford: Blackwell, 2006), 319–76, for more on the interplay between visitor impressions and curatorial intent.
36. See, for instance, Pierre Bourdieu, *Distinction: A Social Critique of the Judgement of Taste*, trans. Richard Nice (London: Routledge, 1984).
37. The Smithsonian Institution exhibition planners also had to take into account each object's suitability for international shipping and setup. Only a very few were rejected on those grounds, however.
38. Geoff Swinney, interview by author, February 7, 2009.
39. Lothar P. Witteborg, *Good Show! A Practical Guide for Temporary Exhibitions* (Washington, DC: Smithsonian Institution Traveling Exhibition Service, 1991), 3.

40. David Dean, *Museum Exhibition: Theory and Practice* (London: Routledge, 1994), 32.
41. See Jules David Prown, "Mind in Matter: An Introduction to Material Culture Theory and Practice," *Winterthur Portfolio* 17, no. 1 (Spring 1982): 1–19.
42. Falk and Dierking, *Museum Experience Revisited.*
43. Kenneth Hudson, *A Social History of Museums: What the Visitors Thought* (London: Macmillan, 1975).
44. Peter Vergo, "The Reticent Object," in *The New Museology*, ed. Peter Vergo (London: Reaktion, 1989), 50.
45. Calder, *Wealth of a Nation.*
46. George Dalgleish, curator of Scottish decorative arts, interview by author, June 10, 2005.
47. George Thomas, Sixth Earl of Albemarle, Will, May 17, 1888, George Dalgleish Files, National Museum of Scotland.
48. The canteen was shown publicly three times before its sale: London, 1931, Loan Exhibit of Scottish Art; London, 1939, Royal Academy Exhibition of Scottish Art; Edinburgh, 1949, Royal Stuart Exhibition. George Dalgleish, "The Silver Travelling Canteen of Prince Charles Edward Stuart," in *Food, Drink, and Travelling Accessories: Essays in Honour of Gosta Berg*, ed. Alexander Fenton and Janken Myrdal (Edinburgh: John Donald, 1988), 168–84.
49. This narrative is most clearly set out in ibid.
50. Patricia Atkins, *Treasures from Scottish Houses: European Decorative Arts, 21st Edinburgh International Festival, Royal Scottish Museum Edinburgh, Aug./Sept. 1967* (Edinburgh: Royal Scottish Museum, 1967), object no. 204.
51. See Ian Jenkins and Kim Sloan, *Vases and Volcanoes: Sir William Hamilton and His Collection* (London: British Museum, 1996).
52. Spencer R. Crews and James E. Sims, "Locating Authenticity: Fragments of a Dialogue," in Karp and Levine, eds., *Exhibiting Cultures: The Politics and Poetics of Display* (Washington, DC: Smithsonian Press, 1991), 159–75.
53. Dean MacCannell, *Empty Meeting Grounds: The Tourist Papers* (London: Routledge, 1992), 44.
54. Anne-Marie Hede and Maree Thyne, "A Journey to the Authentic: Museum Visitors and Their Negotiation of the Inauthentic," *Journal of Marketing Management* 26, nos. 7–8 (2010): 686–705.
55. George Dalgleish, interview by author, June 10, 2005. See also Dalgleish, "The Silver Travelling Canteen of Prince Charles Edward Stuart."
56. Ian Finlay, *Scottish Gold and Silver Work* (Gretna, LA: Pelican, 1999).
57. "Letters, Miss Judith Bannister," London *Times*, January 11, 1984.
58. George Dalgleish and Dallas Mechan, eds., *"I Am Come Home": Treasures of Prince Charles Edward Stuart* (Edinburgh: National Museum of Antiquities of Scotland, 1985), 6.
59. See Calder, *Wealth of a Nation*, 36 (for Jacobite overtones), 73 (for silver).
60. Dalgleish and Mechan, *"I Am Come Home,"* 3.
61. Calder, *Wealth of a Nation*, 70, 83, 104.
62. Ibid., 180.
63. Catherine Holden, director of marketing, NMS, interview by author, March 13, 2007.

Chapter 3: Creating a National Narrative

1. National Heritage (Scotland) Act 1985, passed April 4, 1985, § 4, National Archives, http://www.legislation.gov.uk.
2. Object no. T.1958.117, Accession Records, National Museum of Scotland, Edinburgh (hereafter NMS Archives).
3. Thomas Pennant, *A Tour in Scotland, 1769* (Edinburgh: Birlinn, 2000), 163–64.
4. H. S. Dunn, description of donation, Newcomen Engine, 1903, object no. T.1958.117, Accession Records, April 2006, March 2017, NMS Archives.
5. A. Stowers, Newcomen Society for the Study of the History of Engineering and Technology, to R. W. Plenderleith, Esq., Fellow of the Royal Society of Edinburgh, RSM, December 31, 1958, Accession Records, April 2006, NMS.
6. See Susan Stewart, *On Longing: Narratives of the Miniature, the Gigantic, the Souvenir, the Collection* (Durham, NC: Duke University Press, 1993).
7. John S. Allen, "Newcomen, Thomas (bap. 1664, d. 1729)," in *Oxford Dictionary of National Biography*, ed. H. C. G. Matthew and Brian Harrison (Oxford: Oxford University Press, 2004), 40:602–3.
8. "Museum of Scotland Project Architectural Competition Brief," 1991, 16, D RL REF 069 09411MOS, NMS Archives.
9. The architect's statement is elucidated in Gordon Benson, "The Architect's Vision: Designing for Content and Context," in *Heritage and Museums: Shaping National Identity*, ed. J. M. Fladmark (Shaftesbury, England: Donhead, 2000), 17–28.
10. This came through in all curatorial interviews.
11. David Clarke, "New Things Set in Many Landscapes: Aspects of the Museum of Scotland," *Proceedings of the Society of Antiquaries of Scotland* 128 (1998): 1.
12. Ernest Gellner, *Nations and Nationalism* (Oxford: Blackwell, 1983), 7.
13. Michael Lynch, "The Making of the Museum of Scotland: A Museum of National Memories or Nationalism?" Shannon Lecture, University of Ottawa, September 2003, 3.
14. David Clarke, keeper of archaeology, interview by author, May 23, 2005.
15. George Dalgleish, curator of Scottish decorative arts, interview by author, June 10, 2005.
16. David Clarke, interview by author, May 23, 2005.
17. Gellner, *Nations and Nationalism*, 55.
18. R. G. W Anderson, "Meeting Public Needs," in *A New Museum for Scotland: Papers Presented at a Symposium Held at the Royal Museum of Scotland on 16 October 1990*, ed. R. G. W. Anderson (Edinburgh: National Museums of Scotland, 1990), 42.
19. "The Museum of Scotland Project Exhibition Brief," December 1991, 1, D RL REF 069 09411MOS, NMS Archives.
20. Ibid.
21. Ibid.
22. This largely chronological structure was laid out at the 1990 symposium by R. G. W. Anderson in his paper, "Meeting Public Needs," 42–43.
23. Michael Lynch, Sir William Fraser Professor of Scottish History and Palaeography at the University of Edinburgh, interview by author, June 9, 2005.

24. See Nick Prior, *Museums and Modernity: Art Galleries and the Making of Modern Culture* (Oxford: Berg, 2002), chap. 6, for a discussion of some of these types of hangs.
25. Examples of this can be seen in the National Museum of Antiquities of Scotland or the Pitt-Rivers Museum in Oxford.
26. See Brian O'Doherty, *Inside the White Cube: The Ideology of the Gallery Space* (Berkeley: University of California Press, 1999), for more on this.
27. Hugh Cheape, curator of Scottish history, interview by author, May 23, 2005, February 9, 2007.
28. David Clarke, interview by author, May 24, 2005.
29. G. Y. Craig, "Obituary: Sir Alwyn Williams," (London) *Independent*, April 12, 2004.
30. Alwyn Williams, *A Heritage for Scotland: Scotland's National Museums and Galleries, the Next 25 Years—Report of a Committee Appointed by the Secretary of State for Scotland under the Chairmanship of Dr. Alwyn Williams* (Edinburgh: Her Majesty's Stationary Office, 1981).
31. Ibid., xi.
32. R. B. K. Stevenson, "The Museum, Its Beginnings and Its Development, Part II: The National Museum to 1954," in *The Scottish Antiquarian Tradition: Essays to Mark the Bicentenary of the Society of Antiquaries of Scotland, 1780–1980*, ed. Alan S. Bell (Edinburgh: John Donald, 1981), 156.
33. Williams, "A Heritage for Scotland," 14.
34. Charles McKean, *The Making of the Museum of Scotland* (Edinburgh: NMS Publishing, 2000), 26.
35. Trustees to the Design Committee, 1990, quoted in Benson, "Architect's Vision," 17.
36. See Henri Lefebvre, *The Production of Space*, trans. Donald Nicholson-Smith (Oxford: Basil Blackwell, 1991).
37. Philip Dowson, "The Architect's Role," in Anderson, ed., *A New Museum for Scotland*, 21.
38. Ian Armit, *Towers in the North: The Brochs of Scotland* (Dublin: Tempus, 2003); McKean, *The Making of the Museum of Scotland*, 39, 40.
39. Anthony D. Smith, *Myths and Memories of the Nation* (Oxford: Oxford University Press, 1999), 150.
40. Sir Philip Dowson, quoted in McKean, *The Making of the Museum of Scotland*, 86.
41. Peter Jones, "Overseas Experiences," in Anderson, ed., *A New Museum for Scotland*, 23.
42. Benson, "Architect's Vision," 20.
43. Charles McKean, "A House for Identity: National Shrine or Distorting Mirror?" in Fladmark, ed., *Heritage and Museums*, 140.
44. David Caldwell, keeper of Scotland and Europe, interview by author, May 23, 2005, January 29, 2007.
45. George Dalgleish, interview by author, June 10, 2005.
46. Personal experience of ten "Introduction to the Museum of Scotland" tours taken between January and March 2005.
47. Hugh Pearman, "Tower of Scotland," (London) *Sunday Times*, November 15, 1998.

48. George Dalgleish, interview by author, June 10, 2005.
49. For more on this role of the museum, see Clarke, "New Things Set in Many Landscapes," 2.
50. Hugh Cheape, interview by author, February 9, 2007.
51. George Dalgleish, interview by author, June 10, 2005.

Chapter 4: Objects Connecting Nations

1. Peter Rowley-Conwy, "The Concept of Prehistory and the Invention of the Terms 'Prehistoric' and 'Prehistorian': The Scandinavian Origin, 1833–1850," *European Journal of Archaeology* 9, no. 1 (2006): 103–30.
2. Carol Duncan and Alan Wallach, "The Universal Survey Museum," *Art History* 3 (1980): 448–69.
3. For more on this, see, for example, Ernest Gellner, *Nations and Nationalism* (Oxford: Blackwell, 1983), and Rogers Brubaker, *Nationalism Reframed: Nationhood and the National Question in the New Europe* (Cambridge: Cambridge University Press: 1996).
4. For more on this idea, see Benedict Anderson, *Imagined Communities: Reflections on the Origin and Spread of Nationalism*, 2nd ed. (London: Verso, 1991), chap. 10.
5. Emma Barker, "Exhibiting the Canon: The Blockbuster Show," in *Contemporary Cultures of Display*, ed. Emma Barker (London: Yale University Press, 1999), 127–46; David A. Garvin, "Blockbusters: The Economics of Mass Entertainment," *Journal of Cultural Economics* 5, no. 1 (June 1981): 1–20.
6. John Miller, "The Show You Love to Hate: A Psychology of the Mega-Exhibition," in *Thinking about Exhibitions*, ed. Bruce W. Ferguson et al. (London: Routledge, 1996), 269–74.
7. Shelia Watson, ed., *Museums and Their Communities* (New York: Routledge, 2007). Books like that cover the contested and sometimes controversial nature of recent temporary exhibitions.
8. Gleb Struve, "Russian Friends and Correspondents of Sir Walter Scott," *Comparative Literature* 2 (Autumn 1950): 307–26.
9. Mikhail Piotrovsky, *Beyond the Palace Walls: Islamic Art from the State Hermitage Museum* (Edinburgh: National Museums of Scotland, 2006); Lund Humphries, *Nicholas and Alexandra: The Last Tsar and Tsarina* (Edinburgh: Lund Humphries, 2005).
10. Catherine Holden, director of marketing, NMS, interview by author, March 13, 2007.
11. Sylvie Cameron and Laurent Lapierre, "Company Profile: Mikhaïl Piotrovsky and the State Hermitage Museum," *International Journal of Arts Management* 10, no. 1 (2007): 65–77, http://www.jstor.org.
12. Geraldine Norman, *The Hermitage: The Biography of a Great Museum* (London: Fromm, 1997), 11.
13. "Nicholas and Alexandra," *NMS Explore: The Magazine for Supporters of NMS*, Summer 2005, 6–7.
14. Laurie Hanquinet and Mike Savage, "'Educative Leisure' and the Art Museum," *Museum and Society* 10, no. 1 (2012): 42–59.

15. See Susan Stewart, *On Longing: Narratives of the Miniature, the Gigantic, the Souvenir, the Collection* (Durham, NC: Duke University Press, 1993), and Barker, "Exhibiting the Canon."
16. That exhibition ran from December 10, 2008, to March 29, 2009.
17. Norman, *Hermitage*, 35.
18. Hilary Young, *The Genius of Wedgwood* (London: Antique Collectors' Club, 1995).
19. David Bindman, "The Genius of Wedgewood, London, Victoria and Albert Museum," *Burlington Magazine* 137 (August 1995): 635–57.
20. Norman, *Hermitage*, 28–29, 23.
21. Ibid., 1–4.
22. Robert K. Massie, *Nicholas and Alexandra* (New York: Random House, 1967), 111–12.
23. Norman, *Hermitage*, 36–37.
24. Massie, *Nicholas and Alexandra*, 230.
25. Jane Carmichael, director of collections, NMS, interview by author, February 16, 2007.
26. Anthony Summers and Tom Mangold, *The File on the Tsar: The Fate of the Romanovs—Dramatic New Evidence* (London: Harper and Row, 1976). This book came out of a BBC documentary in the 1970s that investigated the disappearance and death of the tsar and his family.
27. There are at least eight films or television productions about the last Romanovs: *Rasputin and the Empress* (1933), *Anastasia* (1956), *Rasputin: The Mad Monk* (1966), *Nicholas and Alexandra* (1971), *Fall of Eagles* (1974), *Anastasia: Mystery of Anna* (1983), *Rasputin* (1996), and the animated *Anastasia* (1997).
28. Jane Carmichael, interview by author, February 16, 2007.
29. Stuart Johnstone, "Russian Revelations: Memories of the Last Tsar and His Family," *Dundee Evening Telegraph*, July 21, 2005.
30. See the exhibition website for *Nicholas and Alexandra*, http://www.nicholasandalexandra.com.
31. Broughton International, www.broughtonmasterpiece.com. Taken down circa June 2008.
32. Ibid.
33. Gordon Rintoul, foreword, in Humphries, *Nicholas and Alexandra*, x–xi.
34. Jane Carmichael, interview by author, February 16, 2007.
35. Iain Wilson, "Russia Opens Door on Tragic Tale: Nicholas and Alexandra Treasures Head for Edinburgh," *Glasgow Herald*, April 11, 2005.
36. Jane Carmichael, interview by author, February 16, 2007.
37. Rintoul, foreword, x.
38. Ibid., xi.
39. Wilson, "Russia Opens Door on Tragic Tale."
40. Nick Zangwill, "Against the Sociology of the Aesthetic," *Cultural Values* 6 (2002): 443–52; George Dickie, "Art and Value," *British Journal of Aesthetics* 40 (April 2000): 228–41.
41. This dichotomy is most noticeable when the portrait gallery and the art gallery are close by, such as in the case of the British National Portrait Gallery and the National Gallery next door to each other in Trafalgar Square. The American National Portrait Gallery and the Museum of American Art actually share a building, making the split in interpretation even easier to see.

42. Humphries, *Nicholas and Alexandra*, 64.
43. Ibid., 150. Object no. E37, National Museums of Scotland (NMS), Edinburgh.
44. Caroline Jessop, "From Russia with Love," *Scottish Field*, August 1, 2005, 64.
45. Tsar Nicolas II to Queen Victoria, November 16, 1894, quoted in Humphries, *Nicholas and Alexandra*, 66.
46. "Why a Picture of Former Russian Ruler Nicholas II Travels with Scots Soldiers in Training—and on the Battlefield: How a Tsar Became a Guards Icon," *Edinburgh Evening News*, July 8, 2005.
47. Humphries, *Nicholas and Alexandra*.
48. "Why a Picture of Former Russian Ruler Nicholas II Travels with Scots Soldiers in Training."
49. Humphries, *Nicholas and Alexandra*, 119.
50. Peter Gill et al., "Identification of the Remains of the Romanov Family by DNA Analysis," *Nature Genetics* 6 (1994): 130–35.
51. John Curtis Perry and Constantine Pleshakov, *The Flight of the Romanovs: A Family Saga* (Old Saybrook, CT: Konecky and Konecky, 1999), chap. 16.
52. Humphries, *Nicholas and Alexandra*, 116–19.
53. "Lost Romanov Bones 'Identified,'" BBC News, September 28, 2007; "Russia Dig Finds 'Tsar's Family,'" BBC News, August 24, 2007.
54. "Why a Picture of Former Russian Ruler Nicholas II Travels with Scots Soldiers in Training."
55. Humphries, *Nicholas and Alexandra*, 120.
56. "Why a Picture of Former Russian Ruler Nicholas II Travels with Scots Soldiers in Training."
57. Of nineteen reviews, twelve mentioned the Fabergé regalia; eight of those had a picture of it.
58. *Nicholas and Alexandra*, artifact label D14, NMS. See also Humphries, *Nicholas and Alexandra*, 138.
59. *Nicholas and Alexandra*, artifact label D14, NMS.
60. Stewart, *On Longing*.
61. Duncan Forgan, "Glittering Tsar of a Show Will Crown Them All," *Edinburgh Evening News*, July 15, 2005.
62. "Why the Russian Revolution Had to Happen," *Sunday Herald*, July 24, 2005.
63. Humphries, *Nicholas and Alexandra*, 140.
64. Sam Halsted, "Bloody Shirt the Tsar Attraction at City Show," *Edinburgh Evening News*, February 2, 2005. Nicholas was actually twenty-two at the time of the attack. For more on the incident, see George Alexander Lensen, "The Attempt on the Life of Nicholas II in Japan," *Russian Review* 20 (July 1961): 232–53.
65. *NMS Review 06: Looking Back, Looking Forward*, 2, 4.
66. See, for example, the rhetoric used in Piotrovsky, *Beyond the Palace Walls*.
67. Rintoul, foreword, vii.
68. Catherine Holden, interview by author, March 13, 2007; Jane Carmichael, interview by author, February 16, 2007.
69. Catherine Holden, interview by author, March 13, 2007.
70. See, for example, Tony Bennett, *The Birth of the Museum: History, Theory, Politics* (New York: Routledge, 1995); Carol Duncan, *Civilizing Rituals: Inside Public Art Museums* (New York: Routledge, 1995); and Nick Prior, *Museums and Modernity:*

Art Galleries and the Making of Modern Culture (London: Bloomsbury, 2002). All of these use the ideas of *field* and *habitus* from Pierre Bourdieu.
71. Jane Carmichael, interview by author, February 16, 2007.
72. Piotrovsky, *Beyond the Palace Walls*.
73. Ibid., 222–30.
74. Lothar P. Witteborg, *Good Show: A Practical Guide for Temporary Exhibitions* (Washington, DC: Smithsonian Institution, 1991).
75. Jane Carmichael, interview by author, February 16, 2007.
76. Rintoul, foreword, viii.
77. For more, see Dean MacCannell, *The Tourist: A New Theory of the Leisure Class* (Berkeley: University of California Press, 1999), and Walter Benjamin, "The Work of Art in the Age of Mechanical Reproduction," in *Illuminations: Walter Benjamin*, ed. Hannah Arendt (London: Pimlico, 1999).
78. Benjamin, "The *Work of Art*," 218–19.
79. Catherine Holden, interview by author, March 13, 2007.
80. From personal observations made during multiple fieldwork and pleasure visits to sites, 2006–16.
81. See Humphries, *Nicholas and Alexandra*, and Edwards Park, *Treasures from the Smithsonian at the Royal Scottish Museum* (London: Smithsonian Institution Press, 1984).
82. See Jenni Calder, ed., *Wealth of a Nation in the National Museums of Scotland* (Glasgow: Richard Drew Publishing, 1989), and Piotrovsky, *Beyond the Palace Walls*.
83. "'The Wealth of a Nation' Review," in *National Museums of Scotland, Annual Report, April 1989–March 1990* (Edinburgh: National Museums of Scotland, 1990) 7.
84. Lesley Taylor, "Nicholas and Alexandra: Creating the Catalogue," *NMS Explore: The Magazine for Supporters of NMS*, Autumn 2005, 8.
85. "Treasures from the US," *Scotsman*, August 11, 1984; Ralph Rinzler to Executive Committee Members, memorandum, "Interim Report on Edinburgh Festival Participation," box 25/28, Smithsonian Institution Traveling Exhibition Service, Exhibition Records, ca. 1977–99, 00–069, Smithsonian Institution, Washington, DC.
86. Marjorie Swann, *Curiosities and Text: The Culture of Collecting in Early Modern England* (Philadelphia: University of Pennsylvania Press, 2001), 9.
87. Eilean Hooper-Greenhill, *Museums and the Shaping of Knowledge* (New York: Routledge, 1992), 182.
88. See, for example, the catalogue of the Victoria and Albert's British Galleries: Michael Snodin and John Styles, *Design and the Decorative Arts: Britain 1500–1900* (London: V&A, 2001).
89. *Catherine the Great: An Enlightened Empress* ran from July 13 to October 21, 2012.

Chapter 5: Objects Unifying the Nation

1. For more on emigration and the Scottish diaspora, see Jeanette M. Brock, *The Mobile Scot: A Study of Emigration and Migration, 1861–1911* (Edinburgh: John

Donald, 1999); T. M. Devine, *To the Ends of the Earth: Scotland's Global Diaspora, 1750–2010* (Washington, DC: Smithsonian Books, 2011); and Tanja Bueltmann, Andrew Hinson, and Graeme Morton, *The Scottish Diaspora* (Edinburgh: Edinburgh University Press, 2013).

2. For more on this phrase, see Angus Calder, *Revolving Culture: Notes from the Scottish Republic* (London: I. B. Tauris, 1994), and Ian Brown, *From Tartan to Tartanry: Scottish Culture, History, and Myth* (Edinburgh: Edinburgh University Press, 2012).
3. "Highland 2007," Scotland.org, October 22, 2012, http://www.scotland.org.
4. See Tom Nairn, *Faces of Nationalism: Janus Revisited* (London: Verso, 1997); *After Britain: New Labour and the Return of Scotland* (London: Granta, 2000); and *Pariah: Misfortunes of the British Kingdom* (London: Verso, 2002).
5. See Ernest Gellner, *Nations and Nationalism* (Oxford: Blackwell, 1983).
6. For more on the role of the elite in nation building, see Miroslav Hroch, *Social Preconditions of Nationalist Revival: A Comparative Analysis of the Social Composition of Patriotic Groups among the Smaller European Nations* (New York: Columbia University Press, 1985).
7. Highlands and Islands Enterprise, http://www.hie.co.uk; VisitHighlands, http://www.visithighlands.com.
8. Inverness had a population of 67, 230 at the 2011 census. The whole Highlands and Islands parliamentary region had 445,177. This contrasts with Glasgow's 593,245 and Edinburgh's 476,626 numbers. All figures from "Welcome to Scotland's Census: Scotland Census 2011," http://www.scotlandscensus.gov.uk.
9. "European Commission—Culture," European Commission, http://ec.europa.eu.
10. Glasgow 1990, the last British winner, experienced a series of positive results from its participation. See Margaret Ryan, "Boost Continue from Culture Win," BBC News Online, October 30, 2002, http://news.bbc.co.uk.
11. See http://www.liverpool08.com.
12. *Highland 2007: The Year Scotland Celebrates Highland Culture, Has Been Launched*, Scottish government news release, January 12, 2007, http://www.gov.scot.
13. For more on this intriguing word, see Angela Morris, David McCrone, and Richard Kiely, *Scotland—The Brand: The Making of Scottish Heritage* (Edinburgh: Edinburgh University Press, 1995), and Calder, *Revolving Culture*.
14. Thomas Pennant, *A Tour in Scotland 1769* (Edinburgh: Birlinn, 2000); Samuel Johnson and James Boswell, *A Journey to the Western Isles of Scotland and A Journey of a Tour to the Hebrides* (1775/1786; London: Penguin Classics, 1984).
15. Murray G. H. Pittock, *Inventing and Resisting Britain: Cultural Identities in Britain and Ireland, 1685–1789* (London: Palgrave Macmillan, 1997), 32.
16. Walter Scott, *Waverley; or, 'Tis Sixty Years Since* (Edinburgh: Archibald Constable, 1814).
17. Gellner, *Nations and Nationalism*; Benedict Anderson, *Imagined Communities: Reflections on the Origin and Spread of Nationalism*, 2nd ed. (London: Verso, 1991).
18. For more on this, see Murray Pittock, ed., *The Reception of Walter Scott in Europe* (London: Bloomsbury Academic, 2006), and Ann Rigney, *The Afterlives of Walter Scott: Memory on the Move* (Oxford: Oxford University Press, 2012).
19. Murray G. H. Pittock, *Celtic Identity and the British Image* (Manchester: Manchester University Press, 1999), 43.

20. *A Narrative of the Visit of George IV to Scotland in August 1822 by an Eyewitness to Most of the Scenes Which Were Then Exhibited* (Edinburgh: Macredie, Skelly, 1822), 35.
21. John Prebble, *The King's Jaunt: George IV in Scotland, August 1822; "One and Twenty Daft Days to Go"* (Edinburgh: Birlinn, 2000), 262.
22. Pittock, *Celtic Identity and the British Image*, 88.
23. David McCrone, *Understanding Scotland: The Sociology of a Stateless Nation* (London: Routledge, 1992), 57.
24. Murray G. H. Pittock, *Scottish Nationality* (Basingstoke, Eng.: Palgrave, 2001), 85.
25. Pittock, *Celtic Identity and the British Image*, 87.
26. See works such as Dean MacCannell, *Empty Meeting Grounds: The Tourist Papers* (London: Routledge, 1992); Dean MacCannell, *The Tourist: A New Theory of the Leisure Class* (Berkeley: University of California Press, 1999); Tom Selwyn, ed., *The Tourist Image: Myths and Myth-Making in Tourism* (New York: Wiley, 1996); and Chris Rojek and John Urry, eds., *Touring Cultures: Transformations of Travel and Theory* (London: Routledge, 1997).
27. For more on this, see Richard Cooke, "The Home-ly Kailyard Nation: Nineteenth-Century Narratives of the Highland and the Myth of Merrie Auld Scotland," *ELH* 66, no. 4 (1999): 1053–73, and Andrew Nash, *Kailyard and Scottish Literature* (Amsterdam: Rodopi, 2007).
28. McCrone, *Understanding Scotland*, 200
29. "History and Heritage," VisitHighlands, http://www.visithighlands.com.
30. Craig Fees, "Tourism and the Politics of Authenticity in a North Cotswold Town," in Selwyn, ed., *The Tourist Image*, 130.
31. See Raymond Williams, *The Country and the City* (London: Vintage, 1973), 297.
32. One of the stated aims of Highland 2007 was the return of a Scottish/Highland diaspora and others from "key target areas across the world." See "Vision, Aims, and Objectives," Highland 2007, http://www.highland2007.com.
33. MacCannell, *The Tourist*; George Ritzer and Allen Liska, "'McDisneyization' and Post-Tourism: Complementary Perspectives on Contemporary Tourism," in Rojek and Urry, eds., *Touring Cultures*, 107.
34. Sharon MacDonald, *Reimagining Culture: History, Identities, and the Gaelic Renaissance* (Oxford: Bloomsbury Academic, 1997), 6, 36.
35. See David W. Moore, *The Other British Isles: A History of Shetland, Orkney, the Hebrides, Isle of Man, Anglesey, Scilly, Isle of Wight and the Channel Islands* (Jefferson, NC: McFarland, 2005), and Adam Grydehøj, "Ethnicity and the Origins of Local Identity in Shetland, UK—Part I: Picts, Vikings, Fairies, Finns, and Aryans," *Journal of Marine and Island Cultures* 2, no. 1 (2013): 39–48.
36. For more on this, see Eric Richards, *Patrick Sellar and the Highland Clearances: Homicide, Eviction, and the Price of Progress* (Edinburgh: Polygon, 1999); Robert Mathieson, *The Survival of the Unfittest: The Highland Clearances and the End of Isolation* (Edinburgh: John Donald, 2000); and Eric Richards, *The Highland Clearances*, 2nd ed. (Edinburgh: Birlinn, 2008).
37. Not a lot of work has been done about temporary exhibitions and how they differ from permanent ones. Museum management and design texts address how to design them and manage their installation and budgeting, such as in David Dean, *Museum Exhibition: Theory and Practice* (London: Routledge, 2002),

82, 85; Philip Hughes, *Exhibition Design* (London: Laurence King, 2010), 180, 186–91, 204, 214; and Barry Lord and Maria Piacente, eds., *Manual of Museum Exhibitions*, 2nd ed. (London: Rowman and Littlefield, 2014), 197–216. A very early survey of the concept from 1951 is reprinted in Grace L. McCann Morley, "Museums and Temporary Exhibitions," *Museum International* 53, no. 4 (October–December 2001): 56–59.
38. "FAQ," Smithsonian Institution Traveling Exhibition Service Press Service, http://www.sites.si.edu.
39. For more on the theory of objects and global movement, see Celia Lury and Scott Lash, *Global Culture Industry: The Mediation of Things* (Cambridge: Polity, 2007), esp. chap. 2.
40. Mentioned by David Caldwell, keeper of Scotland and Europe, interview by author, May 25, 2005, January 29, 2007; Hugh Cheape, curator of Scottish history, interview by author, May 23, 2005, February 9, 2007; and George Dalgleish, curator of Scottish decorative arts, interview by author, June 10, 2005.
41. Hugh Cheape, interview by author, February 9, 2007.
42. "Highland 2007 on the Horizon," Scottish Executive, August 4, 2005, http://www.scotland.gov.uk.
43. See the later discussion of the Lewis Chessmen and arguments over where they belong.
44. Gordon Rintoul, quoted in "Highland 2007 on the Horizon."
45. Alison Magee, chair of Highland 2007 and convener of the Highland Council, quoted in ibid.
46. The touring schedule was Inverness, January 13–March 17, 2007; Glasgow, April 6–June 10, 2007; Edinburgh, June 29–September 2, 2007; and Stornoway, September 21–December 1, 2007.
47. Inverness Museum and Art Gallery, http://www.invernessmuseum.com; Museum Nan Eilean, http://www.cne-siar.gov.uk.
48. Hugh Cheape, interview by author, February 9, 2007.
49. It is designated as a legal deposit library, which give it these rights under the Legal Deposit Libraries Act of 2003. See "Legal Deposit Libraries Act 2003," http://www.legislation.gov.uk.
50. "National Galleries of Scotland, Who We Are," https://www.nationalgalleries.org.
51. For more on this, see Nick Prior, *Museums and Modernity: Art Galleries and the Making of Modern Culture* (Oxford: Berg, 2002).
52. Hugh Cheape, interview by author, February 9, 2007.
53. Jack McConnell, "Highland 2007," Scottish Executive, January 12, 2007, http://www.scotland.gov.uk.
54. Hugh Cheape, interview by author, February 9, 2007.
55. Ibid.
56. Walter Benjamin, *The Work of Art in the Age of Mechanical Reproduction*, in *Illuminations: Walter Benjamin*, ed. Hannah Arendt (London: Pimlico, 1999); MacCannell, *The Tourist*.
57. James Hunter, *Fonn 's Duthchas: Land and Legacy, The Scottish Highlands: A Contested Country, Gaidhealtachd Alba: Tir fo Dheasbad* (Edinburgh: National Museums of Scotland, 2006), 41, 70, 109, 30, 113.

58. Fredric Madden, "Historical Remarks of the Introduction of the Game of Chess into Europe, and on the Ancient Chessmen Discovered in the Isle of Lewis," *Archaeologica* 24 (1832): 212.
59. Daniel Wilson, *The Archaeology and Prehistoric Annals of Scotland* (Edinburgh: Sutherland and Knox, 1851), 567.
60. "Donations to and Purchases for the Museum," *Proceedings of the Society of Antiquaries of Scotland* 23 (1888–89): 9.
61. Ibid., 10.
62. Madden, "Historical Remarks of the Introduction of the Game of Chess into Europe," 203–91; David H. Caldwell, Mark A. Hall, and Caroline M. Wilkinson, *The Lewis Chessmen Unmasked* (Edinburgh: National Museums Scotland, 2010); David Caldwell and Mark A. Hall, eds., *The Lewis Chessmen: New Perspectives* (Edinburgh: National Museums Scotland, 2015).
63. "Donations to and Purchases for the Museum," *Proceedings of the Society of Antiquaries of Scotland* 23 (1888–89): 11.
64. Hugh Cheape, interview by author, May 23, 2005.
65. Scotinform Ltd., "Royal Museum Project Evaluation of Galleries Draft Report," September 2012, 2. 069(411) NMS 2012, National Museums of Scotland Archives, Edinburgh (hereafter NMS Archives).
66. Arifa Akbar, "Salmond Makes First Move in Battle to Win Back Lewis Chessmen," (London) *Independent*, December 26, 2007; Paul Kelbie, "Salmond Gambit for Return of Chessmen: First Minister Supports Celtic League's Call for the Restitution of Treasures," (Manchester) *Observer*, January 6, 2008. See also Margaret Hodge, "Lewis Chessmen Are Pawns in Salmond's Political Game," Scotsman Online, January 27, 2008, http://www.scotsman.com.
67. The tour started at the NMS, May 21–September 19, 2010, then went to Aberdeen Art Gallery (October 7, 2010–January 8, 2011), Shetland Museum and Archives (January 29–March 27, 2011), and Museum Nan Eilean (April 15–September 12, 2011). See "New Tour for Lewis Chessmen," National Museums of Scotland, press release, October 1, 2009, NMS Press Cuttings Folder, Fall 2009, NMS Archives.
68. Bendor Grosvner, "Letter from Edinburgh: Art and a 'Yes' Vote," *Art History News*, September 1, 2014, http://www.arthistorynews.com.
69. Hunter, *Fonn's Duthchas*, 118.
70. These criteria come from Hugh Cheape, interview by author, February 9, 2007.
71. Hunter, *Fonn's Duthchas*, 72.
72. Object no. H.1991.54.1, Accession Record, NMS Archives.
73. For more on how fashions moved from class to class, see Charlotte Gere and Judy Rudoe, *Jewellery in the Age of Queen Victoria: A Mirror to the World* (London: British Museum Press, 2010).
74. It is worth noting here the connections with Nicholas II and Alexandra of Russia, who were a large part of chapter 4. George was a first cousin of Nicholas II, and May was also related to the pair. Queen Victoria was close to all four and had a hand in orchestrating both marriages. For more, see Anne Edwards, *Matriarch: Queen Mary and the House of Windsor*, repr. ed. (London: Rowman and Littlefield, 2014).

75. Hunter, *Fonn's Duthchas*, 78.
76. David Trachtenberg and Thomas Keith, *Mauchline Ware: A Collector's Guide* (London: Antique Collectors Club, 1999).
77. Joel Myerson and Daniel Shealy, "Three Contemporary Accounts of Louisa May Alcott, with Glimpses of Other Concord Notables," *New England Quarterly* 59, no. 1 (1986): 109–22.
78. Hugh Cheape, interview by author, February 9, 2007.
79. George Dalgleish, *Silver: Made in Scotland* (Edinburgh: National Museums of Scotland, 2008), 39.
80. "Donations to and Purchases for the Museum," *Proceedings of the Society of Antiquaries of Scotland* 103 (1970–71): 244.
81. Robert B. K. Stevenson, "The Cadboll Cup," *Proceedings of the Society of Antiquaries of Scotland* 104 (1972): 306.
82. Dalgleish, *Silver*, 39.
83. Norman Macpherson, "Notice of a Finely Ornamented Chalice of Silver," *Proceedings of the Society of Antiquaries of Scotland* 22 (1888): 423–32.
84. Dalgleish, *Silver*, 39.
85. The Lussit/Ugadale Brooch, H.NGD 11, NMS Archives.
86. Macpherson, "Notice."
87. Hugh McKerrell, "Chemical Analysis of the Cadboll Cup and the Watson Mazer," *Proceedings of the Society of Antiquaries of Scotland* 104 (1970–71): 309–15.
88. Dalgleish, *Silver*, 40.
89. Stevenson, "Cadboll Cup," 307.
90. George Dalgleish, interview by author, June 10, 2005.
91. Hugh Cheape, interview by author, February 9, 2007.
92. Homecoming Scotland 2009 was a yearlong program of events, similar in structure to Highland 2007, organized primarily by VisitScotland and the Scottish government and focused on attracting diaspora audiences. The national institutions were not officially involved in the program, though several temporary display cases were mounted to honor Robert Burns and the homecoming year at the entrance to the NMS. Although focused on the whole nation rather than a specific region, the similarities in rhetoric between Highland 2007 and Homecoming 2009 are striking. According to official advertising, tourists should "join us to celebrate the 250th anniversary of Robert Burns' birth, Scottish contributions to golf and whisky, plus our great minds and innovations and rich culture and heritage." Homecoming Scotland 2009, http://www.homecomingscotland.com.

Chapter 6: Changing Nation, Changing Museum

1. Catherine Holden, director of marketing, National Museums Scotland, interview by author, March 13, 2007.
2. Lynn Jones Research, *Museum of Scotland/Royal Museum Visitor Survey 2003, Final Report*, January 2004, 069(411) Edi NMS/V 2004, 1, National Museums of Scotland Archives, Edinburgh (hereafter NMS Archives).
3. Catherine Holden, interview by author, March 13, 2007.

4. Bonita M. Kolb, *Marketing Cultural Organizations: New Strategies for Attracting Audiences to Classical Music, Dance, Museums, Theatre, and Opera* (Dublin: Oak Tree Press, 2000), 144.
5. Yvla French and Sue Runyard, *Marketing and Public Relations for Museums, Galleries, Cultural and Heritage Attractions* (London: Routledge, 2011), 74.
6. Catherine Holden, interview by author, March 13, 2007.
7. Dr. Alwyn Williams, *A Heritage for Scotland: Scotland's National Museums and Galleries, the Next 25 Years—Report of a Committee Appointed by the Secretary of State for Scotland under the Chairmanship of Dr. Alwyn Williams* (Edinburgh: Her Majesty's Stationary Office, 1981), 13.
8. *National Museums Scotland Brand Guidelines* (Edinburgh: National Museums of Scotland, 2006), 13, NMS Archive. This source was unnumbered in the original, so page numbers were assigned by the author.
9. Quoted in Ernest Gellner, *Nations and Nationalism* (Oxford: Blackwell, 1983), 3.
10. Michael Billig, *Banal Nationalism* (London: Sage, 1995), 11.
11. Catherine Holden, interview by author, March 13, 2007.
12. Ibid.
13. Williams, "A Heritage for Scotland," 12–13.
14. Tim Cornwell, "'Royal' Museum Title Consigned to History," *Scotsman*, October 14, 2006, http://heritage.scotsman.com.
15. Phil Miller, "Museum Drops Its Royal Title to Avoid Confusion among Visitors; Queen Gives Her Seal of Approval to Changing Name of Building after 102 Years," (Glasgow) *Herald*, October 14, 2006.
16. *National Museums Scotland Brand Guidelines*, 12. The rebranding was done by Hat-Trick Design Consultants.
17. Ibid., 1.
18. For more on the role of design in identity, see Forty, *Objects of Desire: Design and Society since 1750.* (London: Thames and Hudson, 1986), esp. chap. 10.
19. See Alan Wallach and Carol Duncan, "The Universal Survey Museum," *Art History* 3, no. 4 (1980): 448–69.
20. Catherine Holden, interview by author, March 13, 2007.
21. Ibid.
22. Ibid.
23. Ibid.
24. Personal observation, autumn 2007–11, repeated November 2014 and April 2017.
25. This object is an authentic replica because while it is not the authentic casket, which is still located in Westminster Abbey, it is the authentic plaster cast copy that was made under the orders of James IV and I to have shipped up to his mother's subjects in Scotland. Object IL.2001.192, NMS Archives.
26. Walter Seton of Abercorn, *The Penicuik Jewels of Mary Queen of Scots* (London: Philip Allan, 1923).
27. Rosalind K. Marshall, ed., *Dynasty: The Royal House of Stewart* (Edinburgh: National Galleries of Scotland, 1990), 48.
28. Object H.NA 421–22, NMS Archives. See also "Donations to the Museum," *Proceedings of the Society of Antiquaries of Scotland* 57 (1923–24): 17. See also a letter and note of Charles Kirkpatrick Sharpe, n.d., Ms 627, NMS Archives.

29. "Donations to the Museum," *Proceedings of the Society of Antiquaries of Scotland* 57 (1923–24): 17.
30. Stuart Maxwell, "The Queen Mary Cameo Jewel Purchased for Museum," *Proceedings of the Society of Antiquaries of Scotland* 93 (1959–60): 244, 245.
31. Ibid., 245.
32. Rosalind K. Marshall, *Queen of Scots* (Edinburgh: Her Majesty's Stationery Office, 1986), 105.
33. Marshall, *Dynasty*, 47.
34. For more on Petrie, see W. M. Flinders Petrie, *Seventy Years in Archaeology*, repr. ed. (1931; Cambridge: Cambridge University Press, 2013), and Margaret S. Drower, *Flinders Petrie: A Life in Archaeology*, 2nd ed. (Madison: University of Wisconsin Press, 1995).
35. James J. Dobbie, "The Excavation of Memphis: Letter to the Editor," *Scotsman*, November 2, 1907, 11.
36. See Thomas Hoving, *Tutakhamun: The Untold Story*, repr. ed. (1978; New York: Cooper Square Press, 2002); Melani McAlister, "The Common Heritage of Mankind: Race, Nation, and Masculinity in the King Tut Exhibit," *Representations* 54 (Spring 1996): 80–103; and Elliot Colla, *Conflicted Antiquities: Egyptology, Egyptomania, Egyptian Modernity* (Durham, NC: Duke University Press, 2007).
37. Dobbie, "Excavation of Memphis," 11.
38. "The Royal Scottish Museum: Need for Additional Accommodation," *Scotsman*, December 17, 1910, 10.
39. These were then reported on by the press. See, for example, "Recent Excavations in Egypt," *Scotsman*, October 26, 1909, 5. Members of the Society of Antiquaries of Scotland also went to explore the excavations themselves and reported back in the press; see William Bryce, "Recent Antiquarian Discoveries in Egypt," *Scotsman*, February 23, 1903, 7.
40. "Royal Scottish Museum."
41. See Geoff Swinney, "Furnishing a Museum: Nineteenth-Century Exhibition Casing in the Royal Museum, Edinburgh," *Furniture History Society* 39 (2003): 121–30. See also Christopher Whitehead, *Museums and the Construction of Disciplines: Art and Archaeology in Nineteenth-Century Britain* (London: Bloomsbury Academic, 2009).
42. Cyril Aldred, *Scenes from Ancient Egypt in the Royal Scottish Museum Edinburgh* (Edinburgh: Royal Scottish Museum, 1979). However, this 2003 renovation was always intended to be temporary, as the Royal Museum Project was already on the horizon.
43. This remains true even when they are moved for temporary exhibitions, as they were for 2012's *Fascinating Mummies* (with the Rijksmuseum in Amsterdam, February–May 2012) and 2017's *The Tomb: Ancient Egyptian Burial* (March 31–September 3, 2017).
44. Personal observation, autumn 2007.
45. "Boxed Gold Marketing 'Brochure' Issued to All Trustees," unpaginated, 069(411) Edi RMP 2011, box 2, RMP.2011.0016, 13, NMS Archives.
46. "Royal Museum Project," National Museums Scotland, http://www.nms.ac.uk.
47. "The Royal Museum Project: Making a World of Difference," A4 Brochure, unpaginated, 069(411) Edi RMP 2011, box 2, RMP.2011.0022, NMS Archives.
48. Catherine Holden, interview by author, March 13, 2007.

49. "Boxed Gold Marketing 'Brochure.'"
50. Ibid.
51. Gordon Rintoul, quoted in Janet Christie, "Wonders of the World: After Three Years and 46M the National Museum of Scotland Is Set to Fling Open Its Doors to a Wide-Eyed Public," *Scotsman*, July 23, 2011, 7.
52. Tim Cornwell, "Nothing Stands Still for Our Museums," *Scotsman*, July 29, 2011, 33.
53. Phil Miller, "Revamped Museum Is Hailed as New Symbol of a Nation: Displays 'Re-Affirm Scottish Identity,'" (Glasgow) *Herald*, July 28, 2011.
54. All details from object A.1895.395, NMS Catalogue.
55. "The Royal Museum of Scotland: A Voyage of Discovery," *Scotsman*, September 21, 2009, http://www.scotsman.com.
56. Scotinform, *Royal Museum Project Evaluation of Galleries Executive Summary*, November 2012, 069(411) NMS 2012, 5, NMS Archives.
57. Ibid., 4, 1.
58. Gordon Rintoul, "Foreword," in *Scotland to the World: Treasures from the National Museum of Scotland*, ed. David Souden (Edinburgh: NMS Enterprises, 2016), vii.
59. For more on this, see Benedict Anderson, *Imagined Communities: Reflections on the Origin and Spread of Nationalism*, 2nd ed. (London: Verso, 1991).
60. Of these, 83 percent were repeat visitors, and 80 percent were local. "To show the children the Royal Museum" was the first listed reason to come. Lynn Jones Research, *Royal Museum Visitor Survey, December 2002–February 2003 Final Report*, March 2003, 069(411) Edi NMS V 2003. 2, NMS Archives.
61. Ballantyne Mackay Consultants, *Royal Museum Visitor Consultation Research Report*, November 2003, 069(411) Edi RMP, box 1, 2012 0026, 6, 33, NMS Archives.
62. Geoff Swinney, "Collecting Legacies: National Identity and the Worldwide Collections of National Museums Scotland," *Review of Scottish Culture* 26 (2014): 132.
63. See the British Museum, the Louvre, and the Hermitage, for example, which make no statements about the national history of the nation in which they are located.
64. Benson + Forsyth, *Museum of Scotland: Benson + Forsyth* (London: August Media/Benson + Forsyth, 1999), 32.

Conclusion

1. Katrin Bennhold, "Amid Divisions in U.K. over 'Brexit,' Nicola Sturgeon Calls for New Referendum on Scottish Independence," *New York Times*, March 13, 2017, https://www.nytimes.com.
2. Object H.MEQ.1584, National Museums of Scotland (NMS), Edinburgh.
3. "EU Referendum Results," BBC News, http://www.bbc.co.uk.
4. Exhibition text, *Scotland: A Changing Nation*, August 16, 2008; emphasis added.
5. The advertising campaign with this tagline ran from the mid-1970s to the early 1990s. Barr Soft Drinks, "A National Drink, 1954–1989," timeline, http://www.agbarr.co.uk.
6. "Edinburgh Agreement," Scottish Government, October 15, 2012, http://www.gov.scot.

Index

Aberdeen, 156–57
abolition of slavery, 42
Act of Proscription, 9, 140–41
Act of Union (1707), 7–8, 11, 83, 85, 137, 159–60, 169. *See also* Union of the Crowns
"Act to Establish the 'Smithsonian Institution' for the Increase and Diffusion of Knowledge Among Men, An," 30
Albemarle family, 71–73, 75
Albemarle, Third Earl of (George Keppel), 71, 73
Albemarle, Sixth Earl of (George Thomas), 71
Albert, Prince, 12, 14
Albert Victor, Prince, 159–60
Alcott, Louisa May, 161
Alexander III, 121
Alexandra (wife of Nicholas II), 109–10, 113–17, 119, 219n74
Alexei (child of Nicholas and Alexandra), 117
Alfred (Victoria's son), 114
Americanness, 32, 36, 43–46
Anderson, Benedict, 17
Anderson, Joseph, 55–57, 86
Anderson, Robert, 57, 64, 88–89
Andrew, Saint, statue of, 58–61, 75–76, 189
Anstruther, 185
Antiquarian Museum, 15
art exhibitions vs. history exhibitions, 125
art galleries vs. portrait galleries, 113, 213n41
artifacts. *See* objects of history
Atiu, wooden feast bowl from, 185
audience engagement, 175
audience response, 104
authenticity of objects of history, 69, 72–73, 84, 162

authenticity of tourist experiences, 146

Balmoral Castle, 13–14, 114–16, 122, 135, 142–43, 146, 159
Balmorality, 140
banal nationalism, 45, 170
Bannister, Judith, 74
Barrie, Maureen, 114
Battle of Bannockburn, 54, 57–58
Benjamin, Walter, 128
Benson, Gordon, 90
Benson + Forsyth (architects), 82, 95–96
Beyond the Palace Walls: Islamic Art from the State Hermitage Museum (exhibition), 102, 122–31, 136
Billig, Michael, 45, 170
biscuit-tin tartanry, 135, 143
blockbuster exhibitions, 19–20, 50–51, 105–6, 122, 132–33, 176, 181
blockbuster icons, 119–20
Board of the National Museums of Scotland, 49
Bolsheviks, 104–5, 108–9, 117
Boswell, James, 140–41
Bourdieu, Pierre, 112
Brander, John, 185
brecbennoch of Saint Columba, 55–58
Brexit, 191, 196
British Army, 9, 116
British Empire, 7
British Museum (London), 16–17, 102–4, 128, 155–56, 174, 180
Britishness, 9
British School of Archaeology, 180
British state, 7, 191
brochs, Scottish, 96–97, 99
Broughton International, 109
Bryden, David, 62–63
Buchan, Eleventh Earl of (David Stewart Erskine), 10–11, 14, 86, 88, 200n20

Burns, Robert, 104, 220n92
Bury, George Viscount. *See* Albemarle, Third Earl of

Cadboll Cup, 161–65
Cairngorm Mountains, 159
Caldwell, David, 62–63, 98
Caledonian Society of Moscow, 118
Callinish, standing stones of, 96
cameo of Mary, Queen of Scots, 177–80
Cameron, Charles, 111
Caprington Colliery, 78–80, 82–83
capsule exhibitions, 126
Carmichael, Jane, 125
Carron Ironworks, 79–80, 83
Catherine II, Empress (Catherine the Great), 105, 107–8, 111
Catherine the Great: An Enlightened Empress (exhibition), 133
Catholic-Protestant tensions in Scotland, 7–8
celebrity wood souvenirs, 161
Celtic Church, 56
Celtic decoration and ornamentation, 54–56, 155, 162–64
Celtic house shrine, 53–54
Chamber's Street Museum. *See* Royal Scottish Museum
Chambers Street site, 94
Cheape, Hugh, 92, 99, 151, 164
Child, Julia, 38–39
Chinese terra cotta army, 104
Christie's auction house, 69, 71–73
City of Culture program, 139, 216n10
Clarke, David, 85
Clashach golden sandstone, 96–97
Clerk family of Penicuik, 178
Clydeside, 96
coal industry in Scotland, 81, 83
coffin of Mary, Queen of Scots, 178, 221n25
Cold War, 26
Columba, Saint, 53–58, 60
Committee for the National Museums and Galleries of Scotland, 93
Conservative Party, 22
constructivists, 112
Cook, Thomas, 140
"Cornucopia" case in *The Wealth of a Nation*, 63

Corporation of Kilmarnock, 81
Culloden Moor and Battle of Culloden, 8–9, 71–72, 75, 140
Cumberland, Duke of, 71, 140
curatorial intent, 6

Dalgleish, George, 86, 100
Danish National Museum of Antiquity, 14
Darsie, George, 185
David, Antonio, 154
Davis, Jefferson, 42
Declaration of Arbroath, 177
deixis, 170
Denison, Alfred. *See* Londesborough, First Baron
design of museum exhibits and display cases, 91–92
Devine, Tom, 183–84
devolution referendum (1997), 85, 136–38, 169, 188
diaspora, Scottish/Highland, 135, 146, 150, 165, 192, 217n32, 220n92
Dick Institute Museum, 81
Dillon, Mary, 40
diorama-based museums, 89
Discourse Delivered at a Meeting for the Purpose of Promoting the Institution of a Society for the Investigation of the History of Scotland and Its Antiquities (Erskine), 10–11
Discoveries gallery, 186–87
Diversity cases in *Treasures from the Smithsonian*, 40
Dobbie, James J., 180–81
Dowson, Sir Philip, 95
Dress Act, 9
Duncan, Carol, 174
Dunlop, Frank, 21, 23, 25–27, 36–37
Dunstaffnage Castle, 96

Edinburgh: as center of Enlightenment philosophy and thought, 9–10; Hermitage's visit to, 111; Highlands' separation from, 149; King George IV's visit to, 141–42; Lewis Chessmen exhibition and, 156–57; New Town of, 12, 16, 94; Old Town of, 94; in panoramic painting of Jubilee, 115; population of, 216n8; public executions in, 14;

Smithsonian exhibition designed for, 22, 26–27, 31, 35, 111; Smithson's visit to, 23–26, 111; Society of Antiquaries and museum in, 12; summer festival season in, 101–2, 105

Edinburgh Agreement, 195

Edinburgh Castle, 107

Edinburgh-Glasgow axis, 138, 145

Edinburgh International Festival, 86, 106; 1967, 71–72; 1984, 20–21, 23, 25–27, 31, 39, 46, 50; 1989, 48, 50. *See also* summer festival season

Edinburgh Museum of Science and Art, xi, 4

Edward, Prince of Wales, 116

Egyptology collection, 180–83, 220nn42–43

Elgin Marbles, 103

Elizabeth, Empress, 108

Elizabeth I, Queen, 7

Elizabeth II, Queen, 25

England, 7, 13

English language, 146

Enlightenment, 9–10, 12, 18, 25, 49–50

Erik the chessman, 1–2, 155

Erskine, David Stewart. *See* Buchan, Eleventh Earl of

ethnography, 4

ethnoscape, 96

Evans, Godfrey, 114

exhibition catalogues: as artifacts, 132, 197; for *Beyond the Palace Walls*, 104, 123, 126, 129–31; Cadboll Cup and, 163; for *Fonn's Duthchas*, 157–59; for *Nicholas and Alexandra*, 104, 107, 109, 112, 119, 121, 129–31; novel catalogue, 129–30; scientific catalogue, 130–31; for *Treasures from the Smithsonian*, 23–24, 31–33, 129, 131–32; for *The Wealth of a Nation*, 51, 62, 67–68, 76, 130–31

Exhibition Review Committee, 89–90

exhibitions, 7, 19–21, 49, 60, 64, 197. *See also* blockbuster exhibitions; temporary exhibitions; traveling exhibitions

Fabergé Company, 119–20

Facing the Sea gallery space, 192

Findlay, John Richie, 16

Findlay Building, 16

Fingal (son of Ossian), 10–11

Fonn's Duthchas: Land and Legacy (exhibition), 135–36, 138, 146–65

Forsyth, Alan, 90

Forsyth, David, 185

Fort, Karen, 44

"Forty-Five" (Jacobite rebellion), 8

France, 74–75, 164

Franklin, Benjamin, 23, 25, 40–45

French decoration, 163–65

French language, 146

French Revolution, 42

Frog Service (china set), 107–8

Gaelic Renaissance, 146

Garland, Judy, 32, 45

Gellner, Ernest, 3, 87

George, Prince (Duke of York), 159–60, 219n74

George IV, King, 13, 86, 140–42

George V, King, 114

Glasgow, 96, 138, 144, 145, 150, 216n8

Glasgow 1990, 216n10

Glasgow Exhibition (1888), 114

globalized narratives, 33, 35

Golden Jubilee, Queen Victoria's, 112–14

Goode, James, 39

Gotzkowsky, Johann Ernst, 108

Grant family of Monymusk, 55–56

Great Britain, 7, 9–10, 22–26, 39, 104, 111, 114–15. *See also* United Kingdom

Great Exhibition of 1851, 4, 20, 46

Greenblatt, Stephen, 60–61

Grossman, Angus, 184–85

guillotine, 14

Hadrian's Wall, 8

Hamilton, William, 72

hangs in art galleries, 91

Hebrides, 146, 156

Heritable Jurisdictions Act, 9

Heritage for Scotland, A (Williams Committee), 93

Heritage Lottery Fund, 73–74, 139, 184

Highland 2007: Cadboll Cup and, 161–62, 164–65; *Fonn's Duthchas* and, 135–36, 138, 148–50, 152–53, 158, 161, 164–65; goals of, 135–36, 217n32; Highlands and modern

Highland 2007 (*continued*)
  Scotland, 138–40; Homecoming Scotland 2009 compared to, 220n92; modern Highlands and, 144–46; Scottish National Party and, 137
Highland cattle, portrait of, 154
Highland Clearances, 147, 153
Highland games, 134
Highlands and Islands Enterprise, 138–39
Highlands and Islands parliamentary district, 138, 150, 157–58, 216n8
Highland Scotland. *See* Scottish Highlands and Highlanders
history exhibitions vs. art exhibitions, 125
Holden, Catherine, 170–71, 175, 176, 184
Hollywood, 33, 109, 134, 140, 144
Homecoming Scotland 2009, 165, 220n92
Hungarian National Museum, 18

iconic objects: American, 120, 128; in *Beyond the Palace Walls*, 127; blockbuster icons, 119–20; collaboration with other institutions and, 104; context and temporary exhibitions, 44–46; exhibition catalogues as, 132; in *Fonn's Duthchas*, 153–64; of Highlands, 142–44; mass of collections as, 182–83; in Museum of Scotland, 77–79, 81, 88, 92, 172–73; national identity creation and, 194; in National Museum of Scotland, 175–83; National Museum of Scotland as, 189–90; in National Museums of Scotland, 154–58, 161; national narratives and, 67, 69; of New York City, 143; in *Nicholas and Alexandra*, 112–22; objects elevated to status of, 176–77; paintings, 113–15; of Paris, 143; religious icons, 115, 118–19, 128; Smithsonian approach and, 39; speaking for selves, 112, 175; treasures, 44–45, 75–76; in universal survey museums, 102; in *The Wealth of a Nation*, 52–53, 58, 61, 65, 69. *See also* national icons
imperial regalia, miniature replica of, 119–20

industrialization in Scotland, 80–83
Industrial Museum of Scotland, xi, 4, 20
industrial museums, 4
International Exhibition in Paris, 119
Invergordon Castle, 162
Inverness, 138–40, 145, 150, 216n8
Inverness Museum and Art Gallery, 150, 152
Ireland, 7, 13, 17
Irn-Bru, 193
Islamic art and culture, 122–29
Islamic tiles, 128–29
Isle of Lewis, 150, 155–57
isolationism in Russia, 104–5

Jackson, Andrew, 28
Jacobites and Jacobite rebellion: defeat at Battle of Culloden, 8–9, 11, 71, 140–41, 144; *Fonn's Duthchas* and, 154; *Scotland Transformed* galleries and, 83; Scottish nationhood and, 88, 195; silver canteen set and, 69–71, 73–75; split in Scottish identities and, 134
James I, King of England, 7
James VI, King of Scotland, 7
Japan, 121
jewels of Mary, Queen of Scots, 177–80

Kailyard vision of Scotland, 144
Kelvingrove Art Gallery and Museum, 150–52
Keppel, George (Lord Bury and Third Earl of Albemarle), 71, 73
Kermit the Frog, 33
Kildonan gold rush, 160
Kingdom of the Scots (gallery), 54–55, 60, 156, 177
King's Laws, 9
knowledge, production and consumption of, 65

Labour Party, 137
Latour, Bruno, 112
Leith Harbor, 115
Lewis Chessmen, 1–2, 154–58, 162, 176, 197
liberty cap of walking stick, 42
Londesborough, First Baron (Alfred Denison), 155–56

London *Times*, 74
Louvre (Paris), 16, 102, 105, 174
Lowland Scotland, 134, 140, 142
Lynch, Michael, 91
Lyon in Mourning, The, 154

MacCannell, Dean, 72
MacDonald, Flora, 154
Macie, Elizabeth Keate Hungerford, 28
Macie, James Lewis, 28
Mackay, Alan, 71
Maclean, Will, 154
Macleod family of Lewis, 162–63
MacPherson, James, 141
Macpherson, Norman, 164
Magnificence of the Tsars (exhibition), 107
Magnusson, Magnus, 51
"Maiden" beheading machine, 14
Maria (child of Nicholas and Alexandra), 117
Mary, Queen of Scots, 7–8, 177–80, 221n25
Mary of Teck (May), 159–60, 219n74
Mauchlinware, 161
McClelland, Donald, 31, 34, 37, 42
McConnell, Jack, 153
militaristic Scot image, 144
monarchy, story of, 120
Monymusk Reliquary: as *brecbennoch* of Saint Columba, 55–58, 208n19; context and story of, 69; at Museum of Scotland entrance, 54–55, 177, 189; provenance of, 56, 179; statue of Saint Andrew and, 60–61; as treasure of the nation, 75–76; use in medieval Scotland, 161; in *The Wealth of a Nation*, 53–58
Morton, Graeme, 9
Mound in Edinburgh, 12–13, 15
Mowbray, Giles, 178
multivocality of objects of history, 64–65, 67–68, 112, 143–44, 194, 197
museum mark, 172–73
Museum Nan Eilean, 150, 152, 157–58
Museum of Antiquities, 15, 91
Museum of Science and Art, 20
Museum of Scotland: building space, 93–100; Cadboll Cup and, 162, 164–65; competing ideas of, 77–78, 83–84; confusing space in, 175; devolution referendum and, 85–86; iconic objects in, 77–79, 81, 88, 92, 172–73; as iconic place, 84–85, 87–88, 96–99; Lewis Chessmen and, 156; logo of, 172; marketing and, 165; mission of, 166, 170; Monymusk Reliquary at entrance of, 54–55, 177, 189; narrative of, 90–92, 97–98; national added to name of, xii, 170–71; National Galleries collections displayed in, 152; National Heritage (Scotland) Act and, 48–49; national identity and, 87, 136, 188; Newcomen engine at, 78–84; as object-centered project, 88–90, 92, 175; opening of, xi, 5, 166, 169, 187–88; rebranding and, 173, 177, 186–89, 192–93; RSM identity and, 4–5; silver canteen and, 75; statue of Saint Andrew and, 60; Union Brooch and, 159–60; visitor studies at, 167; *The Wealth of a Nation* exhibition and case for, 50–51, 53, 58, 66
Museum of Scotland Exhibition Brief, 89–90
Museum of Scotland Project, 89–91
Museum of Scottish Country Life, 166
Museum of the Society of Antiquaries, xi
museum partnerships, 6–7
museums: exhibitions in, 7; names of, 15–16; narratives of, 3, 19, 196–98; nationalism politics and, 7. *See also* national museums; *specific museum names*
myth, 141

Nairn, Tom, 137
narrative-based museums, 89
narratives of museums, 3, 19, 196–98
nation, as term, 3–4
National Archives of Scotland, 170
National Art Collections Fund, 162, 178–79
National Galleries of Scotland, 138, 151–54, 162, 170
National Gallery, 13
National Heritage (Scotland) Act, x, 48–49, 77
National Heritage Memorial Fund, 74
national icons, 32–35, 37–39, 41–46,

national icons (*continued*)
  53–61, 65–66, 69, 111–12. *See also* iconic objects
national identity: exhibition catalogues and, 129–30; national museums and, 17–18, 85–87, 100, 102, 198; vs. universal identity, 4–5; universal survey institutions and, 1–2
national identity of Scotland: artifacts and, 61–62, 194; changing of, 191; Highland 2007 and *Fonn's Duthchas*, 135–38, 149, 153–54; Highlands as part of, 141–44, 153; Monymusk Reliquary and, 57; museum names and brand identity and, 167, 170–72; national museum and, 4–6, 17–18, 85–87, 95–96, 100, 188–89, 195–96; split in, 134; unionist nationalism and, 9–11; Union with England and, x, 7–8, 11. *See also* Scottishness
national identity of the United States, 29, 48. *See also* Americanness
National Institute for the Promotion of Science, 29–30
National Institutions, 170
nationalism, 3, 5–7, 134, 137–38, 195
National Library of Scotland, 138, 151–54, 170
National Museum in Prague, 18
National Museum Krakow, 18
National Museum of Antiquities of Scotland (NMAS): Cadboll Cup and, 162, 164; case for national museum and, 18, 86; creation and opening of, xi, 4, 15; Egyptian collection in, 182, 222n42; formation of the National Museums of Scotland and, xi, 4–5, 49, 77; inadequate display of artifacts in, 61–62; Monymusk Reliquary and, 57; Museum of Scotland to replace, 76, 91, 94; naming of, 15–17; RSM compared to, 46; Saint Andrew statue at, 59; silver canteen set and, 69, 71, 75; Smithsonian exhibition and, 27; *The Wealth of a Nation* and, 51; Wilson's cataloguing of objects in, 14–17
National Museum of Costume Scotland, xi, 168, 171

National Museum of Flight Scotland, xi, 166, 168
National Museum of Rural Life, xi
National Museum of Scotland: creation of, xii, 5, 168–69, 174, 187–89; Egyptology collection in, 180–83; as iconic object for Scotland, 189–90; Lewis Chessmen and, 1–2; modern history in, 192–93; national identity and, 4–6, 188–89, 195–96; Newcomen engine at, 78–84; new icons in, 175–80, 182, 189; objects in entrance of, 189; rebranding in, 173–87, 191–95; Saint Andrew statue and, 59; temporary exhibitions at, 21
national museums: national identity and, 17–18, 85–87, 100, 102; national stories/narratives and, 3–4, 6, 17–19, 66–69; nation-building and, 17–18; need for, 183–84; objects chosen for, 32; temporary exhibitions at, 21–27
National Museums of Scotland: brand identity confusion, 166–68; collection of materials held by, 62, 87, 90, 149; creation of, xi, 4–5, 49, 77; *Fonn's Duthchas* and, 138, 150–52, 159, 162; iconic objects in, 154–59, 161; institutions falling under umbrella of, 103, 166–67; international connections of, 101–33; Monymusk Reliquary and, 55; Museum of Scotland design and, 95; rebranding of, 168–69; renamed National Museums Scotland, xii; silver canteen set and, 74; *The Wealth of a Nation* and, 48, 62–64, 76
National Museums Scotland, xii, 168–73, 184
national narrative of Scotland, creating, 77–100; building museum space, 93–100; nation and museum, 84–93; Newcomen engine, 78–84
national narratives and museums, 3–4, 6, 17–19, 66–69
National War Museum, xi, 168
nation and state, 169–70
nation-building, 17–18
nations, objects connecting. *See* objects connecting Russia and Scotland

natural history collections, 4
New Building Working Committee, 94–95
Newcomen, Thomas, 79, 81–82
Newcomen engine, 78–84, 197
Newcomen Society, 81
Nicholas and Alexandra: The Last Imperial Family of Tsarist Russia (exhibition), 109–11, 118
Nicholas and Alexandra: The Last Tsar and Tsarina (exhibition), 102, 106–13, 115, 118–25, 129–31, 133
Nicholas II, 108–9, 113–19, 121, 219n74
NMAH. *See* Smithsonian National Museum of American History
NMAS. *See* National Museum of Antiquities of Scotland
Norse language and culture, 146, 156–57
novel catalogue, 129–32

objectivists, 112
objects connecting Russia and Scotland, 101–33; *Beyond the Palace Walls*, 122–27; collaborative outcomes, 132–33; making contacts and building bridges, 104–6; miniature imperial regalia, 119–20; national icons, 111–12; *Nicholas and Alexandra*, 106–11; panoramic painting of Golden Jubilee, 112–15; rarities, commodities, and icons, 127–32; religious icon of Nicholas II, 115–19; Tsarevich's shirt, 120–22
objects of history: authenticity of, 69, 72–73, 84, 162; in *Beyond the Palace Walls*, 123, 126–29; chosen for national museums, 32; in *Fonn's Duthchas*, 146–64; mass of collections of, 180–83; multivocality of, 64–65, 67–68, 112, 143–44, 194, 197; museum narrative and, 197–98; museum partnerships and, 6; in National Galleries of Scotland, 151–52; in National Library of Scotland, 151; in *Nicholas and Alexandra*, 112, 127; placement in museums and, 1–3; provenance of, 56, 69–76, 112, 179; rebranding of, 176–80; resonance and wonder of, 60–61; space and, 39–40, 61–64; stories told by, 88–90, 92, 112; in temporary and traveling exhibitions, 19–23, 39–41, 68–69, 148–51; in *Treasures from the Smithsonian*, 31–37, 40–46, 60–61; in *The Wealth of a Nation*, 51–53, 61. *See also* iconic objects
objects unifying Scotland, 134–65; devolution and, 136–38; *Fonn's Duthchas*, 135–36, 138, 146–64; Highlands and modern Scotland, 138–40; Highlands throughout history, 140–44; modern Highlands, 144–46
Old Hermitage, 108
Olga (child of Nicholas and Alexandra), 116
Oliphant, Ebenezer, 69–70, 73, 75
Orkney, 138, 146
Ossian, poems of, 10–11, 141
Ottoman tent, eighteenth century, 127–28

panoramic painting of Golden Jubilee, 112–15
Penicuik Jewels, 178–79
Pennant, Thomas, 80, 140–41
Peterhof, 108
Peter the Great, 108
Petrie, William Flinders, 180–82
Piasetsky, Pavel Yakovlevich, 114
Pictish cross, 177, 189
Plea for a National Museum and Botanic Garden to Be Founded on the Smithsonian Institution at the City of Washington, A, 30
Poems of Ossian, The (MacPherson), 141
politics and nationhood, 194–95
Polk, James K., 20
portrait galleries vs. art galleries, 113, 213n41
Proceedings of the Society of Antiquaries of Scotland, 14–15, 155–56
Proscription Acts. *See* Act of Proscription
provenance of objects of history, 56, 69–76, 112, 179
public institution, museum's move toward, 12–15

Reagan, Ronald, 26
reception theory, 6

Red Clydeside, 144
religious icons, 115, 118–19, 128
Renaissance, 164–65
resonance and wonder of objects, 60–61
Rifkind, Malcolm, 55
Rintoul, Gordon, 111, 123–24, 150, 185
Rinzler, Ralph, 27
Ripley, S. Dillon, 25–27, 31
Ririe, Roderick, 155
"Rising" (Jacobite rebellion), 8
rococo art of chasing, 73–74
Romanov family, 109, 117–19, 121
Romantic era, 104
romantic past, 141–42, 145–46, 161
Royal Botanical Gardens at Kew, 128
Royal Institution building (Royal Scottish Academy), 15
Royal Museum Master Plan, 5
Royal Museum of Scotland: exhibitions from State Hermitage Museum and, 105; exploration encouraged in, 176; Museum of Scotland and, xi–xii, 5; National Museum of Scotland creation and, xii, 171–72; rebranding and, 172–74, 189; renovated, xii, 183–86; RSM rebranded as, xi, 20; as universal survey museum, 103; visitors to, 176, 188, 223n60; *The Wealth of a Nation* exhibition at, 20, 52, 55. *See also* Royal Scottish Museum
Royal Museum Project, 183–86
Royal Scots Dragoon Guards, 117
Royal Scots Greys, 116–18
Royal Scottish Academy, 15
Royal Scottish Museum (RSM): case for national museum and, 86; Egyptian collection in, 180–82, 222n42; founding of, xi, 20; logo of, 172; many names of, xi, 4, 20; mission of, 166; Museum of Scotland and, 94; National Museum of Scotland creation and, xii, 168–69, 171, 173–74; National Museums of Scotland brand confusion and, 168, 188; National Museums of Scotland creation and, xi, 4–5, 49, 77; Newcomen engine and, 81; rebranded as Royal Museum of Scotland, xi, 20; revamping of, 183–86, 191; silver canteen set and, 69, 71; Smithsonian's visit to, 25, 111; South Seas collectables in, 185; symposium held at (1990), 88, 96; as *Treasures from the Smithsonian* host, 21–23, 27, 35–37, 46–48; visitor studies at, 167. *See also* Royal Museum of Scotland
Royal Society of Edinburgh, 13, 15, 180
Royal Society of London, 28
Royal Stewart tartan, 141–42
RSM. *See* Royal Scottish Museum
ruby slippers, from *The Wizard of Oz*, 32–35, 44, 205n48, 206n84
Rush, Richard, 28–29
Russia, 16. *See also* objects connecting Russia and Scotland

Sackler, Arthur M., 26–27, 203n28
Saint Andrew's Cross flag, 172
Salmond, Alex, 156
sarcophagi, 182–83
Scandinavia, 7, 14, 101, 146, 156
scientific catalogue, 130–31
Scotch pebbles, 159–61
Scotland: Catholic-Protestant tensions in, 7–8; connections with Russia, 102–33; connections with United States, 23–25, 39, 44, 104; differences from rest of Great Britain, 22, 112; exhibition for, and about, 48–76; history of, 7–11, 16; national narrative of, 77–100; unionist nationalism in, 9–11
Scotland, changes in nation and museum, 166–90; Egypt in Scotland, 180–83; icons inside museum, 173–75; image of the nation, 172–73; Mary's jewels, 175–80; naming the national museum, 168–72; Royal Museum Project, 183–86; Scotland and the world, 186–90
Scotland—A Changing Nation (display), 192
Scotland Transformed exhibits in Museum of Scotland, 79, 83
Scots language, 146
Scott, Walter, 72, 86, 104, 140–42, 154
Scottish Army, 122. *See also* Royal Scots Greys
Scottish Executive (Scottish Government), 139, 161–62, 184, 195

Index

Scottish Gaelic, 55, 134, 142, 146–47
Scottish Galleries, 189
Scottish Highlands and Highlanders, 134–65; Battle of Culloden and, 8–9; creation of modern, 144–46; devolution and, 136–38; *Fonn's Duthchas*, 135–36, 138, 146–54, 157–62, 164; Highland 2007 and, 135–40, 144–46, 148–50, 152–53, 158, 161, 164–65; modern Scotland and, 138–40; Queen Victoria and, 134–35, 142; Russian elite's affinity for, 104; throughout history, 140–44
Scottish independence from Britain, 137, 157, 169, 191, 194–96
Scottish museum. See Royal Scottish Museum
Scottish National Party (SNP), 22, 137, 156, 169, 194–95
Scottish National Portrait Gallery, 179
Scottishness: defeat at Culloden and, 9; emphasizing, 191–94; *Fonn's Duthchas* and, 149; Highlandism and, 136, 141–43; the national museum evolution and, 6, 17, 46; of the Newcomen engine, 82; new NMS brand and, 186–87, 195; of silver canteen set, 73; in *The Wealth of a Nation*, 76, 135
Scottish & Newcastle (brewing company), 111
Scottish Parliament, 85–86, 136–37
Scottish Sporting Hall of Fame, 192
Scottish United Services Museum, 166
Serbian National Museum, 18
serendipitous discovery, 82–83
seriation, theory of, 14
shabtis, 182–83
Shambellie House Museum of Costume, 166, 168
Sharpe, Charles Kirkpatrick, 155
Shetland, 138, 146, 156–57
silver canteen set, 69–76, 165, 191, 209n48
silversmiths in eighteenth century, 74–75
Simpson, James, 63
SITES. See Smithsonian Institution Traveling Exhibition Service
Smellie, William, 11
Smith, Adam, 49–50, 52
Smith, Anthony, 96

Smithson, James, 23–26, 28–30, 37, 111
Smithsonian Institution (Washington, DC), 22–47; building of, 27–30, 204n38; concepts and contents, 30–32, 204n43; exhibitionary outcomes in Scotland, 46–47; Franklin's and Washington's walking stick, 41–45; name of, 16; objects chosen from, for exhibition, 32–35, 65; presenting abroad, 35–39; traveling exhibitions of, 148; treasures from, 39–41; *Treasures from the Smithsonian* created as traveling exhibit from, 19–27
Smithsonian Institution Traveling Exhibition Service (SITES), 34, 37, 39, 148
Smithsonian National Air and Space Museum, 40, 43
Smithsonian National Museum of African Art, 40
Smithsonian National Museum of American History (NMAH), 32, 34, 38, 40–43, 196, 205n48
Smithsonian National Museum of Natural History, 43
Smithsonian National Portrait Gallery, 16, 40
SNP. See Scottish National Party
Soane, John, 72
Society of Antiquaries of Scotland: Cadboll Cup and, 164; formation of, 11, 88, 93–94, 195; formation of Museum of the Society of Antiquaries and search for space, 11–15, 84, 86; Lewis Chessmen and, 155–56; Monymusk Reliquary and, 55; NMAS created by, xi, 4–5, 15–17
South Pacific, 185, 192
Soviet Union, 104–5, 117
St. Andrew: Will He Ever See the Light? (pamphlet), 58–62
State Hermitage Museum in Russia, 16, 101–33
steam engine, 80
Stevenson, Robert B. K., 164
Stewart, Charles Edward, and Stewart dynasty, 8–9, 69–75, 140, 154, 165, 178, 191
Stewart, Mary. See Mary, Queen of Scots
Stornoway, Isle of Lewis, 150, 155–57
Sturgeon, Nicola, 191

summer festival season, 101–2, 105
Swinney, Geoff, 62–63
Synopsis of the Museum of the Society of Antiquaries of Scotland, 14–15

tartans, 9, 13, 134–35, 141–44, 187
Tebble, Norman, 27, 36–37
technology of modern life, 137
temporary exhibitions: authenticity and, 73; collaborative, 101–33; exhibition catalogues for, 132; gift shop contents and, 128; museum narratives and, 19, 197; at National Library of Scotland, 151; national narratives and, 66–69; nations as objects in, 135–36; nations represented in, 64–66; object-centered, 130; permanent exhibitions compared to, 60, 65–66, 217n37; purposes and appeal of, 19, 21–27, 48, 52, 76, 124, 128, 148; traveling exhibitions compared to, 147, 150; tsars as subjects of, 107. *See also specific temporary exhibition names*
terrorist attacks, 123
Thatcher, Margaret, 22–23, 26
Thomas, George. *See* Albemarle, Sixth Earl of 71
Thomsen, Christian, 14
Thorkelin, Grimur, 14
Thornton, William, 24–25
Timeline of Museum Names, xi–xii
Titaua, Princess, 185, 192
tourism and tourists: City of Culture program and, 139; Edinburgh International Festival and, 25; Highlandism and, 142–43; in modern Highlands, 144–46; National Museum of Scotland creation and, 187; National Museum of Scotland naming and, 172; Newcomen engine and, 80, 83; Scottish past and, 88; *Treasures from the Smithsonian* and, 33. *See also* Highland 2007
Tower of London, 107
"Transport Collection" in *The Wealth of a Nation*, 76
traveling exhibitions: iconic objects in, 154; of Lewis Chessmen, 156–57; museum narratives and, 19; temporary exhibitions compared to, 147, 150. *See also Fonn's Duthchas*

Treasures from Scottish Houses (exhibition), 71–72
Treasures from the Smithsonian Institution at the Royal Scottish Museum (exhibition): *Beyond the Palace Walls* compared to, 123, 126, 128; connections between America and Scotland and, 23, 39; creation of, 20, 35–39; display cases in, 39–40; Edinburgh International Festival and, 21, 23; exhibitionary outcomes, 46–47; exhibition catalogues for, 23–24, 31–33, 129, 131–32; *Fonn's Duthchas* compared to, 136; Franklin's and Washington's walking stick in, 41–45; location chosen for, 26–27; Museum of Scotland and, 101; *Nicholas and Alexandra* compared to, 110; ruby slippers in, 32–35, 45; Smithsonian echoed in, 27–28; *Treasures of the Smithsonian* and, 19; *The Wealth of a Nation* and, 48, 50–53, 60–61, 63–64. *See also* Smithsonian Institution
Treasures of American History (exhibition), 43
Treasures of the Smithsonian (book), 19, 31–32, 35–36, 43
Tsarevich's shirt, 120–22
tsarist history, 106–7, 117, 119–22. *See also* Nicholas II
Tsarskoe Selo (palace), 108
Turkish tiles, 128–29
Tutankhamen, King, 106, 181

Uig, 156
umete, 185
Union Brooch, 158–61
unionist nationalism, 9–11
Union of the Crowns (1603), 7, 9, 141. *See also* Act of Union
Union of the Parliaments, 159
United Kingdom: collections of Society of Antiquaries and, 15; DNA testing of Romanov family remains in, 117; Edinburgh Agreement and, 195; exhibitions from State Hermitage Museum and, 105; Highland 2007 funding and, 139; Jacobites and, 134, 140; Lewis Chessmen and, 155–56; pulled out of European Union, 191; RSM overshadowed by

London museums in, 22; Scotland's separateness and, 142; Scottish Highlands reclaimed for, 134–35; union of nations and, 7; Union of the Crowns and, 141. *See also* Great Britain

United States: connections with Britain, 23–26, 39, 44, 104; national icons of, 32–35, 37–39, 41–45; national identity of, 29, 48; national narrative of, 68; *Nicholas and Alexandra* exhibition in, 109–11; Smithsonian's cultural role in, 38–39; Smithson's bequest to, 28–29

universal identity vs. national identity, 4–5

universal survey museums or institutions, 102–3, 120, 133, 174

University of Edinburgh, 13, 94

Versailles, 108
vexillum, 56
Victoria, Queen, and Victorianism: Golden Jubilee, 112–14; Mary of Teck and, 159–60, 219n74; Nicholas II and Alexandra and, 116, 219n74; Scotch pebble brooch and, 159–61; Scottish Highlands and Highlanders and, 13, 134–35, 140, 142–44, 146; Wilson's *Synopsis* sent to, 14

Victoria and Albert Museum, 74, 107, 128, 162

Victorians and Edwardians (gallery), 159
Viking culture, 145, 156
VisitHighlands, 138
visitor perception, 6
Voltaire, 108

Wales, 7, 17
walking stick of Franklin and Washington, 41–45, 206n80
Wallach, Alan, 174
War of Independence, 41
Wars of Scottish Independence, 57

Washington, George, 41–45
Watt, James, 80
Waverley (Scott), 141, 154
Wealth of a Nation in the National Museums of Scotland, The (exhibition), 48–76; exhibition catalogues for, 130–31; *Fonn's Duthchas* compared to, 136; framing, 51–53; Museum of Scotland and, 101; narratives of the nation and, 66–69; national icons in, 53–61; national identity and, 136; objects selected for, 65, 208n37; political undertone of, 49–51; provenance and, 69–76; space of a nation and, 61–64; temporary nations and, 64–66

Wealth of Nations, The (Smith), 49–50, 52

Weber, Max, 169
Wedgwood, Josiah, 107
Wedgwood china, 107–8
Welby, Lieutenant-Colonel, 116
Western Isles, 138, 146
West Highland character, 162, 164
Westren, Peter MacGregor, 159
white cube museum design, 91–92, 208n29
William I, 53–54
Williams, Sir Alwyn, 93
Williams Committee, 93–94, 169
Wilson, Daniel, 13–14, 16–17, 86, 88, 91, 101
Windows on the World (display), 191
Winter Palace in St. Petersburg, 105, 108, 119
Wizard of Oz, The (film), 32–33, 45
wonder and resonance of objects, 60–61
wooden feast bowl, 185
Worsaae, Jens, 14

"Year of Highland Culture, The". *See* Highland 2007
York, Duchess of, 159–60

www.ingramcontent.com/pod-product-compliance
Lightning Source LLC
Chambersburg PA
CBHW020122240426

43673CB00038B/568